THE ORTHODOX BAPTISTERY OF RAVENNA

Yale Publications in the History of Art, 18

George Kubler, *Editor*

The ORTHODOX BAPTISTERY OF RAVENNA

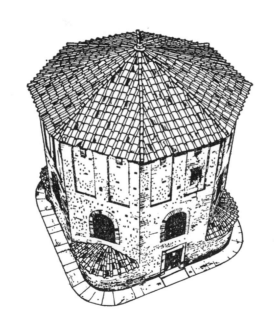

SPIRO K. KOSTOF

NEW HAVEN AND LONDON, YALE UNIVERSITY PRESS, 1965

Στοὺς γονεῖς μου

Μέλπω καὶ Κώστα Κωστώφ

PREFACE

The need for a critical monograph on the Orthodox Baptistery (S. Giovanni in Fonte) became apparent during a graduate seminar at Yale University in 1959–60, which was concerned with special problems of Ravennate art of the fifth and sixth centuries. A study with the general scope of the present book was proposed as a dissertation project to the Department of the History of Art at Yale, and was prepared in the next two years under the supervision of Professor William L. MacDonald. This book is a revised version of the dissertation. Its aims are set forth in the first chapter.

My first close acquaintance with the Orthodox Baptistery was made during a visit to Ravenna in the summer of 1959. A second extended visit in the summer and fall of 1960 was rendered possible by a grant-in-aid from Yale; for this, and for a subsequent grant to assist in the completion of the manuscript, I should like to express my gratitude. I returned to Ravenna in 1963 to complete the research. My work at each of these visits was greatly facilitated and enriched through the generosity of the local authorities, without whose sanction and kindness the book in its present form could not have been prepared. It is with special pleasure that I acknowledge the cooperation of Dottore Arrico Buonomo, Superintendent of Monuments for Ravenna; Monsignor Mario Mazzotti, archivist of the Archivio Arcivescovile; Don. D. DeMarchi, rector of the parish of S. Giovanni in Fonte; and Dottore Giuseppe Cortesi, librarian of the Biblioteca Classense, and his staff. I am particularly indebted to Monsignor Mazzotti, who not only made available the archival material under his care but put at my disposal his personal files and his unmatched knowledge of the monuments of the city. For the three pleasant and fruitful weeks that I spent in the American Academy at Rome in the fall of 1960, my gratitude goes to its director, Mr. Richard Kimball, and to Professor Frank E. Brown.

In its various forms, the manuscript has been read by Professors Richard Krautheimer, Carroll L. V. Meeks, Sumner McKnight Crosby, and Edzard Baumann, and also by Professor George Kubler, Editor of the History of Art Series at Yale: I am thankful to each one of them. The building was surveyed and measured under my direction by Signori Emilio Mariani and Luciano Giambelli, formerly students of architecture at the University of Milan. Their careful drawings are a major contribution to this study, and the photographs which Signore Mariani was able to make while the scaffolding was up have aided me appreciably in its writing and illustration. Mr. Bernard M. Boyle has been good enough to take time from his own work in order to prepare the drawings reproduced on Figures 8, 10, 12, 36, 64, 74, and 128. The sources of the remaining illustrations are acknowledged in the List of Illustrations. (Special permission to reproduce the photographs from the Deutsches Archäologisches Institut in Rome was granted by Professor F. W. Deichmann, in whose book *Frühchristliche Bauten und Mosaiken von Ravenna* [Baden-Baden, 1958] they were first published.) The typescript was prepared, with patience and good nature, by Miss Maria Cozzolino.

To Professor William L. MacDonald, true teacher and generous friend, I owe much more than my professional training. My deepest gratitude goes to him and to his wife for their selfless interest since my early days as a foreign student in this country.

S. K. K.

New Haven, Connecticut
1965

CONTENTS

LIST OF ILLUSTRATIONS

Frontispiece. The mosaics of the cupola, detail

ABBREVIATIONS

AA	*Archäologischer Anzeiger, Beiblatt zum Jahrbuch des deutschen archäologischen Instituts*
AB	*Art Bulletin*
AJA	*American Journal of Archaeology*
Atti per la Romagna	*Atti e memorie della reale deputazione di storia patria per le provincie di Romagna*
BAC	*Bullettino di archeologia cristiana*
Berti, *Sull'antico duomo*	G. Berti, *Sull'Antico Duomo di Ravenna e il battistero e l'episcopio e il Tricolo* (Ravenna, 1880)
"Bona patrimonia"	"Bona patrimonia ecclesiae sancti Johannis in Fonte," MS, Archivio del Battistero
BZ	*Byzantinische Zeitschrift*
Cahiers	*Cahiers archéologiques*
Casalone, "Ricerche"	C. Casalone, "Ricerche sul Battistero della Cattedrale di Ravenna," *Rivista dell'Istituto nazionale d'archeologia e storia dell'arte, 8* (1959)
Ciampini, *Vetera monimenta*	G. G. Ciampini, *Vetera monimenta in quibus praecipuè musiva opera sacrarum* (Rome, 1690–99)
Codex	A. Agnellus, *Codex pontificalis ecclesiae ravennatis*, ed. A. Testi-Rasponi, in *Raccolta degli storici italiani*, II.3, fasc. 196–97 and 200 (Bologna, 1924)
Corsi	*Corsi di cultura sull'arte ravennate e bizantina*
DOP	*Dumbarton Oaks Papers*
FR	*Felix Ravenna*
Holder-Egger	*Agnelli qui et Andreas Liber pontificalis ecclesiae ravennatis*, ed. O. Holder-Egger, in *Monumenta historiae germanica, Scriptores rerum langobardicarum et italicarum* (Hanover, 1878), pp. 265–391
JDAI	*Jahrbuch des (kaiserlichen) deutschen archäologischen Instituts*
JRS	*Journal of Roman Studies*

Lanciani, *Cenni*   F. Lanciani, *Cenni intorno ai monumenti e alle cose più notabili di Ravenna* (Ravenna, 1871)

MAAR   *Memoirs of the American Academy in Rome*

Migne, *PG*   J. P. Migne (ed.), *Patrologiae cursus completus, series graeca* (Paris, 1857–66)

Migne, *PL*   J. P. Migne (ed.), *Patrologiae cursus completus, series latina* (Paris, 1844–65)

PBSR   *Papers of the British School at Rome*

RA   *Revue archéologique*

RAC   *Revue del l'art chrétien*

"Raccolta"   "Raccolta da una miscellanea del Battistero," MS, Biblioteca Classense

RACrist   *Rivista di archeologia cristiana*

Ricci, "S. Giovanni"   C. Ricci, "Il Battistero di S. Giovanni in Fonte," *Atti per la Romagna*, III.7 (1888–89)

Ricci, *Tavole*   C. Ricci, *Tavole storiche dei mosaici di Ravenna* (8 vols. Rome, 1930–37)

RM   *Mittheilungen des deutschen archäologischen Instituts. Römische Abteilung*

Sangiorgi, *Battistero*   C. Sangiorgi, *Il Battistero della Basilica Ursiana di Ravenna* (Ravenna, 1900)

"Varia"   "Varia ad ecclesiam sancti Johannis in Fonte spectantia," MS, Archivio del Battistero

INTRODUCTION

For Ravenna, the years after A.D. 400 were prosperous times. Little is known about the city's earlier history; of the imperial undertakings by Julius Caesar, Augustus, Claudius, and Trajan almost nothing remains standing.[1] But with the transfer of the Roman court by the Emperor Honorius from Milan to Ravenna about A.D. 402, the city was elevated, suddenly, from mere provincial existence to imperial magnificence.

This political distinction had a rapid effect also upon the ecclesiastical prestige of Ravenna. Hitherto strictly under the jurisdiction of the Pope, the church of Ravenna now began to establish itself as a metropolis with several dependent dioceses. The shift was probably already accomplished by the 430s, evidently with the approval of Rome,[2] for Rome was still very much concerned with the power of the see of Milan, which had been the first to challenge papal jurisdiction during the time of Theodosius the Great and St. Ambrose. To remedy this dangerous rift in the province of Emilia the Pope had created about A.D. 400 the metropolis of Aquileia at the territorial expense of Milan. A little later the institution of the vicarage of Gaul further diminished Milan's influence in the Alpine regions. The rise of Ravenna could now deal a final blow to the popularity of Milan which had been due largely to the impact of its great bishop, St. Ambrose.[3]

Papal policy in Northern Italy and the advent of the court, then, were together

1. For the early history of Ravenna up to A.D. 400, see T. Tomai, *Istoria della città di Ravenna* (Pesaro, 1574; 2d ed. Ravenna, 1580); *H. Rubei historiarum ravennatum libri decem* (Venice, 1589); and more recently G. Finsler, *Ravenna in der römischen Kaiserzeit* (Zurich, 1885). Extensive bibliography and summary of the question in G. Bovini, "Le origini di Ravenna e lo sviluppo della città in età romana," *FR*, 70 (1956), 38–60; and 72 (1956), 27–68.

For Roman monuments in Ravenna, see: A. Zirardini, *Degli Antichi Edifici profani di Ravenna* (Faenza, 1726); V. Bedeschi, *Ravenna romana. Il corso del Padenna e le mura di Tiberio Claudio* (Ravenna, 1920); H. Kähler, "Die Porta Aurea di Ravenna," *RM*, 50 (1935), 172–224.

2. The exact date at which Ravenna became an ecclesiastical metropolis is disputed. For summary of arguments and relative bibliography, see R. Massigli, "La création de la métropole ecclésiastique de Ravenne," in *Mélanges d'archéologie et d'histoire de l'École Française de Rome*, *31* (1911), 277–90.

3. These events are admirably reviewed by A. Testi-Rasponi in "La chiesa di Ravenna da Onorio a Teodorico," *FR*, *30* (1925), 5–22. See also A. Baumstark, *Liturgia romana e liturgia nell'Esarcato* (Rome, 1904), pp. 163 ff.

responsible for the spectacular change in the life of Ravenna. An imperial mint began issuing coins there in 403.[4] Also at this time a general program of building was initiated, consonant with the dignity of this new Rome and its church. The faithful had gathered in private places for devotion until then, "in singulis teguriis," as the ninth-century chronicler Agnellus puts it.[5] Only Classis, the port of Ravenna, important since the early days of the Empire and the burial place of the first Ravennate bishops, could boast of a monumental cult building for its Christian community.[6] This was the so-called Basilica Probi, erected probably by Bishop Probus II in the last third of the fourth century.[7] Now, however, the city caught up with and surpassed its port. A new and splendid cathedral dedicated to the Anastasis was raised by Bishop Ursus within the walls, near the Porta Salustra which marked the southeastern extremity of the *cardo*. This Basilica Ursiana, as it was to be called, was an edifice of five aisles divided by fifty-six marble columns and decorated throughout with colored stones and mosaics, a worthy rival to the five-aisled cathedral that St. Ambrose had put up in Milan some twenty years earlier.[8] To its north a baptistery was built, and it too was beautifully adorned.[9] An episcopal palace south of the cathedral provided a proper residence for Ursus and his successors; among these was Bishop Neon, who added to it a new structure called Quinque Accubita, containing a refectory with walls sheathed with an elaborate program of painting:

> He ordered the story of the Psalm which we sing every day, that is, "Praise ye the Lord from the Heavens,"[10] to be depicted on the wall towards the church,

4. See I. Maull, "Le zecche dell'antica Ravenna (402/404–751 D.C.)," *FR, 84* (1961), 79–134; and most recently F. Panvini Rosati, "La produzione della zecca di Ravenna fino alla conquista bizantina della città," *Corsi* (1963), pp. 277–92.

5. "Iste [Ursus] primus hic initiavit tenplum construere Dei, ut plebes christianorum, que in singulis teguriis vagabat, in unum ovile piissimus colegeret pastor," *Codex pontificalis ecclesiae ravennatis*, ed. A. Testi-Rasponi, in *Raccolta degli storici italiani*, 2 part 3, fasc. 196, 197, 200 (Bologna, 1924), p. 65 (henceforth abbreviated as *Codex*). This edition, easily the best one of Agnellus' chronicle, was unfortunately never completed. For the sake of consistency all citations other than those from *Codex* will be made from the earlier edition by O. Holder-Egger, in *Monumenta historiae germanica, Scriptores rerum langobardicarum et italicarum* (Hanover, 1878), pp. 265–391 (hereafter, "Holder-Egger"). There is no English edition of Agnellus; the translation in every case is by me.

6. For the port of Classis, see especially: *Convegno per lo studio della zona archeologica di Classe a mezzo dell'aerofotografia* (Faenza, 1962); and for the early Christian community of Classis: G. B. Rossi, "Il primitivo cimitero cristiano di Ravenna presso S. Apollinare in Classe," *BAC, 3*

(series 9, 1879), 98–117; and F. Lanzoni, *Le Diocesi d'Italia* (Faenza, 1927), pp. 452–54.

7. See summary of present knowledge of the Basilica Probi in R. Farioli, "Ravenna paleocristiana scomparsa," *FR, 82* (1960), esp. pp. 8–9 with notes. Also idem, "Due antichi edifici di culto ancora da rintracciare nel territorio di Classe: La 'Basilica Probi' e la chiesa di S. Severo," *Studi storici, topografici ed archeologici sul "Portus Augusti" di Ravenna e sul territorio classicano* (Faenza, 1961), pp. 87–106.

8. "Lapidibus presissimis parietibus circumdebit, super tocius templi testudinem [apse] tesellis varis diversas figuris compossuit. Omnis autem populus quasi vir unus, spontaneus animus laborabat lectans et gaudens, et de celis Deum cunlaudabat, qui a prosperabatur salus in manibus eorum per intercessionem sui sacerdotis et confesoris," *Codex*, p. 66. For the Basilica Ursiana, see especially G. L. Amadesi, *Metropolitana di Ravenna* (Bologna, 1748); M. Mazzotti, "La cripta della Basilica Ursiana di Ravenna," *FR, 55* (1951), 5–49; G. Bovini, "Qualche appunto sull'antica Cattedrale di Ravenna," *FR, 61* (1953), 59–84.

9. *Codex*, p. 77. See text, p. 11.

10. Psalm 148.

together with the Deluge. And on another wall . . . he caused the story of our Lord Jesus Christ to be depicted in colors, when with five loaves and two fishes He fed, as we read, so many thousands of people . . . And on another wall was depicted the story of the Apostle Peter.[11]

Nor was this all. The fifth-century monuments extant in Ravenna today, superb though they are, afford only feeble testimony to the feverish campaign of building and decorating initiated by Ursus. His immediate successor Peter I Chrysologos, considered by Testi-Rasponi to be as distinguished a bishop as Augustine of Carthage or Ambrose of Milan,[12] founded a cathedral in Classis, the Basilica Petriana, to supersede the earlier Basilica Probi. This cathedral, to quote Agnellus, "was surpassed by no other, either in length or in height."[13] For its own part the imperial court was no less active. In the midst of a new region, which extended beyond the western boundaries of the Roman city, now stood the imperial residence and the palatine church that was sponsored by the Empress Galla Placidia, mother of Valentinian III, and dedicated to the Holy Cross. The Empress possessed an unflagging zeal for building. Her enlightened patronage added appreciably to the artistic interest and activity of the new "Felix Ravenna." The chronicler Agnellus tells us that, having been ordered in a dream to erect a monastic church to St. Zaccharias, she obeyed instantly, and when she arrived at the designated spot she saw the foundations already excavated, as by the will of God. This edifice she completed and adorned magnificently.[14] And she built another church, to St. John the Evangelist, as an offering of thanks for her narrow escape from death during a seastorm on the Aegean; the apse contained portraits of the imperial family to which she belonged.[15]

Most of the monuments from this early phase of Ravenna's renascence were destroyed in subsequent centuries. A few suffered such radical changes in the course of their history that their initial design is irretrievably lost. The Basilica Ursiana itself was razed to the ground in the eighteenth century and replaced by the present cathedral. Of the episcopal complex commenced by Ursus, only the baptistery has come down to our day; the building itself and its sumptuous sheath of interior decoration in mosaic and stucco have survived in good condition for some fifteen hundred

---

11. "Istoriam psalmi, quam cotidie cantamus, idest: 'Laudate dominum de cellis,' una cum cataclismo in pariete, parte ecclesia, pingere iussit; et in alio pariete . . . exornari coloribus fecit istoriam domini nostri Yhesu Christi, quando de V. panibus et duobus piscibus tot milia, legimus, homines saciavit . . . Et in alia fronte depicta storia Petri apostoli," *Codex*, pp. 78–79. See F. Wickhoff, "Das Speisezimmer des Bischofs Neon von Ravenna," *Repertorium für Kunstwissenschaft, 17* (1894), 10–17, for an attempt at reconstructing this program. That the episcopal residence was initially begun by Ursus is understood from *Codex*, p. 68, "De Sancto Urso," ll. 21–23.

12. *FR, 30* (1925), 11. For the order of succes-

sion, compare below, Chap. 2, n. 9.

13. "Nulla eclesia in edificio maior fuit similis illa neque in longitudine, nec in altitudine . . ." *Codex*, p. 71.

14. *Codex*, pp. 117–19.

15. *Codex*, p. 128, 129 n. 1. For the mosaic programs of this and other churches, see E. Müntz, "The Lost Mosaics of Ravenna," *AJA, 1* (1885), 115–30; and more recently, G. Bovini, "Mosaici parietali scomparsi dagli antichi edifici sacri di Ravenna," *FR, 68* (1955), 54–76 and *FR, 69* (1955), 5–20. The church of St. John the Evangelist has been most recently studied by L. Scevola, "La Basilica di San Giovanni Evangelista a Ravenna," *FR, 87* (1963), 5–107.

years. The present study is devoted to this baptistery, the Baptistery of the Orthodox as it is often called to distinguish it from the later Arian building of similar function. It is known also as San Giovanni in Fonte, the Baptistery of the Cathedral, and the Neonian Baptistery after its renovator Bishop Neon of Ravenna.

The significance of the Orthodox Baptistery as an invaluable document from the formative centuries of Christian art cannot be overstressed. The high quality of its figural art alone, a program inferior to no other in this "early medieval Pompeii,"[16] claims the historian's serious attention. Furthermore, its chronological situation at the crossroads of the late antique and early medieval periods furnishes a capital opportunity for the study of the transition from the Imperial Roman to the Christian–Byzantine modes in art and architecture.[17] Finally, the question of Ravenna's precise role in the general development of Christian art in the two centuries after the Peace of the Church could be elucidated by the detailed study of this surviving early monument. In art-historical discussion so far, the practice has been to consider the art of Ravenna for the most part derivative, and to attempt to establish the centers which provided the greatest influence. The city's intimate association with the Italian centers as well as with those of the Eastern Mediterranean during the fifth and sixth centuries makes it difficult to decide on the ultimate source of its art. In the debate of *Orient oder Rom,* which was commenced a half-century ago and which continues to engage scholarly interest, Ravennate monuments have been claimed for both sides. It is well to remember, however, that the history of Ravennate art has had too long and determined a course to be explained solely in terms of transplanted creative energies. The probability needs to be considered seriously that Ravenna, like Alexandria, Constantinople, and Rome, may well have been a generative center in the later fifth and sixth centuries. The case for a discrete native tradition can be substantiated only through the cumulative evidence yielded by thorough examination of each existing monument in this pivotal city of the Early Christian world.

It is with these points in mind that the present work has been undertaken. It attempts to bring together all available material for a comprehensive exposition of the history of the Baptistery. It examines in detail the architecture, and the decorative scheme for which the monument is most famous. Finally, the effort is made to evaluate the Baptistery, first within the immediate context of Ravennate art; and second, within the broader context of the evolution of Byzantine style, whether in its early

---

16. The expression is the late Professor Morey's (*Early Christian Art* [2d ed. Princeton, 1953], p. 157).

17. It may be desirable to clarify from the start some points of terminology regarding periods and styles of art. Throughout the book the term "late antique" is used to refer to (a) the period of time roughly from the early Severans to Julian the Apostate, and (b) the non-Christian art produced during this period within the boundaries of the Roman Empire. The term corresponds also with the more specifically art-historical designation "spätantike," in use among German scholars, and carries the stylistic and formal connotations given to it by them. "Imperial Roman" covers the time and the art from Augustus to the late Antonines. The term "Early Christian" is applied to art with Christian imagery, irrespective of form. Nothing need be said at this point about the semantic complexities of "Byzantine" used as an art-historical term since it will be dealt with later in our discussion (see Chap. 6, esp. p. 134).

but already distinct manifestations in Justinianic art of the sixth century or in its later phases during the so-called Second Golden Age. The detailed consideration of the monument will itself yield, I believe, some valuable hints for comprehending those stylistic traits which W. Zaloziecky, H. Sedlmayr, and others have been investigating so imaginatively in their discussions of the art of the sixth century.[18]

Scholarly interest in the Orthodox Baptistery has been intermittent. Two short early monographs, by Corrado Ricci and Cesare Sangiorgi, 1889 and 1900 respectively, are largely descriptive and have long been outdated.[19] Some articles since then have considered one or another aspect of the monument. Of these a recent comprehensive study by Carla Casalone has attempted to evaluate the state of scholarship on problems of the Baptistery but, unhappily, it is in general a confused and unreliable account that creates new questions along with the specific contributions it makes.[20] The fabric of the building has been studied thoroughly by Monsignor Mario Mazzotti during the last few years; my own account of it is indebted to his careful work.[21] A more complete discussion of the bibliography of the Baptistery appears in a critical note at the end of this book, and the text itself will reveal, directly or indirectly, the relative weight of the authors cited there.

Before setting out on the history of the Orthodox Baptistery, it may be pertinent to add a brief word about similar edifices in Ravenna that preceded and followed it. Baptism prior to the Peace of the Church must have been an open-air ceremony there, a practice common in the early centuries of Christian history. The *Passio Sancti Apollinaris* informs us in fact that this first bishop and patron saint of Ravenna baptized the faithful in a river not far from the city and that "he also baptized in the sea."[22] Agnellus, who relies heavily on the *Passio* for his account of the saint's life, specifies the river as the Bedens, and continues: "he administered baptism, for the first time, in the church of Santa Eufemia which is called Ad Arietem, and where his feet stood that stone gave way and his footmarks were impressed upon it like a seal."[23] Agnellus refers to this church on three other occasions in his chronicle, once in the Life of Bishop Martin and again as "Ad Arietem," and twice as "beata Eufemia que vocatur ad Mare."[24] The building is to be identified almost certainly with the first

---

18. See Chap. 6, pp. 132–35 and nn. 8, 11.

19. C. Ricci, "Il Battistero di S. Giovanni in Fonte," *Atti per la Romagna*, series 3, 7, 268–319 (henceforth abbreviated as Ricci, "S. Giovanni"); C. Sangiorgi, *Il Battistero della Basilica Ursiana di Ravenna* (Ravenna, 1900; henceforth abbreviated as Sangiorgi, *Battistero*). Cf. Bibliographical Note, section 3.

20. C. Casalone, "Ricerche sul Battistero della Cattedrale di Ravenna," *Rivista dell'Istituto nazionale d'archeologia e storia dell'arte*, 8 (1959), 202–68 (henceforth cited as Casalone, "Ricerche").

21. M. Mazzotti, "Il Battistero della Cattedrale di Ravenna: Problemi architettonici e vicende del monumento," *Corsi* (1961), pp. 255–78.

22. For the text of the *Passio*, see L. A. Muratori, *Rerum italicarum scriptores*, I.2, 529–33. For its history and reliability, see E. Will, *Saint Apollinaire de Ravenne* (Paris, 1936), pp. 15 ff. with bibliography; and M. Mazzotti, "Per una nuova datazione della 'Passio S. Apollinaris,'" *Studi Romagnoli, 3* (1952), 123–29.

23. "In basilica beate Eufemie que vocatur Ad Arietem, primitus baptismum fecit, et ubi pedibus stetit, liquefactus est ille lapis et vestigia quasi signum inpresa sunt," *Codex*, p. 23 and n. 2.

24. The relevant passages are the following: (a) "Edificata est iam dicta basilica iuxta ardicam beate Eufemie que vocatur Ad mare, qua nunc demolitam esse videmus," *Codex*, pp. 36–37, in the Life of

baptistery of Ravenna, built adjacent to the Basilica Probi of Classis mentioned above. Its consecration to the sainted woman of Chalcedon must have come only after Classis was given a new baptistery by Bishop Peter II (494–after 518) as an addition to the Basilica Petriana which his earlier namesake Peter I Chrysologos had begun in the second quarter of the fifth century. But the memory of the first baptistery survived after its transformation into a church, and in fact S. Eufemia came to be considered as commemorating the very spot near the Adriatic Sea where St. Apollinaris himself administered baptism.[25]

The exact location and form of this initial baptistery are unknown; it was already destroyed by the time of Agnellus' account in the ninth century. It was followed by our own Orthodox Baptistery, within Ravenna proper, in the first half of the fifth century. The Baptistery of the Basilica Petriana, built by Bishop Peter II, must then be third in chronological order. Agnellus describes it as a large structure of square plan, with "double walls," probably a reference to an exterior ambulatory. Archbishop Victor (538–45) added to its decoration, and on two interior arches he inscribed the words SALVO DOMNO and PAPA VICTORE. Under the font was situated the tomb of the founder of the baptistery, Bishop Peter II.[26]

These three baptismal buildings attached to their churches—S. Eufemia to the Basilica Probi, the Orthodox Baptistery to the cathedral of Ursus, and the baptistery of Classis to the cathedral of Peter I Chrysologos—were all designed to serve the orthodox faith of the metropolis. The Gothic rule of Theodoric, however, was devoted to the heretical persuasion of Arianism. Their cathedral, the "Anastasis gothorum," built in the early sixth century in conscious emulation of the "Anastasis catholicorum." i.e. the Basilica Ursiana, also was equipped with an independent

---

Bishop Probus I. (b) "et sepultus est, ut asserunt quidam, in ardica beati Probi confessoris in civitate dudum Classis. In arca magna saxea ibidem positus fuit, iuxta ecclesia beatae Euphemiae, quae vocatur ad mare . . . quae nunc demolita est," Agnellus, ed. Holder-Egger ("De sancto Petro seniori"), p. 341. (c) "Munivit hic antistes ecclesiam beatae Eufemiae quae vocatur Ad Arietem, quam olim aqua dominabatur," ed. Holder-Egger ("De sancto Martino"), p. 387.

25. For a summary of our present knowledge of this first Ravennate baptistery, see R. Farioli, "Ravenna paleocristiana scomparsa," *FR, 82* (1960), 9–10, and nn.

26. This description comes from two passages: (a) "Edificavit hic beatisimus [Peter II] fontem in civitate Classis iuxta eclesiam que vocatur Petriana, quam Petrus antistes [Chrysologos] fundavit. Qui fons mira magnitudinis, duplicibus muris et altis menibus structis artmedice artis," *Codex*, p. 148. (b) "Fontem vero tetragonum, quem beatissimus Petrus Grisologus [sic] hedificavit in civitate Classis iuxta eclesiam Petrianam, iste [Bishop Victor] ornavit, et in medio cameris, parte virorum, subtus arcum orbita modica, in qua usque hodie

continetur ita: SALVO DOMNO—ex alio parte mulierum alia orbitella, ut supra, ex auratis literis invicem ex parte se respicientes a legentibus invenitur sic: PAPA VICTORE," *Codex*, pp. 183–84. See also *Codex*, pp. 73–75, for a description of the tomb as seen by Agnellus.

Among baptismal constructions in Ravenna, the Arian Baptistery is a certain example of "duplicibus muris." The possibility of such an ambulatory for the Orthodox Baptistery is discussed below, p. 39. The reference to the "art of arithmetic" (*artmedice artis*) is too general to throw any light on methods of construction in early Christian times. Where exactly were the arches with the inscriptions? *Medio cameris* almost certainly refers to the central body of the building which contained the font; and the *orbitellae* must be two of the arches that supported the vault over the font. Very interesting is the distinction made by Agnellus between "the side for men" and "the side for women" (*parte virorum . . . parte mulierum*). Testi-Rasponi believes that this statement confirms the existence of the ambulatory (*Codex*, p. 184 n. 2), but the distinction may refer simply to the practice in Agnellus' own time rather than Bishop Victor's.

baptismal hall.[27] This baptistery for the Arians of Ravenna was duly purified of heresy and reconciled to the Orthodox faith by Archbishop Agnellus (557–70), together with a number of other churches, after the downfall of the Goths.[28] As a result of the unification of the Church at this time, the Arian baptistery lost its reason for existence. It became the church for a group of Greek monks, assuming the designation of Santa Maria in Cosmedin.

Finally, among the Arian buildings purified by Archbishop Agnellus there was also the baptistery of the Gothic palatine church of St. Martin, later Sant'Apollinare Nuovo. Its exact position and appearance are unknown.[29]

A brief description of the Orthodox Baptistery at this point will be useful to clarify for its various parts the nomenclature to be used in the course of this study. Each part will, of course, be described at length in later chapters. The building has an octagonal body and four ground niches which yield, externally, a square plan with rounded corners (*Fig.* 14). Over the niches is a row of windows, one for every side of the octagon. Over these in turn the brick masonry is decorated with a band of blind arcading. This exterior ordering terminates in a tile roof surmounted by a simple cross (which in June 1963 replaced a seventh-century bronze cross, to be discussed later).

The interior scheme is a complex one, and can probably be best described with the aid of a diagrammatic drawing (*Fig.* 41). Architecturally the scheme consists of a cupola resting on two stories of arcades. The decoration, on the other hand, is arranged in four superposed tiers, and the medallion with the baptism of Christ in the center of the cupola. These tiers will be called Zones I through IV, and for the sake of convenience the medallion will be referred to as Zone V.

Zone I corresponds to the lower story of arcades. Eight broad arches spring from an equal number of columns placed at the corners of the octagon. A, B, C, and D on the diagram refer to the sides of the octagon where the niches mentioned above are to be found. These alternate with the flat sides, which have a paneling of *opus sectile* and are designated by A′, B′, C′, and D′. Over the arcades themselves is a mosaic border of acanthus *rinceaux,* and eight prophets, also in mosaic, which I have numbered 1 to 8 in counterclockwise sequence beginning at the present entrance to the Baptistery (Side D′).

Zone II corresponds to the second story of interior arcades and the eight windows.

27. The bibliography of the Arian Baptistery is listed by G. Bovini in "Principale bibliografia su Ravenna romana, paleocristiana e paleobizantina," *Corsi* (1962), p. 30. The best illustrative material is in F. W. Deichmann, *Frühchristliche Bauten und Mosaiken von Ravenna* (Baden-Baden, 1958), Pls. 249–73. The "Anastasis gothorum" is identifiable as the present church of Spirito Santo. See M. Mazzotti, "La 'Anastasis gothorum,'" *FR, 75* (1957), 25–62; and also idem, "L'Anastasis gothorum ed il suo battistero," *Corsi* (1957), fasc. 1, pp. 57–66.

28. *Codex,* pp. 216 ff. Especially: "Et ubi nunc est monasterium sancta et semper virginis intemerate Marie, fontes predicta martiris eclesia fuerunt . . ."

29. "Fontesque beati Martini eclesia ipse [Bishop Agnellus] reconciliavit et tesellis decoravit," *Codex,* p. 221. Testi-Rasponi's suggestion that yet another baptistery may have existed within the body of the Church of the Holy Cross (Santa Croce), built by Galla Placidia as mentioned on p. 3, is conjectural. Even if correct, it would not be an independent baptismal hall of the kind we are considering here (*Codex,* p. 119 n. 9).

Each side of the octagon at the level of Zone II is labeled with the same letter as that given to the corresponding side in Zone I (A, A′, B, B′, etc.). Here, however, each of the eight main arches is subdivided into a triple set of smaller arches, the central ones containing the windows. In the small arches flanking the windows there are aedicules in stucco containing single figures of prophets, also in stucco. There are sixteen prophets in Zone II (two to each side of the octagon), and they have been numbered again in counterclockwise sequence from the present door of the Baptistery.

Zones III through *V* are subdivisions of the mosaic scheme of the cupola. Zone III is made up of eight panels, corresponding to the sides of Zones I and II, and similarly labeled A, A′, B, B′, etc. This zone of mosaics features a framework of architectural motifs in which are placed thrones surmounted by crosses (Panels A, B, C, D) alternating with altars surmounted by open gospels (Panels A′, B′, C′, D′). Above this zone we see the twelve apostles bearing crowns and marching in two separate files of six, led by Sts. Peter and Paul (Zone IV). The apostles are marked on the diagram a, b, c, d, e, f, etc. in counterclockwise sequence beginning with St. Peter. Finally, the cupola scheme culminates in the central medallion containing the scene of the baptism of Christ (Zone V).

THE HISTORY OF
THE ORTHODOX BAPTISTERY

The fifteen-hundred-year history of the Orthodox Baptistery can be drafted from two main classes of materials: written tradition and the archaeological evidence derived from a close study of the building's fabric. We are concerned in this chapter with the first of these classes which can be grouped, for convenience, under four headings.

Historical notices. Early descriptions of the Baptistery are included by most of Ravenna's native chroniclers in their compilations of local events, accounts of major families, stories of monuments, and even legends and miracles. Of these chroniclers the earliest is the indispensable, but by no means always reliable, Agnellus (ninth century), already cited above. Others are Girolamo Rossi (sixteenth century); Girolamo Fabri and Serafino Pasolini (seventeenth century); and Antonio Zirardini, Francesco Beltrami, and Benedetto Fiandrini (eighteenth century).[1]

Epigraphy. The reconstruction of the Baptistery's early history is aided by the several inscriptions that appear on parts of the building itself. Aside from the famous but no longer extant dedicatory verses of Bishop Neon, there are three monograms in the niches of Zone I, an inscription incised on the bronze cross which until recently surmounted the roof (and now is displayed on a capital in Niche A), and another inscription on the architrave of the present door.

Documents. For the past five hundred years of the monument's history this is by far the most important category. Church documents—accounts of archiepiscopal visitations, inventories, expense accounts, and official and private letters—are housed in

---

1. G. Rossi, *Historiarum ravennatum libri* (Venice, 1589); G. Fabri, *Le Sagre Memorie di Ravenna antica* (Venice, 1664); S. Pasolini, *Lustri ravennati dall'anno seicento doppo l'Universal Diluvio fino all'anno mile di Nostra Salute* (Bologna, 1678); A. Zirardini, *Degli Antichi Edifici profani di Ravenna* (Faenza, 1726); F. Beltrami, *Il Forestiere instruito delle cose notabili della città di Ravenna e suburbane della medesima* (Ravenna, 1783); B. Fiandrini, "Annali ravennati dalla fondazione della città fino alla fine del secolo XVIII" (Ravenna, 1794), MS in the Biblioteca Classense.

two separate archives: the Archivio Arcivescovile in the archiepiscopal palace, and the Archivio del Battistero in the rectory for the parish of San Giovanni in Fonte. Most of these documents can be consulted in their original form. Some have been preserved secondhand by conscientious clergymen in manuscript collections, of which the "Raccolta da una miscellanea del Battistero," kept in the Biblioteca Classense, should be especially noted.[2] (In Appendix 2 the more important church documents have been transcribed in chronological order and will be referred to by their designated numbers in the subsequent discussion.)

In addition, the Superintendency of Monuments at Ravenna (with offices at San Vitale) preserves drawings and photographs of the more recent repairs and restorations officially undertaken.

Travel books and vedute. Compared to more celebrated cities like Rome and Florence, Ravenna received little attention from early visitors to Italy. In the eyes of the uninitiated traveler, her ruins were neither sufficiently spectacular nor numerous enough to justify a visit. Mentions of the Orthodox Baptistery in early travel books are therefore rare. Then too, the period of ridicule and scorn for things Byzantine, led by eighteenth-century French authors like Montesquieu and Voltaire, had its effect on the more informed traveler.[3] H. Taine, who visited Ravenna during his Italian sojourn of 1864, found no word of praise for its nonclassic art. The Christian artist of the Orthodox Baptistery, he wrote, probably had some pagan model to look at, "but his eyes, dimmed by the tyranny of mystical ideas, followed the contours [of his model] which his hand, tremulous and heavy, could not and dared not trace but inadequately."[4]

The earliest substantial description of the Baptistery is that written by Giovanni Giustino Ciampini in the late seventeenth century.[5] His work deserves better than to be classed with popular travel books; it is in fact one of the first serious books on Early Christian mosaics. For us its significance lies in the fact that it includes some engravings designed to illustrate his description. These and a very crude engraving by Vincenzo Coronelli, reproduced in an early eighteenth-century edition of Fabri's *Ravenna ricercata*, appear to be the only illustrations of the Baptistery published before 1800.[6]

To the group of early vedute belong also two drawings (one extant in the Archivio Arcivescovile, the other, almost identical, preserved in an old photograph [*Fig. 37*]),

---

2. A note in Ricci's *Tavole* (2, 11 n. 2) states that there are two copies of this compilation. The note gives the title of the work and then continues: "ms. nell'Archivio del Battistero medesimo, e copia presso noi." I have been unable to locate the second copy.

3. See, for example, A. A. Vasiliev, *History of the Byzantine Empire* (Madison, 1952), pp. 6 ff.

4. *Voyage en Italie* (Paris, 1866), 2, 285: "Peut-être l'artiste chrétien avait-il sous les yeux quelque peinture païenne, et ses yeux, obscurcis par la tyran-nie des idées mystiques, suivaient des contours que sa main tremblotante, appesantie, ne pouvait et n'osait plus tracer qu'à demi."

5. *Vetera monimenta in quibus praecipuè musiva opera sacrarum* (Rome, 1690–99), pp. 233–38; reprinted with the same engravings in a second edition, Rome, 1747.

6. G. Fabri, *Ravenna ricercata o vero compendio istorico delle cose più notabili dell'antica città di Ravenna*, n.p., n.d. [1707]. The first edition was published in Bologna, 1678.

which depict the interior of the building as it should have appeared at the end of the eighteenth century. In the following century, especially after 1850, illustrative prints of the Baptistery became frequent, and in 1880 the first color plate of the interior decoration was published.[7]

ORIGINS AND EARLY HISTORY

Neon's inscription

The written history of the Baptistery begins with Agnellus in the ninth century. In his "Life of Bishop Neon" he provides us with the only direct reference to the building and its decoration:

> Fontes Ursiana ecclesia pulcerime decoravit. Musiva et auratis tesselis apostolorum immagines et nomina camera circumfinxit, parietes promiscuis lapidibus cinxit. Nomen ipsius lapideis descriptum est helementis.
>
> CEDE VETUS NOMEN, NOVITATI CEDE VETUSTAS.
> PULCRIUS ECCE NITET RENOVATI GLORIA FONTIS.
> MAGNANIMUS HUNC NANQUE NEOM SUMMUSQUE SACERDOS
> EXQUOLUIT, PULCRO CONPONENS OMNIA CULTU.[8]

This might be rendered into English as follows:

> He [Neon] beautifully decorated the Baptistery of the Basilica Ursiana. With mosaics and golden tesserae he fashioned the images and the names of the apostles around the vault, and covered the walls with various stones. His name is inscribed in mosaic [?].
>
> Old name, begone; antiquity, yield to the new.
> The glory of the renovated font now gleams with greater beauty.
> For the noble and highest priest Neon
> Adorned it, arranging all most splendidly.

Setting aside for the moment Agnellus' introductory comments, let us concentrate on the inscription itself. Clearly, it was a commemorative verse intended to record a major renovation of the Baptistery by Bishop Neon. It can be inferred therefore that the Baptistery already existed when Neon commenced his episcopate, and that Neon carried out some alterations in order to make it more beautiful.

When precisely was the Baptistery erected? The *terminus ante* is the year of Neon's accession to the episcopal throne of Ravenna (about 451). Since the Baptistry should be thought of as a constituent element in the great cathedral complex launched by Ursus, the *terminus post* must be some time during his episcopate. Ursus' dates,

---

7. For early prints, see Bibliographical Note, Section 5; the color plate is in H. Koehler, *Polychrome Meisterwerke der monumentalen Kunst in* *Italien vom V. bis XVI. Jahrhundert* (Leipzig, 1880), Pl. 1.

8. *Codex*, pp. 77–78.

however, are controversial. One group of scholars agrees on 389 or 396 as the year of his death, while Testi-Rasponi favors a later date, 426 or 429.[9] An Ursonion attribution of the Baptistery furthermore is not necessarily warranted. The possibility should not be overlooked that the Baptistery, although intended from the start, was not completed, or even begun, in Ursus' episcopate but some time between his death and the accession of Neon.[10] In view of these uncertainties, the date for the initial structure can be no more specific than the first half of the fifth century, the fifty or sixty years prior to the beginning of Neon's episcopate.

This initial stage of the monument's history was further confused by a theory first set forth by Corrado Ricci in 1889, which was generally accepted by subsequent stu-

9. See Testi-Rasponi, "Note marginali al 'Liber pontificalis' di Agnello ravennate, XI," *Atti per la Romagna, 3.28* (1910), 281 ff.; and idem, "Note agnelliane, III. I vescovi ravennati del V secolo," *FR, 18* (1915), 773–78. The earlier date has been championed, against his theory, by E. Stein, "Beiträge zur Geschichte von Ravenna in spätrömischer und byzantinischer Zeit. I. Chronologie der ravennatischen Bischöfe vom Ende des vierten bis zur Mitte des achten Jahrhunderts," *Klio, 16* (1920), 40 ff.; and after him by A. W. Byvanck in *Mededeelingen van het Nederlandsch Historisch Instituut te Rome, 8* (1928), 61–73. Cf. also H. L. Gonin, *Excerpta agnelliana* (Utrecht [1933]), "Introduction." The controversy centers around the statement in Agnellus that Bishop Ursus died on an Easter day which fell on the thirteenth of April: "Post hec vero omnia consumata et edificia pleniter constructa, infirmitatem modicam sensit corporis, quasi eructuans reddidit spiritum Idus Aprilis. In tale pace et tranquilitate vitam finivit in die sancte Resurectionis" (*Codex*, p. 68 and n. 9). Easter fell in April in the years 389, 396, 398, 402, 410, 413, 415, 418, 424, 426, and 429. Up to Testi-Rasponi's day, 389 was the favorite choice. This however left a gap of sixty years between the death of Ursus and the next solid piece of evidence, a letter from Peter Chrysologos to Eutyches, dated 449 (Migne, *PL, 52,* col. 71). Holder-Egger, in his edition, fills the gap with two dubious bishops, another Peter and a John I. Testi-Rasponi's refutation of Holder-Egger, and therefore also of the later Stein who depends on him, seems to me to be justified. Historical facts are also more in accordance with the later date for Ursus' pontificate: that the great building activity initiated by him (see above, p. 2) should belong to the years after the transfer of the capital to Ravenna (A.D. 402) seems more logical on all counts. A similar stand in favor of Testi-Rasponi has previously been taken by other, mostly Italian, scholars, among them C. Casalone ("Ricerche," p. 204) and G. Bovini (*FR, 61* [1953], 60). A table of parallel chronologies for the fifth century follows for the sake of comparison.

Bishops	Testi-Rasponi	Stein	Byvanck	Gonin
Ursus	d. 426 or 429	d. 396	369/70–396	undecided
[John I]		396–after 431	ca. 400–ca. 432	
Petrus I	ca. 429–451	after 432–450	ca. 433–450/51	ca. 432–451
Neon	ca. 451–after 459	24 Oct. 458*	ca. 451–ca. 475	451–ca. 473
Exuperantius	?–477	d. 26 May 477	ca. 475–477	ca. 473–477
John II	477–494	477–494	477–494	477–494
Petrus II	494–after 518	494–520	494–520	494–519

* Date of letter from Pope Leo the Great to Neon (Migne, *PL, 54,* col. 1191).

10. Zirardini seems to be the first to start the idea of an Ursonian construction: "Ab Urso episcopo aedificatum credere par est" (n. 1 above, Chap. 1, p. 3). Beltrami explains that since Ursus built the cathedral, it can be assumed that he also built the Baptistery (n. 1 above, p. 30). From then on this view is commonly held. Adriana Ghezzo suggests in her recent article (*FR, 86* [1962], 7–8) that proof of such an attribution is found in Agnellus' "Life of Ursus," where it is said, "post hec vero omnia consumata et edificia pleniter constructa" (*Codex*, p. 68). Now since the "Life" credits Ursus specifically with the construction of one building only (the cathedral) the plural *edificia*, she reasons, must imply other structures as well, most likely the Baptistery. But why not the episcopal palace which is first mentioned by Agnellus in the "Life of Ursus," and which was certainly not extant before him? "Habitabat autem sanctisimus vir [Ursus] infra episcopium . . . mira magnitudine et tota edificiali madicho constructa . . ." (*Codex*, p. 68).

dents and went unchallenged until recently, having found its way into the handbooks. Ricci maintained that the Baptistery originally had been a *laconicum* (sweating room) within a Roman bath complex, that it was transformed by Bishop Neon into a Christian cult building, and that the "cede vetus nomen" in the Neonian inscription implied just such an alteration of a pagan edifice. He proposed to read *exsolvit* (i.e. unbound, set free) for *exquoluit* (corrupt form of *excolvit*, i.e. adorned), and took *conponens* to mean "redeeming or arranging." His translation therefore reads: "For the magnanimous and highest priest Neon freed it [the Baptistery], setting it in order for the generous or glorious worship."[11]

The arguments proffered by Ricci to substantiate his theory can be listed as follows:

(1) Roman baths of undetermined date existed in the area where the Basilica Ursiana was later built. Neon altered one room into a baptistery, and Archbishop Victor (538–45), as is recorded in Agnellus, renovated and decorated the remaining parts of these baths.

(2) Excavations conducted by F. Lanciani disclosed an antique floor 3 meters below the present floor of the Baptistery.[12] Since the original pavement of the so-called Mausoleum of Galla Placidia lies only 1.43 meters below the modern one, the original pavement of San Vitale only 0.96 meter below, and that of the Arian Baptistery only 2 meters below, it must be deduced that the antique floor of the Orthodox Baptistery, being deeper, belongs to a much earlier date than the fifth–sixth centuries when these other buildings were erected; that is to say, it belongs to Roman times.

(3) There is analogical evidence from other Christian baptisteries which were similarly transformed from pagan bath units.

(4) The octagonal plan of the Orthodox Baptistery with the four original entrances and the four corner niches has parallels in the architecture of Roman baths.

(5) Names given to baths by the Greeks (λουτρόν, κολυμβήθρα) and by the Romans (*balneum, piscina, baptisterium*) correspond to the names applied by the Christians to their baptismal structures.

It is to be noted that arguments (3), (4), and (5) are only secondary to the specific instance of the Orthodox Baptistery. Against (3) it could be pointed out that evidence also exists that some Christian baptisteries were *not* transformed from Roman bath

---

11. "S. Giovanni," p. 271: "poichè il magnanimo e sommo sacerdote Neone lo liberò, ordinandolo a generoso o glorioso culto." For another early interpretation of "cede vetus nomen," see G. Berti, *Sull'Antico Duomo di Ravenna e il battistero e l'Episcopio e il Tricolo* (Ravenna, 1880; hereafter cited as Berti, *Sull'antico duomo*), pp. 48–49, where the meaning is understood to be that the building could no longer be called after its founder, Ursus, but necessarily after Neon, its renovator.

Five years after Ricci's article appeared, F. X. Kraus first agreed in print with the bath theory, concluding that "Die Abhandlung ist besonders lehrreich für die Beziehungen der christlichen Taufkirchen zu den Bädern der Alten," *Repertorium für Kunstwissenschaft, 17* (1894), 56. By 1931 Ricci could boast that his theory "quale abbiam dato più di quarant'anni or sono . . . è stato accolto da quanti, in seguito, hanno scritto intorno a quel battistero," and lists the names of Kraus, Sangiorgi, Testi-Rasponi, Galassi, and Gerola (*Tavole, 2* [Rome, 1931], 4 and n. 3). Lavagnino goes a step farther and claims that "recenti scavi ne [of the Baptistery] hanno dimostrato l'origine pagana"! (*L'Arte medioevale* [Turin, 1949], p. 84).

12. See Lanciani, *Cenni intorno ai monumenti e alle cose più notabili di Ravenna* (Ravenna, 1871; hereafter *Cenni*), pp. 7–8; and *BAC, 4* (1866), 73; also below, pp. 26, 36.

units, that in fact the practice is the exception rather than the rule. In reference to (4), research since Ricci's day has shown the architectural typology of baptisteries to be more complex than was once believed (see Chapter 3). The plan of the Orthodox Baptistery belongs, as we shall see, in a broad typological family that includes octagonal chambers in Roman villas and baths as well as Roman mausolea. As for (5), it is explained by the fact that the sacrament of baptism was a form of bathing, with a deeply religious significance, and that therefore to the late antique mind current nomenclature for baths would be, by association, also applicable to baptisteries. There are other examples of Roman secular terms which were borrowed and sanctified by the early Christians: *basilica* is the classic instance. Such terminology almost always refers to functional, not formal, relationships between pagan antecedents and Christian descendants.

The prior existence of Roman baths in the cathedral area and the question of superposed floors are the only two immediate arguments in Ricci's case. It is of course not impossible that, before Ursus' campaign of building, the area of his episcopal complex should be occupied by a Roman thermal establishment. Part of the Roman city wall was disclosed in recent excavations under the apse of the Basilica Ursiana, but Monsignor Mazzotti's recent objection to the existence of baths because of this proximity to the city walls is unjustified.[13] What is more essential is the complete lack of archaeological evidence for such early baths in this area. Literary evidence is also inconclusive. The most useful and earliest reference to baths is in Agnellus' account of Archbishop Victor's episcopate (538–45), quoted by Ricci in support of his theory, as mentioned above:

> And he [Archbishop Victor] restored the baths which were adjacent to the church [i.e. the Basilica Ursiana] and attached to the walls of the episcopium where he resided.[14]

From this it is inferred that the baths were built before Victor and that they were built to abut on the walls of the episcopal residence. Almost certainly the "episcopium" here spoken of is the same that had been under construction since the days of Ursus, the one to which Neon added the Quinque Accubita with its richly painted refectory (p. 2). The baths which Victor restored must have stood, as did the episcopium, south of the cathedral (*Fig.* 12) and need date no earlier than the time of Ursus. Testi-Rasponi suggested, however, that the episcopium here referred to may have been a later one, north of the cathedral, toward the present Via d'Azeglio. Indeed in this region there was an "aditum balnei," to judge from two mentions in documents from the eleventh and twelfth centuries.[15] Unfortunately, the suggestion

---

13. M. Mazzotti, "Il Battistero della Cattedrale di Ravenna," *Corsi* (1961), p. 256.

14. "Refecitque balneum iuxta domum ecclesie, herens parietibus muri episcopi, ubi residebat" (*Codex*, p. 183). Other references to baths in Agnellus are too general to be of help: e.g. in the "Life of Bishop Thedorus" ("De Sancto Theodoro"), ed. Holder-Egger, p. 356.

15. *Codex*, p. 183 n. 1. The documents date from 1003 and 1186 and are cited, respectively, in A. Zirardini, *Degli Antichi Edifici profani di Ravenna* (modern ed., Ravenna, 1908–09; originally Faenza, 1726), p. 179; and M. Fantuzzi, *Monumenti ravennati de' secoli di mezzo per la maggior parte inediti*, 2 (Venice, 1801–04), 156.

for this additional episcopium is entirely gratuitous. From the end of the fifth to the middle of the sixth century the bishops of Ravenna, including Victor, were occupied with the construction of Tricolli, the magnificent episcopal palace conceived as an enlargement of the earlier Ursonian residence. It is improbable that only a short distance from the cathedral and in the opposite direction a second palace should be undertaken. But even allowing for this different situation of the episcopium, we still remain completely in the dark as to the date of the baths built adjacent to it and renovated by Victor in the early sixth century, and we have no reason to assume that they were of Roman date.

This leads to the final argument set forth by Ricci—the question of superposed floors. It should be pointed out that the rise of level due to alluvial deposits has not been the same in all sections of Ravenna. Ricci himself had to face this problem when he realized that the original pavement of the Arian Baptistery, built about A.D. 500, was 2 meters below the present ground level, whereas the pavement of the "Mausoleum of Galla Placidia," built half a century earlier, was only 1.43 meters below. Ricci was therefore forced to postulate that the Arian Baptistery was also converted from a pre-existing bathing hall that belonged to the house of "Drocdone," another dubious proposition.[16]

The answer to the specific instance of the Orthodox Baptistery was given by Monsignor Mazzotti during his recent excavation in the crypt of the Basilica Ursiana, when he affirmed that the original fifth-century pavement of the cathedral lay 3.55 meters under the present eighteenth-century pavement. It will be remembered that Lanciani found the earliest pavement of the Baptistery 3 meters below the modern ground level. By Ricci's logic, therefore, Baptistery and cathedral, now that they are proved to have been originally about at the same ground level, must be considered contemporaneous constructions.[17]

This discussion can now be concluded by returning to our point of departure, the Neonian inscription preserved by Agnellus. If Ricci's case for a pagan origin of the Orthodox Baptistery is untenable, what can be said about the special reading that he chose to give to the inscription?

Exquoluit. The only variant for this word in the surviving manuscripts of Agnellus is *excoluit.* Ricci's reading of *exsolvit,* presumably in the Codex of the Biblioteca Estense in Modena, is mistaken.

Conponens. Although *componere* could sometimes mean "to quiet, settle, reconcile," it is not commonly used, in Ravennate texts at any rate, to refer to the redemption of a pagan or heretical building to the orthodox faith. *Reconciliare* is the

---

16. Ricci deduced this from Agnellus' comment: "Infra urbem vero Ravenam, ecclesiam sancti Theodori non longe a domo Drocdonis, qua domus una cum balneo et sancti Appolenaris monasterio," etc. (*Codex,* p. 217). The passage reveals nothing about the date of the baths. Their location is not easy to determine either. Testi-Rasponi thinks the baths were "di fianco e dietro la basilica [church of Spirito Santo]," and calls the identification of the

antique wall near the Arian Baptistery as the remains of Drocdone's house, a "grossolano errore" (ibid., p. 217 n. 6).

17. M. Mazzotti, "La cripta della Basilica Ursiana," *FR,* 55 (1951), 44 ff., and bibliography cited there. A similar conclusion was reached much earlier by the author of an unpublished note entitled "Relazione sulla profondità del pavimento," in "Raccolta," pp. 32 ff.

standard verb in such cases; it is repeatedly used in the "Life of Archbishop Agnellus" (557–70), under whom Ravenna was purged of Arianism and many Arian churches purified of their heresy. The passage describing the purification of the church of St. Martin (later Sant'Apollinare Nuovo) clearly distinguishes the meaning of the two verbs: "Igitur *reconciliavit* beatisimus Agnellus pontifex . . . eclesia sancti Martini confesoris, quam Theodoricus rex fundavit . . . et pavimentum lithostratis mira *composuit*." (Then his Holiness Archbishop Agnellus *purified* the church of St. Martin the Confessor, which King Theodoric had built . . . and *adorned* [literally "arranged, disposed"] its pavement wonderfully with tesselated stones.)[18]

Cultu. The word *cultus* can of course mean either "physical shape, care, adornment," or "worship, faith." In our inscription however, "pulcro conponens omnia cultu," given the meaning of *conponens* as discussed above, should be taken to refer to form rather than faith. The phrasing might be compared to the epigraph that Archbishop Victor placed on the baths that he renovated:

VICTOR APOSTOLICA TUTUS VIRTUTE SACERDOS
BALNEA PARVA PRIUS PRISCO VETUSTA LABORE
DEPONENTE, MIRAQUE TAMEN NOVITATE REFECIT,
PULCRIOR UT CULTUS MAIORQUE RESURGAT AB IMO.[19]

Here too the adjective *pulcrior* (more beautiful) in reference to *cultus* has clearly a physical, not a spiritual, connotation.

Vetustas–novitas. Ricci's interpretation of this dichotomy in the Neonian verse as referring to the Christianization of a pagan monument is improbable. In Victor's inscription just cited the same relationship of the old and the new denotes specifically the restoration of a secular building. At least in two other instances similar wording is applied to religious buildings simply to denote restoration. One was an inscription at the church of S. Pietro in Vincoli, the first line of which closely resembles the beginning of our own Neonian verse and carries no pagan frame of reference:

CEDE PRIUS NOMEN NOVITATI CEDE VETUSTAS[20]

This line was also put together from fragments of an inscription discovered in a church in Numidia.[21]

---

18. *Codex*, p. 218. The italics are mine.
19. *Codex*, p. 183.
20. The inscription, which used to be above the west door, commemorated the reconstruction of the church by Sixtus III; for the full text see G. B. de Rossi, *Inscriptiones christianae urbis Romae*, 2.1 (Rome, 1888), p. 110 no. 67; also ibid., p. 134. Ricci himself observed that the Neonian inscription "ripete quasi testualmente il primo verso di quella di Sisto III per i ristauri di S. Pietro in Vincoli a Roma" (*Tavole, 2, 4*), but he seemed unaware

that this fact contradicted his special reading of the Neonian inscription.
21. See G. B. de Rossi, "Epigrafe di una chiesa dedicata agli apostoli Pietro e Paolo," *BAC* (1878), pp. 14–22. That the church was reconstructed over an earlier one is made clear by the third line of the same inscription: HAEC PETRI PAULIQUE SEDES CRISTO LIBENTE RESURSIT. For a similar use of "vetustas-novitas" see also Paulinus of Nola, *Carmen 8, 203* ff. (R. C. Goldschmidt, *Paulinus' Churches at Nola* [Amsterdam, 1940], pp. 82–83).

The foregoing discussion has shown, I believe, that Ricci's theory regarding the early history of the Orthodox Baptistery is unfounded. Without the support of further evidence, there seems no just cause to doubt that it was originally destined as a Christian cult building, nor to set its date any earlier than the episcopate of Ursus.

Three points remain to be considered regarding the Neonian inscription: its form, its exact location, and the date of its disappearance from the monument.

The form of the inscription must be deduced from the phrase *lapideis helementis* in Agnellus' descriptive remarks which precede the transcription of the verses. Ricci takes it to mean that the inscription was incised on stone or on marble.[22] Sangiorgi prefers to read "letters in mosaic."[23] Testi-Rasponi, while understanding "mosaics," suggests that the phrase refers to Neon's monogram in Niche C of Zone I.[24] I think it quite unlikely that *lapideis helementis* refers to anything but the inscription which immediately follows it. *Lapideis* does not ordinarily mean "in mosaic." When this form of inscription is being discussed Agnellus is usually explicit (*auratis tesselis nomina; literis aureis; tessellis exaratum*[25]). Incised inscriptions are understood either from the context (for example in his transcription of epitaphs) or because an explicative word makes the sense clear (*literis marmore exaratis*[26]). In the case of the Orthodox Baptistery the meaning of the Agnellian phrase remains ambiguous. I prefer "mosaic" for the reasons that such an inscription would be more in keeping with the rest of the decoration, and also because one early chronicler, S. Pasolini in the seventeenth century when the removal of the inscription was of more recent memory, explicitly speaks of "the four verses which are in mosaic."[27] Textually the reading may also be permissible since, in one other passage of Agnellus, during the description of the interior decoration of Sant'Apollinare Nuovo, a similar use of *lapideis* almost certainly refers to mosaics.[28]

The placement of the inscription is also uncertain. More than once in the eighteenth century it was described as being "over the door, on the inside."[29] The inscription was then no longer extant, and one can only accept this late statement on faith. It is not unlikely, however, that Neon's verses were placed inside, over the present door where the *opus sectile* of Side D′ is now seen. This arrangement would be in

---

22. *Tavole, 2, 3.*

23. *Battistero,* p. 39, where he goes as far as to say that the letters were "a mosaico dorato sopra fondo parimente a mosaico di color turchino carico."

24. *Codex,* p. 77 n. 14.

25. Cf. *Codex,* p. 77 line 7; p. 97 line 39; p. 183 line 30; p. 184 line 46; etc.

26. *Codex,* p. 224 line 114.

27. Pasolini (above, n. 1), p. 124: "quattro versi che vi sono in musaico." I do not see the relevance of Ricci's strange comment: "scrivendo egli [Pasolini] a tavolino, sulla scorta delle storie di Girolamo Rossi, senza, cioè, curarsi di controllare nel monumento, equivocava" (*Tavole, 2, 3*); especially since Rossi's very short description of the Baptistery con-

tains no statement as to the form of the Neonian inscription. Ricci's comment must derive from Ciampini, *Vetera monimenta,* p. 234: "Seraphinus Pasolini, qui in aliquibus pene ad verbum Hieronymi [G. Rossi] spectator est . . ."

28. "In tribunali vero . . . super fenestras invenietis ex lapideis litteritis exaratum ita . . ." (*Codex,* p. 219).

29. Sangiorgi, *Battistero,* p. 41, quotes two such descriptions from the inventories of the rector Prospero Grossi. Cf. also Document 9 of Jan. 22, 1741. Fifty years later B. Fiandrini (above, n. 1), 2, 264, arbitrarily comments that Neon's verses were "incisi sull'architrave della porta."

accord with a number of other Early Christian monuments which had similarly placed inscriptions, for example Santa Croce in Ravenna and Santa Sabina in Rome.[30]

In 1664 Girolamo Fabri wrote: "Neon renovated [the Orthodox Baptistery] as is proved by the four verses that once could be read here."[31] How much earlier than this the inscription disappeared is impossible to say. Most probably, it was destroyed when the door of the Baptistery was raised in the sixteenth century.

The period after Neon

From the death of Bishop Neon to about 1500 very little is on record concerning the state of the Baptistery. It is inevitable that some restorations or renovations should have been undertaken during this silent millenium. At some time, indeed, the exterior wall was raised to its present height; at some time one, or even two, of the corner niches was destroyed because of encroaching structures. Yet one finds no note of these changes in the written sources. This lack of adequate information has impelled the students of the Baptistery to infer too much from the few scraps of evidence that we do possess for this period.

Maximian's monogram. One such piece of evidence is a monogram in mosaic on the arch of Niche D in Zone I (*Fig.* 105), which is one of three set in the middle of the scriptural inscriptions that run on the niche arches of Sides A, C, and D. (Side B of Zone I has an inscription but no monogram [*Fig.* 103].) The inscriptions themselves will be discussed in a later chapter, but monograms are dealt with at this point so far as they can be considered indicative of work carried out in the Baptistery.

It should be said initially that the greater part of the mosaic of Zone I has been drastically restored in modern times. Of the inscriptions under discussion only minor sections retain their original fifth-century form.[32] The same applies to the monograms. Any conclusions that may be derived from their presence must remain tentative in view of their substantial restoration by Felice Kibel in the early 1860s.

Of the three monograms, that on Side C (*Fig.* 104) has caused the least concern. It can easily be read as "Neon Episcopus Dei famulus" (Bishop Neon, servant of God). Given Neon's interest in the Baptistery it is not surprising that this monogram should appear as part of the interior decoration. The second monogram (*Fig.* 106), however, was restored by Kibel in its entirety. Testi-Rasponi, who was close to the scene for at least half a century, pronounced it "guastato nel restauro."[33] In its present form, the letters P T E S and O can be discerned; it has been read as "Episcopus" (Ricci) and "Petrus Episcopus" (Barbier de Montault, Casalone) and has been thought to refer to Bishop Peter I Chrysologos.[34] Long before Kibel's restoration,

30. For S. Croce, no longer extant, see *Codex*, p. 121: "Et in fronte ipsius tenpli, introeuntes pili ianuas . . ."

31. Page 214 (see above, n. 1): "Neone . . . lo rinovò come dimostrano i quattri versi che già cui si leggevano."

32. Cf. Ricci, *Tavole*, 2, Pls. 14 ff.

33. *Codex*, Pl. 1 opposite p. 78.

34. Ricci, "S. Giovanni," p. 300; X. Barbier de Montault, "Baptistère de la Cathédrale," *RAC* (1896), p. 85; Casalone, "Ricerche," p. 209.

however, Ciampini reported it as a composite of the letters B N E S[35] (*Fig.* 26). It seems certain, therefore, that we shall be unable to decipher this particular monogram accurately.

The third monogram has been read as "Maximianus" by more than one scholar, and has been identified with Archbishop Maximian, the well-known pastor of Ravenna in the sixth century, who is a prominent figure beside the Emperor Justinian in one of the mosaic panels in the bema of San Vitale. From this identification it has been assumed that Maximian carried out work of restoration in the Baptistry a century after the completion of its form by Bishop Neon. The present arrangement of Zone II in a series of triple arches has been attributed, first in an unpublished thesis by Gino Gamberini and subsequently by C. Casalone, to this Maximianic renovation.[36]

It appears to this writer that the faith placed in this one monogram is largely unwarranted. The accuracy with which it has been restored, for one thing, is not beyond question.[37] Neither can the identification be considered irreproachable. The monogram does not compare well with two other surviving monograms of Archbishop Maximian, one on the celebrated ivory throne and the other on the pulvin from the monastery of Sant'Andrea in Ravenna (*Fig.* 27). These show both forks of the M crossed, thus forming two distinct A's, whereas the monogram of the Baptistery has only one fork crossed. More important, the other monograms include the modifying title *episcopus* in their pattern; this one leaves out the title completely.[38] It has already been proposed that a possible reading for the monogram might be "Maximus," used as a modifying epithet for the "Neon Episcopus" of Niche C;[39] perhaps this is a more acceptable rendering. In any case, it should be reiterated that it is imprudent to postulate post-Neonian renovations in the Baptistery on the evidence these heavily restored monograms of Zone I alone might provide.

Archbishop Theodorus' cross (see also Appendix 1). An inscription on the bronze cross which until recently surmounted the roof of the Baptistery commemorates "donations" (*de donis*) offered to God and the Virgin Mary by one Felex and one Stefanus in the time of Archbishop Theodorus (677–88). Beltrami first, and later

---

35. *Vetera monimenta*, Pl. 19.2, and p. 237 where he suggests BEATUS as a probable reading. In the same plate, here reproduced as *Fig.* 26, Ciampini illustrates *two* identical monograms of 'Maximianus," thus omitting altogether the monogram of "Neon Episcopus."

36. I am indebted to Mr. Gamberini of Ravenna for allowing me to read a copy of the thesis, presented to the University of Venice in 1956, and for the kind hospitality he offered me during my stay in Ravenna in the fall of 1960. Casalone, "Ricerche," p. 242. Cf. also my Chap. 3, n. 30.

37. Only about half the monogram, as it exists today, is original: see drawing in G. Gerola, "Il monogramma della cattedra eburnea di Ravenna," *FR, 19* (1915), 810; redrawn in our *Fig.* 27. It is therefore odd that Gerola should use this monogram in his article as evidence for reading the monogram on the famous throne as "Maximianus."

38. Almost all the surviving episcopal monograms in Ravenna include the letters EP in their pattern. If not, the title forms a second monogram, as in the case of the double monogram on a pulvin from the salutatorium or the Domus Felicis, reading "Felix Archiepiscopus" (Testi-Rasponi, *Codex*, Pl. 1).

39. Barbier de Montault (n. 34 above), pp. 85–86; and Sangiorgi, *Battistero*, pp. 109 ff. See also Ricci, *Tavole*, 2, 10, who, having found no trace of Maximianic restoration in the mosaics of the Baptistery, suggests that the monogram should not read "Maximianus."

Ricci, suggested that the inscription implied some restoration in the Baptistery on the part of the archbishop, who is known to have covered the roof of the adjacent cathedral with lead plates.[40] Such an inference is hypothetical. For one thing, the inscription on the cross refers to two private citizens, and the archbishop's name is there only as an indication of date. Then too, it is not absolutely clear whether "de donis" refers only to the cross or to additional gifts as well. Furthermore, although it has always been taken for granted that the cross was destined for the Baptistery, it appears to this writer that the possibility of its belonging initially to another building is not precluded.

Domus Felicis. A document of 1207 provides an indirect reference to the Baptistery, which may pertain to the eighth century. The document speaks of "a house with a garden, next to the house of Felix behind the Baptistery."[41] This house of Felix may be the same one that, according to Agnellus, was built by Archbishop Felix (709–23) three years after his triumphant return from Constantinople where he had been blinded and kept prisoner by Emperor Justinian II.[42]

Medieval restoration. In the twelfth century the written sources record that the apse mosaic of the cathedral was lavishly redone.[43] The hypothesis that the Baptistery mosaics too had their share of restoration at this time rests on no solid ground. Thorough examination of the interior surfaces early in this century has revealed no trace of medieval restoration.[44]

References. A few brief written references constitute all the information we possess of the Baptistery from the thirteenth to the early sixteenth centuries. Parchments in the Archivio Arcivescovile, from the years 1270 to 1351, preserve the names of the rectors of San Giovanni in Fonte, that is, of the Baptistery.[45] Ambrogio Traversari, a visitor to Ravenna in 1431, noted in his "Hodoeporicon": "And we saw also the Baptistery, which is near the Church [i.e. the Basilica Ursiana], of antique and wonderful workmanship."[46] In 1509 Benedict Adam, French ambassador to Pope Julius

40. Beltrami (n. 1 above), p. 71; Ricci, "S. Giovanni," p. 305. For the possibility that the reference is to Pope Theodore I (642–49), see Sangiorgi, *Battistero*, p. 144.

41. "Et preterea Casam cum Horto iuxta domum Felicis post Ecclesiam baptismalem," M. Fantuzzi (n. 15 above), 2, 175, item xcii (Feb. 9, 1207).

42. Ed. Holder-Egger, "De Sancto Felice," esp. p. 373: "Post vero annos tres haedificavit domum infra episcopium quo de suo nomine domum Felicis nominavit."

43. See G. Galassi, *Roma o Bisanzio; Musaici di Ravenna e le origini dell'arte italiana* (Rome, 1952), pp. 250–54; and G. L. Amadesi, *Metropolitana di Ravenna* (Bologna, 1748), p. ix.

44. The hypothesis was expressed by Ricci, "S. Giovanni," p. 305; but cf. his later observation in *Tavole*, 2, 10: "Nè altre tracce di mani medioevali,

palesi nei mosaici di S. Apollinare in Classe, vi si trovano; nemmeno dei mosaicisti che nel secolo XII ornarono l'abside del vicino Duomo."

45. See *Tabularij Metropolitanae Ravennatis index alphabeticus verborum et rerum, 6,* 453, for a list of these references. See also Fantuzzi (above, n. 15), *4,* 380: "(Anno 1270). D.nus presbyter Johannes Ecclesie S. Johannis in Fontibus"; ibid., p. 103: "(Anno 1290). Pr[esbiter] Jo[hannes] Eccl[esie] S. Jo. Bapt. in Fontibus"; 2, 340: "(Anno 1361). D. Johannes Rector S. Joannis in Fontibus." Also M. Mazzotti, "S. Giovanni in Fonte," *L'Argine, 9* (Feb. 26, 1955).

46. A. Dini-Traversari, *Ambrogio Traversari e i suoi tempi* (Florence, 1912), p. 1433: "Vidimus & Baptisterium, Ecclesiae propinquum, antiquo & mirando opere."

II, placed on the architrave of the newly raised Baptistery door his escutcheon, with an eagle and the motto "En Espoir Dieu." This inscription is still in place.[47]

THE PERIOD OF RESTORATIONS

The sixteenth century. To judge from the long series of restorations which began in the 1550s, the Baptistery must have been in a poor state of preservation at that time. In 1566 an archiepiscopal ordinance was issued, following a visit to the Baptistery, to "restore the mosaics and whatever else is devastated" (Document 1).[48] Seven years later, Archbishop Giulio della Rovere ordered (a) that a marble slab be provided for the altar; (b) that two windows be opened, one to the east and another to the west; and (c) that the pavement around the sacristy be repaired (Document 2). Item (b) must refer to Zone II, where some or all of the windows had probably been gradually blocked up. The transformation of the original arched windows into rectangular ones must have begun at this time (cf. Document 7, "vitreas quadratas"). The sacristy in item (c), according to a later note by Giulio Francesco Varneri, rector of the Baptistery in the second half of the eighteenth century, refers to Niche D of Zone I.[49] Rossi's cursory description of the monument in 1589 unhappily contains no mention of this renovation,[50] but a church document of 1591 describes how the building and its figural art threatened to collapse "on account of their antiquity," and how the Baptistery "today stands even more handsome" after proper restoration. However, the document notes that more still remains to be done (Document 3).

The seventeenth century. Descriptions of the Orthodox Baptistery in church documents become common in this century (see Documents 5, 7). The ecclesiastics of Ravenna appear now to have grown aware of the beauty and historical importance of the building, and its rectors show pride in the monument put in their charge. New ornaments for it are planned, among them an elaborate ciborium to be placed over the font (Document 4), which was in fact never realized.

Between 1604 and 1621, by order of Archbishop Aldobrandini, the new Cappella del Sacramento was being built on the north flank of the cathedral.[51] This construction required the demolition of some structures abutting on the Baptistery. One of these was the rector's house. A letter of testimony dated 1673 attests to its demolition

47. This is the same French prelate who was responsible for an identical motto on the marble frame of San Giovanni in Oleo in Rome, and the inscription "Loyalté tout paces" on the tabernacle of Porta San Pancrazio at Bergamo. Cf. A. Nibby, *Roma nel anno 1838, Parte prima moderna, 1* (Rome, 1839), p. 271. Also see Ricci, *Guida di Ravenna* (6th ed. Ravenna, n.d. [1923]), p. 56.

48. The interpretation of the word "capelle" in Document 1 is not clear: it may refer to the cupola or to the Baptistery itself. Probably not much was done to the mosaics at this time except to paint

over some of the areas from which tesserae had fallen. Cf. the later Document 3: "remanserunt nonulle reliquie, que adhuc indigent reparatione modo prout actum fuit in locis, et figuris jam resarcitis ac restauratis."

49. Varneri defines it clearly as "the niche with the monogram of Maximian" ("Raccolta," p. 3).

50. *Hieronymi Rubei historiarum ravennatum libri* (Venice, 1589), p. 110.

51. See Amadesi, *Metropolitana di Ravenna*, p. xvii. Also Berti, *Sull'antico duomo*, p. 49.

and records the building of a new rectory about fourteen feet from the Cappella del Sacramento (Document 8).[52] The plan of the new rectory and its relation to the Baptistery can be seen in an engraving in an early nineteenth-century guidebook to Ravenna; its facade continued the diagonal line of Side A (then without its niche), and Side A′ and a part of Side B were used as enclosing walls for its western section (*Fig.* 12).[53]

Toward the close of the century Ciampini published the first learned account of the Baptistery, as mentioned above. His plan shows the Baptistery with only two of its four corner niches (*Fig.* 26). The engravings of the mosaics are too generalized to permit speculation about the state of their preservation, but it should be noted that Ciampini does make an effort to indicate impaired areas in the decoration.

The eighteenth century. Thanks to the responsible attitude and the zeal of two rectors, Prospero Grossi and Giulio Francesco Varneri, restorations of this century were recorded in detail. An inventory of 1741 sketches the surroundings of the Baptistery (*Fig.* 12): "The Baptistery . . . is placed opposite the lateral entrance of the Cathedral and to the west of it . . . ; to its south is the rectory, to its north the cemetery, and to the east the courtyard of His Holiness the Archbishop" (Document 9). A late nineteenth-century photograph from the files of the Superintendency of Monuments in Ravenna illustrates this cluttered setting (*Fig.* 11). Compare also an unpublished plan of the same time, which shows a warehouse attached to Side C′ on the eastern part of the cemetery (*Fig.* 23). Grossi, however, was more concerned with the adornment of the interior than with the isolation of the monument from impinging structures. He proudly writes of an altarpiece that he himself "painted on canvas in good form," depicting the baptism of Our Lord, and of a cover for the font painted with another baptism and with arabesques "alla chinese." To his eyes the most prized feature of the decoration is the opus sectile, and more than once he speaks admiringly of the disks of porphyry and serpentine and *verde antico*. Parts of the opus sectile were already missing and the vacancies had simply been patched in plaster (Document 10) and painted over "in order to demonstrate in paint the initial nobility of the ornament" (Document 9). But the chief addition during Grossi's period of office was a new timber roof over the cupola. Expense accounts and drawings of the roof were carefully entered in the records.[54] Upon its completion in 1765, a commemorative inscription was incised by one Scaramello upon the bronze cross of Archbishop Theodorus' time (Document 11).

The repairs of Varneri, who took over in the late 1760s, were designed to bring long-term advantages. The door which had been pierced through Niche B to give onto the archbishop's courtyard was now closed off and replaced with a small window.

52. Mazzotti notes that the demolition must have taken place prior to Nov. 28, 1612, the day when the cornerstone of the new chapel was laid (Corsi [1961], p. 263).

53. G. Ribuffi, *Guida di Ravenna* (Ravenna, 1835), page of drawings (unnumbered).

54. In "Bona patrimonia," pp. 65 ff. On a folded double sheet numbered p. 69 is a pen and ink drawing of the roof shown in cross section. On p. 70 verso is a color drawing of the new roof seen from above.

Another door was opened on Side A′, communicating directly with the rectory (Document 12). The lower parts of the building had long been endangered by water which came in through the door or from the central font which was emptied every year at Holy Sabbath, its contents being conducted to the "sacrario," a deep basin attached to Niche D. The custom of filling the font with water, a remnant of the days when baptism was by immersion, was now discontinued by Varneri, who had a new font made, smaller than the original and inserted into it (Documents 12, 15 and *Fig.* 39). The water from the outside, which at times rose to a height of two palms within the Baptistery, was also checked by two large marble steps placed on either side of the main door (Document 23). Furthermore, part of the cemetery wall which abutted on the Baptistery was destroyed. An area around the building was thus opened up to prevent the flow of rain water from the relatively higher ground of the cemetery (Document 15). During these operations, which were conducted under the direction of the architect Camillo Morigia, the remnants of an old wall were excavated, extending from the cemetery wall to the lateral wall of the cathedral (Document 15). Varneri thought these ruins demonstrated that in antiquity a portico joined the Baptistery to the cathedral (cf. p. 38 below).

Still working with Morigia, Varneri tried to raise the architrave of the main door to allow more light to enter, but when the architrave was taken down to be consolidated by iron clamps, the two lateral walls of the door collapsed. Making the best of an unfortunate accident, Varneri had the door raised and moved slightly, in order to place it in the exact center of Side D′ (Document 12).

An earthquake on April 4, 1781, caused damage which required new repairs. Two windows in Zone II were opened up, one on Side A′ and another on Side C′ (Document 13). Varneri wrote on this occasion that there were only two other unblocked windows at the time, "one opposite the door [Side B′ ?] and another over the confessional [Side D′ ?]."[55] These must have been the two windows opened by the archiepiscopal decree of 1573 (Document 2). Varneri then reinforced three arches of Zone II which had been weakened (Document 13), and rid the columns of this zone from the plaster with which they had previously been coated (cf. below, pp. 75–76). The pavement too was raised and renewed, and the prophets of Zone II "were stood up again" (Document 15).[56] The rector noted with satisfaction that all these precautions had proved wise and timely when another earthquake shook the building in July of the same year.[57] And in the records of the next year he entered, not without pride and a touch of self-importance, the visit to the Baptistery of His Royal Highness

---

55. "Raccolta," p. 25: "e cioè quella in faccia alla porta e quella sopra il Confessionale." But cf. Document 7, of 1612, which makes mention of three windows.

56. See also "Raccolta," p. 31, for the pavement: "A questa ben battuta si aggiunge uno saliciato di sassi a posta ordinati in Rimino." This project was completed by Aug. 3, 1789. The reference to the re-erection of the stucco prophets of Zone II is not clear. Are we to suppose that they had fallen during the earthquake? Would this have not been a more serious loss than Varneri's casual remark implies? The prophets today bear no traces of such a major disruption.

57. "Raccolta," p. 25.

Ferdinand (brother of Emperor Joseph II) and Maria Beatrice d'Este his wife.[58]

During the following years Varneri occupied himself with the problem of the mosaics, badly in need of restoration. Zone I was cleaned and restored about 1785 by the painter Pietro Brandolini (Document 14). But work on the cupola mosaics was a much more expensive proposition since it required elaborate scaffolding. Surviving correspondence demonstrates Varneri's efforts to raise the required funds, which included fees of 60 scudi for the architect Morigia and 90 for the painter Brandolini (Documents 16–19, 21). Toward the end of July 1791, with the sanction of the Archbishop of Ravenna, the scaffolding was erected, and Brandolini began his work on August 16 of the same year.

The technique of these restorations has already been discussed by Gerola.[59] Briefly, it consisted in cleaning the original mosaics and covering the destroyed areas with oil paint. The two existing corner niches were also painted, in fresco, but it is difficult to determine how much more this involved than a mere coating for the masonry. The work was completed by August 26, 1793 (Documents 20, 22). An inscribed plaque was affixed to one of the interior walls of Zone I:[60]

> Fontem Sacri Baptismatis
> Quem Ursus Antistes Ecclesie Ravenne
> Aedificatae Basilicae Adiecit
> Seculo Quinto Ineunte
> Neon Successor
> Musivo Opere ac Marmore Exornavit

The nineteenth century. The state of the Baptistery as Varneri left it upon his death in 1793 can be seen in a drawing of the early decades of the following century, preserved only in an old photograph (*Fig.* 37), and in another similar drawing (in light pencil) now at the Archivio Arcivescovile. The rendering is from one of the two corner niches then in existence and looks toward the main door which is shown open. One sees the raised and renovated floor which buries about a third of the height of the Zone I columns and results in unpleasantly squat proportions. In the center is the original font with Varneri's smaller new font set in it, the latter covered by a lid capped by the Lamb of God. The wall of the altar niche is painted with decorative designs simulating intarsia. This and the rosettes of the niche in which the viewer is standing must be the work of the painter Brandolini. The side next to the altar niche is pierced by a door leading to the rectory. The side to the right of this door shows the marble plaque with the Varnerian inscription. At the level of Zone II can be seen three of the four open windows, rectangular in form; the others are still blocked.

58. "Bona patrimonia," p. 155 verso: Sept. 6, 1782.

59. G. Gerola, "La tecnica dei restauri ai mosaici di Ravenna," *Atti per la Romagna, 4.7,* (1917), 139 ff. Brandolini's work was effaced by the subsequent restorations under Felice Kibel and is therefore hard to evaluate. Gerola suggests, however, that many of Kibel's mistakes may be properly traced to Brandolini (ibid., p. 142).

60. See Sangiorgi, *Battistero,* p. 24.

No further work was done for fifty years after Varneri's death. At mid-century a new series of more drastic restorations commenced, executed by two Romans, the painter Felice Kibel and the architect Filippo Lanciani. In Rome the method of restoring mosaics with actual tesserae had already been developed. Kibel and one Salandri were the first to apply this method to the mosaics of Ravenna. The process involved the use of a putty of gypsum and oil as a bedding, and the application to this of fallen or new tesserae. Kibel, who first worked extensively on the mosaics of Sant' Apollinare Nuovo, started his work in the Baptistery, at the level of Zone I, toward the close of 1854.

G. Gerola, in a study published in 1917, examined carefully the deplorable results of the Roman restorer's activity.[61] On June 26, 1856, a large piece of the ancient mosaic (four square meters, according to Gerola) fell from Zone I owing to the carelessness of a worker; this had to be entirely replaced. During 1859–60 Kibel redid the areas previously restored in painting, and in the process a good part of the ancient mosaic was also dismantled and remounted.[62] This impatient and untidy work was completed in March 1864 with the thorough restoration of the scriptural inscriptions on the niche arches of Zone I.

The work of Kibel has now disappeared because of later restorations, but its extent can be estimated from accounts in the Archivio della Prefettura and the Superintendency of Monuments in Ravenna. Sketches of the renewed inscriptions were prepared by Lanciani and published later by Sangiorgi.[63] But even with these one is at a loss to determine Kibel's fidelity to the original mosaics. The technical quality of his work is not in doubt: his patches began falling very soon, and within two decades the restoration of the mosaics had to be reconsidered.[64]

Meanwhile the architectural fabric of the Baptistery was also undergoing repairs. The arches of Zone I were reconstructed by Tommaso Stamigni from Perugia, as is attested by a news item in *L'Adriatico* of January 22, 1861.[65] About the same time

---

61. Gerola (n. 59 above), esp. pp. 139 ff.

62. F. de Dartein wrote at the time: "On restaurait précisément la mosaïque de la voute lorsque, en septembre 1861, j'ai relevé les dessins du Baptistère. Je dois à cette circonstance d'avoir vu la voute à nu et d'être ainsi parfaitement renseigné sur sa structure," *Étude sur l'architecture lombarde et sur les origines de l'architecture romano-byzantine* (Paris, 1865–82), p. 15 n. 1. A note in 1862 informs us that "nel Battistero si è pure testè compito il rivestimento di opera musaica nei rivolti degli otto archi che sostengono la cupola di questo magnifico monumento colla spesa di L. 3430. 92," *Diario di Ravenna per l'anno 1863* (Ravenna, 1862), p. 93. A curious note by Pietro Sulfrini, "Miscellanea di cose spettante a Ravenna," MS in the possession of M. Mazzotti (n.d., item no. 48), speaks of a fire in the Baptistery which "calcined" the surface of the cupola mosaics: "Il medesimo

Kibel, nell'eseguire presentemente (1860) i ristauri del Musaico del Battistero, ha fatto osservare, che tutto quanto (specialmente il bacino della cupola) deve aver subito l'azione di grande incendio: essendo tutto lo smalto calcinato a seguo d'aver perduto quasi ogni colore non chè l'oro. Io stesso, montato sui salchi il 23 Marzo, ho verificato la realtà del fatto." I have been unable to find further information on this point.

63. Sangiorgi, *Battistero*, pp. 101 ff. Republished by Ricci, *Tavole*, 2, 34 ff.

64. Gerola (n. 59 above), pp. 163 ff. For bits that had fallen off by 1883, see C. Ricci in *Fanfulla della Domenica*, year V, no. 46 (Nov. 18, 1883).

65. The same news item reports that this renovation was due to the kindness of his majesty Vittorio Emanuele who had visited the Baptistery during his stay in Ravenna in 1860.

Filippo Lanciani, dispatched to Ravenna by the new Italian Government as inspector of monuments, was on the scene, conducting excavations in and around the Baptistery. These excavations, the first of their kind and vital for information on the original form of the building, were unfortunately not adequately published.[66] One drawing, dated February 10, 1863, and signed by Lanciani himself, shows a ground plan of the Baptistery with the two newly excavated niches which had been demolished at some unknown period in the past but had survived underground to a height of about 2.25 meters from the original pavement (*Fig. 25*). Lanciani's first task was to rebuild these two niches (A and D). He also lowered the main door from the position given to it by Varneri in 1775 (see above, p. 23; and Document 12) and restored the windows of Zone II to their original arched form, on the basis of a surviving brick in the archivolt of the window on Side A'.[67]

The excavations, to be discussed in greater detail in Chapter 3, also disclosed the antique floor of the Baptistery and the bases where the columns of Zone I initially rested (*Figs. 20, 21*). To recreate the proportions originally intended, Lanciani first thought of merely excavating a well around the building down to the initial pavement, but he then conceived a plan which was to start a heated debate lasting for over a decade. This was the notorious "rialzamento" project, that is, raising the Baptistery onto a platform 3.65 meters high. Several sketches exist, illustrating how the project was to be carried out (*Fig. 22*). The Baptistery would first be freed from surrounding buildings, and a well would be excavated all around it to enable the use of proper machinery. Arches were to be opened below ground level in the four flat sides. The danger of disrupting the walls or the mosaics during the operation was to be forestalled by the choice of machines capable of "such slow and unfelt movement" that no harm could possibly come to the building. Once the Baptistery had been raised sufficiently so that the original floor was at the level of the modern ground, the columns of Zone I would be altered to fit the new height of the building. A broad street would be opened where the encroaching structures stood, connecting the Piazza Arcivescovile to the east with the Piazza del Duomo to the west.[68]

For once in its history the Baptistery of Ravenna became a subject of nationwide dispute. Public opinion in the city itself was sharply divided. Part of the press and some of the people in authority sided with "the illustrious hydraulic engineer and archaeologist Commendatore Filippo Lanciani."[69] These urged the state to allot the necessary funds for the operation. By May 5, 1876, 12,000 lire were already allotted,

---

66. Brief summaries in *BAC*, 4 (1886), 73; and Lanciani, *Cenni*, pp. 7–8. Cf. also my Chap. 3, n. 14.

67. Sangiorgi, *Battistero*, p. 44.

68. See a story in the *Monitore delle Romagne*, Feb. 5, 1876, for a summary of this project, whence the "slow and unfelt movement" ("così lento ed insensibile movimento") is quoted. A drawing of the project is here published for the first time (*Fig. 22*). The numbers on the drawing stand for the following: 1, the present floor; 2, the floor on which the columns of Zone I rest; 3, walls of medieval date to support the columns; 4, substructure of the central font; 5, new wall proposed by Lanciani to facilitate the rialzamento; 6, a proposed stair leading down to the original fifth-century pavement; 7, a new iron railing; 8, the rectory.

69. ". . . illustre idraulico, ed archeologo Comm. Filippo Lanciani," from the same story (see previous note).

and the Consiglio comunale was debating the appropriation of another 6,000.[70] The isolation of the Baptistery was also under way. The rectory and some warehouses to the southeast and northwest had been demolished the year before.[71] The walls of the monument were mended with new bricks of the same size as the antique ones, in preparation for the rialzamento.[72] And inside, the opus sectile of Zone I was taken down and stored.[73]

But another faction was strongly opposed to the proceedings on the ground that the smallest mistake might result in irreparable damage to the building and especially its mosaics. Corrado Ricci became the fiery spokesman of the opposition. That the rialzamento would prevent damage from humidity was ridiculous, he wrote. "Let us then raise San Marco in Venice, the Roman buildings in Ostia, Zara, Fiumicino, Anzio ... Let us raise Herculaneum buried several meters below Resina."[74] The dissension managed to spread beyond Italy. In England, a letter in the *Times* from its Roman correspondent protested strongly against the idea.[75] An editorial in the *Architect* volunteered suggestions for preserving the mosaics and objected to the rialzamento on aesthetic grounds: "If the ancient decoration be made to rest on nine feet of brand new work [the building's] unity and harmony will be forever destroyed."[76] After a final flare of debate in 1883, the required approval was denied by the authorities, and the fury subsided as quickly as it had risen.[77] The only visible profit was that the Baptistery now stood free from abutting structures like the warehouse and the rectory, and the necessary impetus had been provided for bringing the project of isolation and renovation to a head.

Some time during the controversy, the Baptistery lost the stucco decoration of the lunettes of Zone II, torn down because it was thought to be the result of a foolish bungle of the seventeenth century, a "balorda raffazzonatura seicentesca."[78] The exact date for this bit of unexpected vandalism cannot be determined. Ricci believes it to have taken place around 1880; Verzone mentions 1887.[79] But a print of the in-

---

70. *Il Ravennate*, May 5, 1876. This paper, like the *Monitore delle Romagne*, was consistently pro-Lanciani and called the project a kind of modern Raising of Lazarus ("Si tratta di rinnovare una specie di miracolo di Lazzaro").

71. See "Bona patrimonia," p. 165 verso.

72. Ricci says this repair took place ca. 1880 ("S. Giovanni," p. 308). A similar date is given by Sulfrini (n. 62 above, item no. 479). Verzone on the other hand, quoting Sangiorgi, writes: "La parte esterna dei muri fu rifatta verso il 1877 adoperando mattoni nuovi della stessa dimensione degli antichi: nè si badò alla chiarezza del cemento" (*L'architettura religiosa*, p. 78 n. 8). Sangiorgi informs us that the bricks for this repair were made in Imola, in three different colors (*Battistero*, p. 143). A further part of the renovation seems to have been the alteration of Grossi's roof. See Sulfrini (n. 62 above, item no. 403): "Nell'agosto 1874 rimovando il tetto del Battistero . . ."; and Ricci, *Guida di Ravenna*

(6th ed. [1923]), p. 56: "Sul vertice del tetto, ricoperto di piombo nel 1874 . . ."

73. Ricci, "S. Giovanni," p. 304.

74. Ibid., p. 318.

75. *The Times*, April 23, 1880.

76. *The Architect*, *23* (1880), 365–66.

77. A. Cavaletto defended the project in the Italian Parliament in March 1883 (*Atti del Parlamento Italiano* [Rome, 1883], 2, 1717–18). See *Il Ravennate*, March 8, 10, 1883. A vicious attack on Cavaletto appears in the Milanese paper *Il Secolo*, March 19–20, 1883.

78. S. Busmanti, *Guida breve per Ravenna antica e moderna* (Ravenna, 1883), p. 93.

79. Ricci, *Guida di Ravenna* (6th ed. [1923]), p. 53; P. Verzone, *L'Architettura religiosa*, p. 78 n. 9. G. Polvara assigns the destruction of the stuccoes to 1830, with no mention of his source (*Arte cristiana*, *23* [1935], 53). The stucco decoration in the apse of Sant'Ambrogio in Milan was similarly destroyed

terior decoration published by Rahn in 1869 shows the stuccoes already demolished, with bare brick wall visible underneath.[80]

The rest of the stucco decoration of Zone II, the prophets in the aedicules, was also being tampered with. Known to have been painted originally in several colors, they now received a modern polychromy, although a monochrome coating seems to have been applied first. An irate commentator remarked in 1890: "It is the fifth or sixth time, or perhaps even the seventh or eighth, that they have altered the color, always from bad to worse."[81] In 1897 Sangiorgi suggested a pattern of polychromy (red for the ground of the prophets, blue for the ground of the lunettes, gold for the architectural members),[82] and a year later it is reported that the painter Enrico Piazza executed a trial painting in one corner of Zone II.[83]

Between 1886 and 1890 the renovation of the mosaics, already falling off, that had been patched up by Felice Kibel, was assigned to his son Ildebrando Kibel and to Carlo Novelli.[84] Properly speaking their work was not restoration. It consisted of applying numerous clamps to consolidate the mosaics with the fabric of the building. At the turn of the century these two men were replaced by Alessandro Azzaroni and Giuseppe Zampiga.

Also in the last years of the nineteenth century the opus sectile of Zone I was brought out of storage to be remounted. This task and the reconstruction of missing parts was referred by the Ministry of Education to the Reale Opificio delle Pietre Dure di Firenze. Careful drawings of the reconstruction, which lasted from 1897 to 1906, survive in the Superintendency of Monuments; two are reproduced (*Figs.* 111, 112). The assignment was not an easy one for the colored marbles had been juggled around more than once, and a group of them was already missing in Prospero Grossi's time, as we have seen (Document 9). The work of the Opificio, however commendable as a piece of reconstruction, should never be taken to represent the fifth-century arrangement.[85] One should be especially aware of the danger of formulating hypotheses, as some recent students have done,[86] about the Neonian renovation of the Baptistery, based on the present superposition of the Zone I arches over the opus sectile.

about 1860 since it was supposed to be Baroque. See W. Lethaby and H. Swainson, *The Church of Sancta Sophia* (London, 1894), p. 291.

80. J. R. Rahn, *Ravenna: Eine kunstgeschichtliche Studie* (Leipzig, 1869), Pl. opposite p. 8.

81. O. Gardella, *L'Atterramento di una parte dell'ardica della Basilica Classense di Ravenna* (Ravenna, 1890), p. 18.

82. In *Corriere di Romagna*, Dec. 16, 1897.

83. Ricci, *Ravenna e i lavori fatti dalla sovrintendenza dei monumenti nel 1898* (Bergamo, 1899), p. 35.

84. For the work of Novelli and Ildebrando Kibel, see Gerola, (above, n. 59), pp. 81 ff., 179–80; also Ricci, *Tavole, 2,* 23 ff. Cf. an unpublished letter from Alessandro Azzaroni to Ricci dated "25-2-31" (now at the Biblioteca Classense), where Novelli

and the younger Kibel are said to have applied "numerissime grappe *solamente*. Nella volta del Battistero, compreso pure i sott'archi superiori, trovo che sono segnate in rosso 67 crocette, grappe collocate dal Novelli e 47 segnate in nero che sono del Kibel. Queste due cifre le trovo negli appunti che si fa (?) sul posto. E questa è la ragione che nelle . . . tavole non risulta con un colore speciale, non avendo rifatto nulla . . ."

85. For a bitter attack on the proficiency of the Opificio and the accuracy of its work, see Gardella, in the *Faro Romagnolo* for Oct. 27, 1897. See also Sangiorgi in *Corriere di Romagna* for April 23, 1898.

86. See for example Verzone, *L'Architettura religiosa,* p. 76. Cf. my Chap. 3, n. 30.

This arrangement cannot be taken to mean that the opus sectile antedates the arches for it has not necessarily retained its original position through the centuries, nor in point of fact do the arches overlap the design of the opus sectile (*Fig.* 110).

The twentieth century. While the impression of the restorations by the two Kibels was still fresh in living memory, an attempt was made early in this century to make good the damage they had done. Azzaroni and Zampiga, entrusted with the new work, seem to have confined their attention to the decorative patterns in the arch soffits of Zones I and II and to retouching formerly restored parts.[87] Their major contribution, however, was the preparation of colored drawings, now at the Superintendency of Monuments, designed to show the principal periods of restoration that the Ravennate mosaics underwent. It is upon these drawings that the monumental work of Corrado Ricci, the *Tavole storiche dei mosaici di Ravenna*, 1930–37, is based. The drawings were prepared in 1903; in Ricci's reproductions F. Kibel's restorations are shown in red, the Azzaroni–Zampiga ones in purple, and the original fifth-century mosaics in black.

In 1904 the columns of Zone I were freed from Varneri's pavement, which buried one third of their height as they rested on an earlier lower pavement. For this purpose a well, about 1.10 meters wide beginning at the wall surfaces, was dug all around the interior of the building, down to the level of the earlier pavement. The iron railing which is still at the edges of Varneri's abbreviated pavement was put in position also at this time (*Fig.* 39).[88]

With the outbreak of World War I, a committee consisting of G. Gerola, C. Ecchia, and the engineer C. Pedretti was appointed to decide upon protective measures against bombing. The four corner niches were filled with sandbags, and the four flat sides were protected from the outside by masonry encasements filled with straw. Between the extrados of the cupola and the roof a strong wooden scaffolding was built, upon which were placed tightly packed bales of seaweed to a height of 1.50 meters. The interior walls were sheathed completely with sandbags, but the eight windows were left free. The intrados of the cupola was also padded with seaweed which would hold any bits of mosaics that might be disengaged.[89] The Baptistery survived the war unharmed but, probably for the first time in its history, the building's function was interrupted: between 1914 and 1918 baptism had to be administered in one of the rooms of the Casa Canonica.[90]

The last and most meticulous restoration took place in 1937–39, during a campaign of consolidation of the major Ravennate monuments and their mosaics. This commendable enterprise was undertaken by the Superintendency of Bologna and was put

87. See Gerola (above, n. 59), pp. 185 ff.; also Ricci, *Tavole*, 2, 25 ff., for documentation.

88. Three drawings seen by me in the Archivio Arcivescovile, but ordinarily kept in the Superintendency of Monuments, illustrate this particular restoration. All three are by a certain Maioli, architect in charge of the work. One drawing shows a ground plan of the Baptistery. The second, signed and dated June 15, 1904, shows a cross section with the railing in place. The third, also dated June 15, 1904, is a precise drawing of the railing itself.

89. See C. Ricci (ed.) in *Bollettino d'arte, 11–12* (1917–18), 265–69, for these details.

90. Note in "Bona patrimonia," p. 166.

under the direction of the architect Corrado Capezzuoli. Detailed photographs and a clear account by Capezzuoli and others assist in following closely every stage of this particular restoration.[91] The first problem was one which had bedeviled the Baptistery since its erection: the presence of water under and around the foundations. A photograph taken after the excavation of a ditch around the exterior walls shows the poor state of the substructure; another illustrates the measures taken to remedy the situation (*Figs.* 18, 19). The lower parts of the walls were renewed and covered with a coat of specially treated concrete, five centimeters thick, to keep the water out. The ditch was refilled with dry soil and covered with a concrete gutter. Inside the building, Varneri's tile pavement was replaced with one of Verona marble. The windows were reglazed with new panes of Thermolux glass.

The method used to consolidate the mosaics is instructive. According to the old system, clamps were used to attach loose areas of mosaic to the bedding. Zampiga, at the beginning of the century, applied a new method whereby the bedding was renewed and the mosaic reset.[92] The danger in this method is the possible alteration in the arrangement of the tesserae during the resetting. To prevent this, the following procedure was used in repairing the Baptistery mosaics in the late 1930s; it was carried out by the Opificio delle Pietre Dure di Firenze with the collaboration of the Scuola del Musaico della Accademia di Belle Arti di Ravenna. The exact impression of a section of mosaic was made on a sensitive paper; the section was then dismounted, the old bedding entirely removed, and new mortar applied. The pattern of the tesserae on the paper was transferred to the new bedding, and the mosaics were then reset (*Fig.* 31). During the work all remnants of previous restorations (stucco and clamps) were removed. Almost the whole of Zone V was dismounted and reset in this way. In Zone IV the renewal was confined to the heads of Apostles Bartholomew, Philip, and James of Zebedee, and some other minor details. The work was interrupted by the Second World War. A bombardment on August 25, 1944, damaged the roof and threatened the mosaics, but again the *tyche* of Ravenna intervened.[93] The roof was repaired after the war, and the consolidation of the mosaics was concluded.

Two projects should, I believe, be considered in the future. One is the proper excavation of the monument, both outside and in, to ascertain the results of Lanciani's work, which were incompletely published a century ago. The second project would be to lower the pavement to its original fifth-century level when that is more definitely established from the new excavations, thus retrieving the proportions intended by its designer. Both of these are difficult and costly propositions, but no more so for our time than were the activities of Giulio Francesco Varneri for his.

---

91. The photographs are in the files of the Superintendency of Monuments. Capezzuoli's account is in *Le Arti, 17* (1938–39), 531–46; see also *FR, 46* (1938), 63–64.

92. *Le Arti, 17* (1938–39), 532. Cf. Th. Whittemore, *The Mosaics of St. Sophia at Istanbul* (Oxford, 1933 ff.), for similar methods of restoration.

93. *FR, 52* (1950), 73.

THE ARCHITECTURE

THE EXTERIOR

The Baptistery of Ravenna, as it stands today after at least a millennium of restorations and alterations, is a small, unprepossessing brick structure north of the present eighteenth-century cathedral and separated from it by the narrow Strada del Battistero (*Figs.* 9, 10, 13, 14). Four semicircular niches, diagonally disposed, expand the octagonal plan into a square with rounded corners. The niches rise to an average height of 2.30 meters from the present ground level and are covered by tile roofs in the shape of truncated cones. Above these sits the octagonal main body of the Baptistery, covered in turn by a tile roof in eight plane segments, its periphery outlined by a saw-tooth cornice in brick.[1] Two courses below this cornice begins a blind arcade in the form of a wide frieze around the upper part of the building. It consists of sixteen double-arched panels, sunk about 0.10 meter into the masonry, two to each side of the octagon. Each panel is 1.40 meters wide and 4.20 meters high from base to the level of the keystones in its double-arched top (*Fig.* 15).

Between the niche story and the frieze of blind arcading, about 4.10 meters from the ground, is the row of eight arched windows. Two other smaller windows at the level of the blind arcade—one on Side B, the other on Side D'—give access to the area between the extrados of the masonry cupola and the roof; in the former, to the southeast, is preserved the original stone sill and arched top. In the right panel of arcading on Side D is a relief showing a horseman, set within the masonry (*Fig.* 125; discussed in Appendix 1). The only door is on Side D'. It is bounded by the stone frame dating from the sixteenth century, with the inscription EN ESPOIR DIEU on the architrave (see pp. 20–21).

Most of the exterior is in good condition, excepting a serious crack on Side D'. The diagonal scars visible in the masonry of Sides B and B' (*Fig.* 13) are due to the old rectory which once abutted on the Baptistery at this point (*Figs.* 11, 12). The

---

1. The same saw-tooth cornice, about 0.25 meter high, is to be found at the eaves of the corner niche on Side B; the other three niches have only a projecting course of plain brick below the roof.

upper parts of the walls are pierced by four more or less regular lines of square holes for the scaffolding. The brick masonry is a patchwork of different dates; the original fifth-century masonry is nowhere in evidence. The newest and most readily identifiable brickwork, seen for example on the niche of Side B, on Side B' up to the window level, and on a good part of Sides C and C', is the work of the restorations of the 1930s (*Fig.* 15).[2] Lanciani's work, notably the rebuilt niches of Sides A and D missing from an unknown date until 1863, is characterized by small half-bricks, mat and apparently reused (*Fig.* 16, left).[3] Distinct from both of these types of brickwork is the frieze of blind arcading built of irregular and friable bricks which have a yellowish tint and thick mortar joinings and are of medieval date, as we shall discuss below (*Fig.* 15, top).

THE INTERIOR

It is no easy matter, within the Baptistery, to extricate structure from the sumptuous and complex decorative scheme which informs it. The interdependence of the two, of container and content, is a distinctive feature of this monument. The isolation of architecture in the present chapter is resorted to only for the sake of more convenient discussion. Briefly described, the architectural system of the interior is a cupola resting on two stories of arcades (*Figs.* 39, 40). The arcade of Zone I rests on impost blocks placed over the capitals of the eight columns at the corners of the octagon. The arcade of Zone II rests on brackets projecting over the imposts of the corner columns of this story. The system of the arcades and the cupola is distinct from the octagonal shell of the exterior walls which serve only as partial buttresses for the thrust exerted by the cupola. In fact, the inner and outer walls do not merge but are attached only at certain points where fissures have been filled with mortar.[4]

The cupola is the only part of the building not of brick. It is constructed of two congruent shells of hollow terra-cotta tubes, about 0.20 meter long, which are fitted one into the other to form concentric rings verging toward the top (*Figs.* 28, 31, 33). The rings of the two shells are neither strictly horizontal nor radial, in respect to the center of the cupola, but are disposed rather with a peculiar inclination such that each inner ring is held in place by two outer rings in V-shaped formation (*Fig.* 32). In the order of construction, the inner rings were probably laid out first, resting in each case on two previous rings, an inner and an outer. By this method an elaborate wood framework could be dispensed with. The rings were grafted together with a fast-drying mortar, and the resultant vault was one of extreme lightness, with an

2. These bricks, of two distinct shades of red, are in two sizes: 0.42 meter wide by 0.06 thick, and 0.28 meter wide by 0.06 thick.

3. They measure 0.15 meter wide and 0.055 thick, with occasional whole bricks measuring 0.30 by 0.055 meter. This nineteenth-century brickwork is also evident in small patches elsewhere in the fabric, especially on the upper portion of the niche on Side C. In the lower parts of this niche, which are probably also of the same type of masonry, the bricks have been blackened as if by fire. Would this

be the fire mentioned by Sulfrini (Chap. 2, n. 62 above)?

The brickwork of the eighteenth century may be exemplified by the two lateral walls of the main door which, it will be recalled, collapsed in 1775 during the raising of the architrave and were rebuilt by Varneri in the same year. The bricks are thin and the courses neatly laid. The tympanum of the blind arch over the architrave is also of this type.

4. Sangiorgi, *Battistero*, p. 16.

outer thrust considerably less than that of a similar vault in brick. The weight was
further reduced in fact by stopping the tubular construction short of the top, about
one meter below the crown (*Figs.* 29, 30). This area, approximately corresponding
to the central portion of the mosaic tondo of the baptism (Zone V), was filled with
rough, porous pumice blocks of a dark color, from the lava beds of Vesuvius. The
mortar used here is exactly the same as that used in the rings of tubes; the two parts
of the cupola must therefore be coeval. A further proof of this is the fact that several
tesserae of fifth-century mosaic were found attached to the mortar of the area made
of pumice blocks. The reason for the change of materials in the construction of the
cupola seems to have been a structural exigency. It may be that the builders wished
to circumvent the difficulty of forming small rings toward the top with the rigid
tubes at hand. In San Vitale, a century later, the builders attempted to complete
the cupola, which is also of tubular construction, without the insertion of an alien
material. This resulted in upper rings built of broken tubes roughly fitted together.
Even so, a hole with a diameter of 0.15 meter was left open at the crown.[5]

Eight holes, partly filled with stucco, are pierced through the fabric of the lower
section of the Baptistery's cupola. They are made by the vertical insertion of hollow
tubes into the two shells, and were undoubtedly part of the initial design of the
cupola. The holes are on axis with the eight windows and are visible above them at
the level of Zone IV.[6] Capezzuoli, their discoverer, attempted to explain them as air
holes, or as a possible way of reaching the intrados from the outside—both dubious
suggestions.[7] It is more probable that they were meant for the cords of the lamps
suspended from above to light the interior, as was suggested by De Angelis d'Ossat.[8]

The diameter of the cupola at its springing line is about 9.60 meters. It fits onto
the octagon by means of eight segmental pendentives of the "merging" kind; i.e.
pendentives whose curve is continuous with that of the cupola. These and the eight
main arches of Zone II were originally also built of tubes, but during the restoration
of Tomasso Stamigni of 1860 (p. 25), large bricks were substituted, designed to add
support to the tubes of the cupola (*Fig.* 31).

---

5. This description of the cupola is derived
largely from G. De Angelis d'Ossat's study, "Nuovi
dati sulle volte costruite con vasi fittili," *Palladio*,
5 (1941), 245–49; now reprinted, with additions
and better illustration, in De Angelis d'Ossat, *Studi
ravennati: Problemi di architettura paleocristiana*
(Faenza, 1962), pp. 137–55. The hollow tubes of
the cupola are 0.14 to 0.16 meter long, with a point
0.06 meter long, yielding a total length of 0.20 to
0.22 meter. Their diameter is 0.07 to 0.08 meter.
Capezzuoli, who was the first to study the structure
of the cupola in detail (during the restorations of
the 1930s), suggested the following explanations for
the change of materials at the top of the cupola: (a)
a possible collapse during its construction, before
the mosaic had been executed; (b) a possible scarcity of terra-cotta tubes; (c) a change in the per-
sonnel, and the ignorance of the new workers in the
method of vaulting by tubes ("Ravenna: Battistero
di Neone. Indagini interessanti, la struttura muraria dell'edificio," *Le Arti*, 2 [1940], 394). All of
these hypotheses are improbable.

6. Their positions are as follows: 1, on the chiton
of the Apostle Thomas; 2, on the candelabrum between the apostles James son of Alphaeus and Matthew; 3, slightly to the left of St. Simon; 4, on the
left leg of St. Bartholomew; 5, just to the right of
St. Philip; 6, just to the left of St. James son of
Zebedee; 7, to the right of St. Peter; 8, to the left
of the candelabrum between Sts. Peter and Paul (on
Paul's side). The position of the tubes used for these
holes is in fact not strictly vertical but inclines
about fifteen degrees toward the interior.

7. Capezzuoli (see n. 5), p. 397.

8. *Studi ravennati*, pp. 148–49.

The brackets on which the main arches of Zone II rest are carved on the sides facing into the Baptistery, each with a cross and some foliage (*Fig. 75*). They in turn rest on the plain pulvin blocks which cap the corner columns of this zone. There are twenty-four columns, about 1.16 meters high (excluding capitals and bases). Of these only those at the corners of the octagon bear any of the load of the cupola. The other sixteen, also capped by plain pulvins, flank the eight windows, and help to support smaller triple arcades set within the tympana of the eight main arches of Zone II.[9] Within this framework of smaller arcades are placed aedicules in stucco relief containing figures of prophets also in stucco (*Figs. 70, 71*). The columns sit on a ledge, 0.35 meter wide, on plain square bases touching the back wall. All but one have Ionic capitals of an ordinary type with two sets of simple volutes; the column to the left of the window on Side B′ has no capital but only a pulvin placed directly over the shaft (*Fig. 40, first column from the left*).[10]

The lower arcade of Zone I is also in brick (*Figs. 104, 109*). Here too the arches rest on pulvin blocks which, however, unlike their equivalents in Zone II, pierce the walls at the corners. They are carved with a pattern of upright leaves in two superposed and interlocking planes (*Figs. 116–21*).[11] The eight columns are dissimilar. The height of the shafts varies between 1.55 and 1.72 meters (or between 1.75 and 1.91 inclusive of their bases). A glance at the ground plan will make it apparent that they are not all accurately placed in the exact angles of the octagon (*Fig. 1*). Two of the shafts are unusual: one, at the corner of Sides C and C′, has a reversed Latin cross in high relief toward the base; the other, at the corner of Sides C′ and D (*Fig. 39, first column from the left*), is only a half column with two wide grooves filled in with mortar.

Of the capitals, two, at corners C′–D and D–D′, are of the kind generally known as Byzantine Corinthian, very common in Early Christian architecture (*Fig. 121*).[12] The other six are composite capitals of the type used in the Baths of Caracalla and in many other late antique buildings. Some of these (at corners A–A′, A′–B, B–B′) have a singular peculiarity: there are five volutes to each capital instead of the usual four, yielding a curious pentagonal section (*Figs. 117–20*). I have been unable to trace other examples of this interesting variant of the composite capital. It is very probable that they were carved specifically for use in a polygonal building. If so, they were certainly designed to stand in mid-space so that they might present a pair of volutes when viewed from any side. The small re-entrant angle formed by the two of the five

---

9. Three of the columns of Zone II are of *bigio*, two of *pavonazzeto*, and the rest of white marble. Cf. below, p. 75.

10. The capital existed originally. It now stands in Niche A and serves as a base for the bronze cross of Archbishop Theodorus' time (see Appendix 1).

11. The pulvins measure about 0.21 meter in height. Their width, on the front facing the interior, varies from 0.41 to 0.47 at the bottom line; at the

top line it is consistently 0.57 meter (except the pulvin at angle A–A′ which has a chipped corner).

12. For the term "Byzantine Corinthian," see A. van Millingen, *Byzantine Churches in Constantinople* (London, 1912), pp. 30–31. For examples of this type of capital, see R. Kautzsch, *Kapitellstudien* (Berlin-Leipzig, 1936), numbers 1, 7, and 88 among others.

volutes closest together would have faced toward the central space, and the remaining three would have fanned out toward the ambulating space in consonance with the lines of their epistyle. That these capitals were not made originally for the Baptistery is, I think, certain. Neither are they suitable for the angles of the eight corners nor is there any possibility for their use in mid-space except around the ancient font, but that, disclosed by Lanciani's excavations (p. 36), was not circled by columns. These unique capitals, therefore, were reused in the Baptistery at a later time, as were all the other capitals of Zone I.[13]

The columns of Zone I are standing at present on a floor which is about half a meter below the modern pavement. They rest on a sustaining wall which is contiguous, but apparently not uninterruptedly, with the bounding wall. The sides of the octagon at this zone are alternately flat and semicircular. The flat sides (A', B', C', and D') have decoration in opus sectile within the tympana of the arches and down to the level of the upper shafts of the columns (*Figs.* 107, 108; p. 28). Below this, bare brickwork shows, with one relieving arch in the masonry of each side. In Side D', the upper part of the door cuts into the opus sectile. The corner niches which open out from Sides A, B, C, and D begin at about 0.80 meter from either angle (*Figs.* 104–06). Their average width is about 3 meters, and their height from the present pavement about 2.60 meters. The broad arches on which the scriptural inscriptions are set rest on marble impost blocks inserted in the masonry; they are carved with much the same ornament as the pulvins over the columns of Zone I.

It will have become apparent from the drawings and the approximate measurements given in the text that the Baptistery is not built in accordance with a design of strict geometric precision. It is not an exaggeration to say that there is no perfectly vertical line in the structure. The whole building in fact leans gently from southeast to northwest. Some of these metric casualties are due to frequent repairs, but it must be remembered that early medieval buildings in general were put together more by experience of the eye than by the dictation of the straightedge. The resulting imprecision endows these buildings with a quality of extemporaneousness that is quite fetching. It also renders suspect attempts on the part of architectural historians to discover ideal systems of geometric proportions or of modules; in fact, such abstract calculation should be discouraged by the actual measurements of the buildings. In the Baptistery, where the sides of the octagon internally vary between 4.48 and 4.86 meters in width and the distance between diagonal corners ranges from 11.24 to 11.47 meters, there seems little point in pursuing any perfect mathematical or geometric system.

---

13. The six composite capitals, though generically quite similar, are certainly not all carved by the same hand. Their date would appear to be third century. Casalone maintains that these capitals were initially made for Zone II, and that during later changes they were moved to Zone I ("Ricerche," p. 215). There is no proof of this. The capitals in fact are 0.41 to 0.43 meter wide, while the bottom width of the pulvins of Zone II, under which they would have had to stand, is about 0.25 meter. Her statement that the capitals with five volutes fit perfectly into their corners is based on an ideal drawing by Gino Gamberini in his unpublished thesis, and is untrue.

STAGES OF BUILDING

The historical account of the Orthodox Baptistery based on written sources (Chapter 2) and the description of its present state have cleared the way for an attempt to reconstruct, on the basis of archaeological evidence, the earliest form given to it by its designers. Ricci's theory concerning the pre-Christian origin of the Baptistery has already been sufficiently discussed to allow the investigation to begin with the fifth century.

1. The Baptistery before Neon

That Bishop Neon undertook a major renovation of the Baptistery some decades after it was first built is attested, it will be recalled, by the commemorative inscription reported in Agnellus' life of the bishop. The problem is to establish, so far as this is possible, the appearance of the Baptistery prior to his episcopate, and then to investigate the nature of his renovation. The examination of written sources has proved to be of little avail in these matters. One can begin therefore with the excavations of Lanciani in the latter nineteenth century. The inadequately published results may be summarized as follows. (1) The discovery of the original pavement, 2.99 meters below the present ground level. (2) The discovery of the lower parts of the two missing niches, which allowed him to reconstruct the ground plan as we have it today. (3) At the level of the antique pavement, the unearthing of some of the pedestals of the original columns of Zone I; and remnants of an early font, round on the inside and made of Greek marbles, on the foundations of which the present octagonal font rests (*Figs.* 20, 21).[14] There were, according to Lanciani, two original doors, on Sides C' and D'.[15] Curiously, the number was raised by subsequent scholars to four, one

---

14. See Lanciani, *Cenni*, pp. 7–8; and *BAC, 4* (1866), 73. Sangiorgi writes that the original floor, at a depth of 2.99 meters below the present one, was discovered before Lanciani's time, first by Camillo Morigia, the architect employed by the rector Giulio Varneri in the second half of the eighteenth century (*Battistero*, p. 19). The only drawing of the excavations published by Lanciani himself is a ground plan which shows no more than the two excavated niches (*BAC, 4* [1866], 73). Later Sangiorgi published two more drawings "conforming to the studies of the engineer Lanciani," which presented reconstructions of the interior and the exterior of the building as it would have looked in the fifth century (*Battistero*, frontispiece and p. 133). I have myself discovered several unpublished sketches, probably made by Lanciani and certainly dating from the excavation years. One shows the superposition of the present central font on the foundations of the antique font (*Fig.* 20); another seems to sketch the pedestals and the antique font on the original pavement, with intermediary arches presumably to facilitate the "rialzamento" (*Fig.* 21; cf. n. 17 below). A third drawing (*Fig.* 24) is a

ground plan of the Baptistery showing the niches as externally polygonal, very probably a study for the reconstruction of the niches, as is the drawing (signed and dated) mentioned above, p. 26. The sketch illustrated here in *Fig.* 22 was prepared for the project of the "rialzamento" (cf. Chap. 2, n. 68). All these drawings are kept at the Superintendency of Monuments at Ravenna, except the one published by Sangiorgi (*Battistero*, frontispiece), which was reported to be in the Biblioteca Classense but which seems now to be lost. One final drawing of the exterior, unavailable to me, was published recently by A. Ghezzo (*FR, 86* [1962], p. 42).

15. Lanciani, *Cenni*, p. 7; also *BAC, 4* (1866), 73, where the two doors are said to be there for a special purpose—perhaps one was used by women, the other by men; or again perhaps the arrangement of the doors and four niches "poteva essere in qualche modo destinata a supplire alla mancanza di locali esterni al battistero (come veggonsi in Salona), dove i battezzandi si preparavano per poi scendere ed immergersi nella fonte." Cf. also G. Martinetti Cardoni, *Ravenna antica* (Faenza, 1875

for each of the flat sides.[16] This revision is based, to my knowledge, on no solid evidence but appears to be due to considerations of symmetry. The four relieving arches visible today below the opus sectile are not original and should not therefore be taken to relate to the initial arrangement of the Baptistery doors.[17] It is noteworthy that the Arian Baptistery, in many ways a conscious copy of the Orthodox, had only two doors.

It would seem also that the original shape of the niches was not made altogether certain from Lanciani's excavations. Early ground plans from Ciampini onward depict them as externally semicircular but beginning a little way in from the angles of the octagon, as they do in fact on the inside of the building (*Fig.* 26).[18] I see no reason to doubt this disposition. Lanciani's studies reflect his indecision on the subject (*Figs.* 24, 25). At one point he considered reconstructing the niches as polygonal externally; this idea was echoed in plans published in some contemporary books.[19] We are never told why in the end he decided on a semicircular form continuous with the flat sides of the octagon.

Two further problems about the external appearance of the Baptistery need to be considered: the existence of a portico connecting it with the cathedral and an ambulatory surrounding the lower part of the building. The dispute about the portico is the older. Its presence was first posited by Berti, and despite Ricci's effort to disprove the claim, it found ready acceptance by subsequent students.[20] The evidence

---

ff.), p. 62: "Aveva due porte (ne fu chiusa una)." The architrave which was found by Varneri on Side A' (Document 12) did not have to belong to an antique door. If it had, Lanciani should have uncovered the foundations. Rather, it must have been part of the door through which the Baptistery communicated with the old rectory demolished in the seventeenth century.

16. Ricci was the first: see "S. Giovanni," p. 272, where he ends a discussion of Lanciani's reasoning for the presence of the two doors (see previous note) by stating that it is immaterial since "le porte sono quattro." He cites no source for this.

17. For example Sangiorgi, *Battistero*, p. 11: "Nei lati della parte bassa sono interpolate . . . quattro porte oggi sepolte. Gli archi di scarico a fior di terra mostrano anche oggidì che le porte si aprivano sui lati Sud-Est, Nord-Est, Nord-Ovest, Sud-Ovest." And more recently, Casalone in "Ricerche," p. 205: "Sotto il deambulatorio [sic; see below, p. 39] si aprivano le quattro porte, architravate e sovrastate da un arco di scarico . . ." The sources in the Baptistery archives are explicit on these arches: "gli archi invisibili fatti alla profondità di circa tre metri, sopra i cigli dei quali si dovevano posare le macchine operatrice di rialzamento, furono eseguiti negli anni inseguenti al 1864" ("Bona patrimonia," note below frontispiece drawing). Cf. also *Figs.* 21, 22. When the project failed to materialize the arches were filled in.

18. See for example a ground plan in "Bona patrimonia" (frontispiece); L. Canina, *Ricerche*

sull'architettura più propria dei tempij cristiani (Rome, 1846), Pl. 104; M.E. Isabelle, *Les Édifices circulaires et les domes classés par ordre chronologique* (Paris, 1855), Pl. 42, reproduced in Cabrol-Leclercq, *Dictionnaire d'archéologie chrétienne et de liturgie* (Paris, 1907 ff.), 2, col. 427, Fig. 1337; H. Hübsch, *Monuments de l'architecture chrétienne* (Paris, 1866), Pl. XIII.13.

19. See F. de Dartein, *Étude sur l'architecture lombarde . . .* (Paris, 1865–82), Pl. I; R. Garrucci, *Storia della arte cristiana nei primi otto secoli della chiesa* (Prato, 1872–81), 4, Pl. 228; C. F. Rogers, "Baptism and Christian Archaeology," *Studia biblica et ecclesiastica*, 5 part 4 (Oxford, 1903), Fig. 63.

20. Berti, *Sull'Antico Duomo*, pp. 49–50, where he believes the porch to have been destroyed during the building of the Cappella del Sacramento in the early seventeenth century. Ricci's dissension is in "S. Giovanni," pp. 311–12. Among those who favor the existence of the portico are Sangiorgi (*Battistero*, p. 137); Verzone (*Architettura religiosa dell'alto medio evo nell'Italia settentrionale* [Milan, 1942], p. 91); Casalone ("Ricerche," p. 75); and most recently Mazzotti (in *Corsi* [1961], p. 264). S. Bottari (in *Corsi* [1960], fasc. 2, p. 2) doubts its existence, on the negative evidence that no trace of it survives today on the wall of the Baptistery door; this of course is not a valid observation, since the wall was redone completely in 1775 (see Document 12).

is not altogether conclusive. Lanciani himself has published no record of such a find, and it is therefore impossible to weigh the value of Sangiorgi's statement thirty years later that Lanciani's studies had proved the presence of this connecting portico.[21] The clearest proof of remains is in Varneri's reports from the eighteenth century. He recorded the uncovering of substantial foundation walls during the repair of the narrow street between the cathedral and the Baptistery, and attributed these to a destroyed portico. The remains extended across the cemetery, terminating at the lateral wall of the cathedral (Document 15). How much of this substructure pertained actually to the old rectory demolished by Archbishop Aldobrandini in the early seventeenth century (p. 21) is of course impossible to tell; but part of it at least could well go back to an earlier stage in the Baptistery's history, especially if Varneri's claim is correct that the uncovered walls were "very ancient" ("antichissimi") and "of the same masonry as the fabric of the Baptistery."[22] Before the time of Varneri, special phraseology used in certain church documents seems in fact to make explicit reference to the portico. The relevant passages follow.

> *November 2, 1367.* Indict. V. Ravenne in guaita Gazi sub porticu ecclesie Sancti Joannis in Fontibus ante ecclesiam Maiorem prope sepulturam Balbis.
>
> *1455.* Ravenne in S. Ravennati Ecclesia sub porticu Baptismatis.
>
> *June 4, 1507.* Actum Ravenna sub porticu Baptismi prope portam Ecclesie Catedralis.
>
> *1516.* S. Joannis in Fontibus sub porticu Ecclesiae Majoris sive Ursiana, ubi Baptismus.
>
> *1606.* Metropolitanae Ecclesiae modico intervallo in septentrionem conjungitur Baptisterium Sancto Joanni Baptistae consecratum.[23]

It appears from these documents, although the contextual meaning of "sub porticu" is not always certain, that some sort of covered porch joined the Baptistery with the north doors of the Basilica Ursiana at least from the fourteenth century onward. After the demolition of intermediate structures between Baptistery and cathedral in the

---

21. "Sappiamo inoltre che l'Ing. Lanciani per istudio fatto sul luogo trovò avanzi e vestigia di un portichetto che doveva unire la Basilica Ursiana al Battistero, e sembrava abbraciare due porte del medesimo, cioè l'odierna e quella a Nord-Ovest; e questo dedusse da un pavimento antico ivi trovato" (*Battistero*, p. 139). This is the only reference to such a find by Lanciani.

22. "della stessa materia della fabbrica del battisterio, il quale tira avanti dal suddetto battisterio a tutta la casa bassa." Document quoted by Mazzotti in *Corsi* (1961), p. 263.

23. The sources of these documents are as follows: 1, Archivio Notarile Ravennate, Memoriale 16, carta 196 verso and 197 recto; 2, idem, Protocollo 20, c. 5 recto; 3, idem, Protocollo 60, c. 262 verso; 4, M. Fantuzzi, *Monumenti ravennati . . .* , 6

(Venice, 1801–04), 237; 5, our Document 5 in Appendix 2. The tradition reported by G. Rossi (*Hieronymi Rubei historiarum ravennatum libri* [Venice, 1589], p. 766) that each child baptized in Ravenna received two names, one at the font and another at the door of the cathedral, has been taken by Berti (*Sull'Antico Duomo*, p. 50) as an argument for the portico; for it is assumed by him that, since the baptized child had to travel from the Baptistery to the cathedral during the ceremony, a covered passage must have existed as shelter from the weather. The deduction is unwarranted and, if true, it must be remembered that the practice relates to Rossi's day, the late sixteenth century, and should not necessarily be pushed all the way back to the fifth.

early seventeenth century for the construction of the Cappella del Sacramento, the references in documents vary enough from the above to connote proximity between the two buildings but not junction.[24]

The theory of an external ambulatory was originated by Testi-Rasponi, who, on the evidence of the words "duplicibus muris" used by Agnellus in describing the baptistery of Classis, suggested that the Orthodox Baptistery too must have had "double walls," that is, an ambulatory.[25] The suggestion was strengthened by the analogy of the Arian Baptistery, where the existence of an external ambulatory has been proved beyond doubt by the excavations of Gerola in the second decade of this century.[26] It did not take long for Testi-Rasponi's tenuous theory to gain acceptance. Casalone's recent study concludes a discussion of the issue with the declaration that "the existence of this element can be said to be certain."[27] Such confidence is entirely gratuitous. It seems improbable in the first place that no traces of the ambulatory would have come to light, if it ever existed, after two complete excavations of the Baptistery's periphery, one by Lanciani for the project of the "rialzamento" and the other in the late 1930s for the consolidation of the substructure. Visually, too, it would be hard to reconcile the four equal niches, which give character to the external mass by playing against the clear planes of the upper octagon, with a continuous ambulatory that would conceal them from view.[28] The case of the Arian Baptistery is quite different. The apsidal niche there is much larger than the other three, and the ambulatory would have served to create an octagon in plan, one side of which would be interrupted by this prominent niche. In this respect the Arian Baptistery is closer to the external disposition of San Vitale than to that of the Orthodox Baptistery.

It has long been recognized that the frieze of blind arcading over the windows, a motif which, in its essential form, is a trademark of Lombard architecture common on North Italian buildings after the ninth century, could not be part of the original design of the Baptistery. After a critical examination of the masonry Gerola, in an article published in 1917, announced that there was a clear discontinuity in the fabric, starting about half a meter below the frieze of arcading. He hypothesized that

24. Note, for example, a document of 1612, where it is said that the Baptistery "metropolitanae proximum adiacet" (quoted by Mazzotti in *Corsi* [1961], p. 264). The porch at the Orthodox Baptistery would not be unprecedented: witness the third baptistery at Aquileia, which was joined to the atrium of the Basilica Popponiana by two lateral porticoes (P. L. Zovatto, *Monumenti paleocristiani di Aquileia e di Grado* [Udine, 1957], pp. 160–66, Fig. 59, and Pl. VI). Also see baptistery at Salona (E. Dyggve, *History of Salonitan Christianity* [Oslo, 1951], pp. 30–33 and Fig. II.25). A porch, rebuilt in the tenth century and again in the Romanesque period, existed between S. Tecla in Milan and its baptistery. See M. Mirabella Roberti "La cattedrale antica di Milano e il suo bat-tistero," *Arte Lombarda*, 8 (1963), 86 ff., and Figs. 1, 2, 19.

25. *Codex*, p. 218.

26. G. Gerola, "Il restauro del Battistero Ariano," *Studien zur Kunst des Ostens* (Hellerau, 1923), pp. 112–29.

27. "Ricerche," p. 204. Her claim that the four doors will have an architectural meaning only if they are understood to communicate with an ambulatory (ibid., p. 205) is invalidated by the fact that there were probably only two doors, as discussed above, pp. 36–37.

28. S. Bottari, in a recent article, objects to the presence of an ambulatory on similar grounds ("Il Battistero della Cattedrale di Ravenna," *Corsi* (1960), fasc. 2, pp. 7–12.

at some unknown date the upper part of the building was rebuilt, with new walls which coated the original masonry and rose to the present height. Attached to the antique part of the perimetric wall, on the inside a little above the lower extrados of the cupola, Gerola uncovered remnants of a stucco cornice, below which could be seen fragments of plaster painted in red. This crucial find made it apparent that before the cupola with its sheath of mosaics was built, the Baptistery was covered by a timber, probably coffered, ceiling which extended above the projecting cornice in stucco.[29] Inexplicably, the import of Gerola's contribution to the history of the monument was almost universally ignored by scholars for forty years; even the truth of his discovery has been doubted.[30] In a recent investigation Mazzotti was able to prove incontrovertibly the accuracy of Gerola's earlier observations. On July 22, 1960, digging below the debris that has accumulated through the centuries between the lower extrados of the cupola and the exterior wall, Mazzotti disclosed, about eight meters above the present pavement, a considerable portion of the stucco cornice at the angle of Sides B and B' (*Fig. 34*).[31] It is 0.11 meter wide and is carved with a simple ribbon motif. Parts of the plaster coating painted in red can clearly be seen at the lower edge of a detached and cleaned fragment of the cornice, now kept at the Archivio Arcivescovile (*Fig. 35*). The cornice appears complete at the top, and it is very likely that not much more came between this and the timber ceiling on the inside. The abrupt change, both of mortar and of module, in the masonry of the perimetric wall is plainly evident 0.42 meter above the cornice (*Fig. 17*). From here to the present roof the masonry is homogeneous, all of it the work of the medieval

---

29. See G. Gerola, "L'alzamento e la cupola del Battistero Neoniano," *Atti del instituto veneto di scienze, lettere ed arti*, 76 (1916–17), 311–21.

30. See Casalone, "Ricerche," p. 209, where she informs the reader that she climbed into the area between the extrados and the modern roof to look for Gerola's cornice and that she found no trace of it. She concludes therefore that the cupola existed from the very beginning. She maintains further that the arcade of Zone I and the triple arches of Zone II are not contemporary with, but are later than, the cupola. According to her, the building had a cupola originally, resting on eight main arches at the level of Zone II. Zone I had no arcade, but eight tall columns capped by a high architrave. At a later time, most probably under Archbishop Maximian, the arcade of Zone I and the triple arches of Zone II were added; at this time the main arches of Zone II were shortened and placed on their present brackets. Consequently, the columns of Zone II also had to be changed and be replaced by the present twenty-four Ionic columns (ibid., pp. 211–15). This complicated chain of supposed alterations and additions loses its validity when the existence of the stucco cornice is taken into account. Casalone's argument is indeed very similar to that presented by G. Gamberini in his un-

published thesis (University of Venice, Scuola Superiore di Architettura, 1956), apparently consulted by Casalone, although she does not include it in her bibliography. (In fact, Casalone's Fig. 9 corresponds almost exactly to a reconstruction drawing in Gamberini's thesis.) The only difference between the two arguments is that Casalone takes the stucco prophets to be Maximianic, while Gamberini dates them to the time of Ursus. An error common to both studies is the emphasis placed on the present location of the opus sectile. (Cf. also E. H. Swift, *Roman Sources of Christian Art* [New York, 1951], p. 133: "the sumptuous *sectile* decorations . . . which antedate the system of wall arches now marring their original uninterrupted friezelike arrangement . . .") No argument can be based on this element of the decoration, as we noted in the previous chapter.

It is not necessary to deal separately with Bettini's similar but earlier hypothesis about the early building history of the Baptistery ("Il Battistero della Cattedrale," *FR*, 52 [1950], 58).

31. Mazzotti, "Il Battistero della Cattedrale di Ravenna," *Corsi* (1961), esp. pp. 264–68. The cornice, which I inspected personally on Oct. 18, 1960, begins at 1.25 meters below the sill of the small arched window of Side B.

alteration. Toward the outside this later brickwork extends in broad bands, roughly equal to the double panels of the frieze of arcading, to about 0.40 meter below the level of the cornice, filling in, with an uneven base line, the much deeper blind arcade with which the exterior seems to have originally terminated (*Fig.* 36). Bits of painted plaster clinging to the cracks of the older masonry may belong to the initial coating of the exterior.

This then, so far as can be deduced from a study of its fabric, was the general form of the Baptistery of the Basilica Ursiana in the early fifth century: a simple octagon in brick with salient niches at the four corners;[32] a row of arched windows above, one on each side of the octagon; and toward the top, a deep blind arcade sunk about 0.35 meter into the masonry (*Fig.* 7). If the evidence of a few traces of plaster in this upper part is to be trusted, the brickwork was not left exposed. The total height of the structure could not have been much more than about 11.50 meters; it was almost certainly capped by a wooden roof.[33] Within, the one inevitable conclusion is that the Baptistery was unvaulted. What existed below the timber ceiling and its painted stucco cornice, however, cannot be determined. It seems clear that the two superposed rows of arcades would be entirely out of place without the cupola. The contrary view of Monsignor Mazzotti, that they originated with the monument and were not added to it subsequently, is unacceptable to this writer.[34] Given the level of the stucco cornice (*Figs.* 8, 36), a ceiling that extended a little way above it would either cut into the tops of the Zone II arches or else be so close upon them as to present an extraordinarily unpleasing interior. It is known furthermore that these arches were initially of tubular construction like the cupola they were meant to support (p. 33) and surely an extension of its structure. The perimetric wall is not married to the masonry of the arcades; at the level of Zone I the arcade is simply indented into the bounding wall for stability.[35] Mazzotti, in defending his view, attaches great importance to the fact that, at the level of the cornice, the wall was one meter deep. Since without the arcades the lower wall measures only 0.60 meter deep, he insists that the building would have been impossibly top-heavy unless it is assumed that only the cupola, and nothing else, was lacking from the initial design; that the perimetric wall, although built prior to the arcades, was in fact built as a function of them. Two points should be raised against this reasoning. First, exactly at the top, where the stucco cornice

---

32. In one of his inventories, the rector Varneri noted that he had discovered an "antique" window in the altar niche (see the last part of Document 15 and note following it). Sangiorgi suggests that each of the four niches might have had one small window, at least by the time of Bishop Neon (*Battistero*, p. 46). This is pure speculation and cannot be ascertained, as he himself concedes, since the niches have been so thoroughly reconstructed in modern times.

33. An alternative possibility would be that the building was hypaethral. This, however, is very unlikely, considering the fact that baptism was ad-

ministered on Easter day, which fell in March or in early April, and that total immersion was the prevalent procedure. One more point should be noted here: if Neon found it necessary to raise the exterior wall because of his new cupola, there is no evidence of this in the masonry.

34. Mazzotti (see n. 31), pp. 268–69.

35. This is clearly the meaning of C. Ricci's note, cited by Mazzotti, curiously, to support his own theory: "Battistero, maggio 1905. Gli archi A [of Zone I] adorni di mosaico penetrano nel muro per 15 centimetri e furono fatti dopo costrutto il muro ottangolare in cui s'innestano . . ."

adheres to the bounding wall, the thickness would have been considerably decreased by the presence of the deep blind arcade toward the outside; and second, from the fact that the thicker wall close to the ceiling would have required some support below it, it does not necessarily follow that this support must be the superposed arcades. Two stories of corner columns, each with its own entablature, would serve equally well and, given the absence of the cupola, would be visually preferable. For the rest, one can do nothing but speculate about the decoration of the walls. Likely as not, they had the usual contemporary ornament on them—opus sectile and painted stucco. The possibility that the stucco prophets of Zone II belonged to this decorative system cannot be entirely overlooked.[36] I believe however that this zone is so much a part of the overall decoration and so intricately involved in the main arcade at this level that it must be contemporary with the mosaics and therefore datable to the second stage in the history of the Baptistery (cf. below, pp. 99 ff.).

2. *The Neonian Baptistery*

It is this simple timber-roofed building, which we have been trying to reconstruct above, that Bishop Neon saw standing beside the cathedral of his predecessor. When he was finally done with it, the previously modest Baptistery had been altered so radically that Neon felt justified in putting up his rather pretentious inscription: "Cede vetus nomen, novitati cede vetustas." From Agnellus' account of his life, Neon emerges as one of the great builders of Ravenna. Not only did he launch ambitious new projects of his own; he completed projects that had been started by his predecessors and left unfinished. "Meet it was," remarks Agnellus, speaking of one of these incomplete projects, the Basilica Petriana, "for the successors to complete their predecessors' work. And when the building had been set up and its roofs were in place, he [Neon] had it painted with diverse colors."[37] And with these lines Agnellus leads up to the renovation of the Orthodox Baptistery.

We are now in a better position to appreciate the extent of this renovation. To Agnellus' eye, as to the eye of the modern visitor, it was the mosaics that were the spectacular novelty. But the framework on which these mosaics were set is no less spectacular. It is obvious that Neon wanted a domed building, but the dome could not simply be placed on the already existing walls since these were not built to bear such a load. The thickness of the exterior walls of the Baptistery, a mere 0.60 meter, is often commented upon by students of medieval architecture. The usual explanation offered is that they could be made so slender because the light tubular cupola exerted little downward pressure and because its thrust was inconsequential.[38] The order of this explanation should now be reversed. It is not the exterior walls that

---

36. So Gerola (above, n. 29), p. 317.

37. *Codex*, p. 77: "unde neccesse erat, successores antecessori opus implere. Dehinc fuerant omnia postquam constructa edificia et sarta tecta tenpli innovata sunt, variis coloribus depingere fecit."

38. See for example G. T. Rivoira, *Lombardic Architecture, Its Origin, Development and Derivatives, I* (London, 1910), 38; also F. de Dartein, *Étude sur l'architecture lombarde, I,* 15.

could *afford* to be thin because of the lightness of the cupola, but rather the cupola which, as a later idea, *had* to be light because of the slenderness of the existing walls.

Even so, however, no chances were taken. The cupola was provided with its own supports which are largely independent of the exterior walls (*Fig.* 8). Ingeniously, these elements took the shape of the superposed arcades. The weight of the cupola was directed downward by the pendentives and partly placed on the brackets of Zone II. The corner columns of Zone II transferred this weight to the columns of Zone I, which in turn resolved it into the ground. In effect, therefore, the resultant building was composed of two separate units: an internal aerial structure in the form of a baldacchino and an external shell which, essentially unconnected with the vault and arcades inside, provided for them a simple, solid sheath.

The term "baldacchino" is appropriate to describe this Neonian interior. Fifth-century baptisteries often had a ciborium of simple or more elaborate design for the central font. In Neon's Baptistery the whole new interior functions as such, a magnificently ornamented ciborium for the font which was the focal point of, indeed the excuse for, this Ravennate monument. It can be inferred from a passage in the Roman *Liber pontificalis* that the Baptistery of the Lateran had undergone a parallel renovation some years before, during the pontificate of Sixtus III (432–40), for the baptistery that Constantine the Great had erected on this site seems to have had no *tegurium,* or cupola. Sixtus put up the eight porphyry columns collected by Constantine; over them he placed a tegurium, and on the epistyle of the columns he had carved a long inscription in verse dealing with the mystery of baptism (*Fig.* 129).[39] Is it not more than coincidence that two decades or so afterward one finds Neon undertaking a very similar renovation for the baptistery of his own city, a renovation utilizing those same elements of columns, tegurium, and inscription? And is it not a proper testimony to Neon's interest in the most crucial sacrament of early Christian times that the only document of his episcopate is a letter to him by Leo the Great in answer to Neon's query about the baptism of those returning from captivity among heretics?[40]

3. Medieval Renovation

More than any other feature, what characterizes the external appearance of the Orthodox Baptistery is the frieze of slender double arches, two to each side of the octagon, sunk into the upper masonry (*Figs.* 3, 4, 15). Long considered a part of the Neonian additions to the pre-existing structure, it was often singled out by scholars, with astonishment or enthusiasm, as a precursor of so-called "deuterobyzantine" or, in Puig y Cadafalch's terminology, "first romanesque" architecture.[41] There is no

---

39. For an excellent discussion of this renovation see P. Underwood, "The Fountain of Life in Manuscripts of the Gospels," *DOP, 5* (1950), 53 ff.

40. Migne, *PL, 54,* col. 1191, letter no. CLXVI: "Ad Neonem Ravennatem episcopum."

41. A Neonian date was favored by Sangiorgi

(*Battistero,* pp. 15–18); Rivoira (n. 38 above; p. 257); and C. Calzecchi ("Sviluppi e influssi dell'architettura ravennate de V e VI secolo in Italia," *FR, 47* [1938], 5–21). Puig y Cadafalch himself was noncommittal but said that, if Neonian, "cet emploi du thème décoratif serait le plus ancien connu"

question today that this frieze belongs to, and does not so dramatically antedate, this later development of medieval building. The fabric of thin yellowish bricks whose ratio to the mortar is about 3 to 2, and the quality of the mortar itself with its content of large, colored pebbles, clearly distinguish the handsome arcade from the very different fifth-century masonry seen on the inside, above and below the stucco cornice uncovered by Gerola. The type and proportions of the double arches find no parallel in the classic period of Ravenna's Christian buildings, that is, of the fifth and sixth centuries. No example, it would seem, survives before the late eighth century of the motif of a triangular brick inserted in the juncture of the two small arches that form the units of the frieze. Here at the Baptistery the unusually large size of this feature and its division into a lozenge and two complementary triangles places it in an advanced stage of the development of this particular motif.[42] The kind of small arched window seen on Side B' appears on no other monument of Ravenna prior to the ninth century (*Fig.* 13).[43] Despite the pioneer research of Gerola and G. Galassi,[44] the chronology of this later medieval architecture in the Emilia-Romagna is not as yet refined enough to allow a precise dating for the arcade at the Baptistery; to attempt it would involve one in a complex question that lies beyond the scope of this study. Galassi's decision upon a general date of about the tenth century is an intelligent one.[45]

Roughly the same date was reached more recently by Mazzotti, who approached the problem from another angle.[46] Lanciani's excavations apparently had disclosed not only the antique pavement 3 meters below the present ground level, but also

---

(*La Géographie et les origines du premier art roman* [Paris, 1935], p. 113). Gerola wavered between a Romanesque and a fifth-century date; he first decided on the latter (n. 29 above; p. 320), but later had a change of mind ("L'architettura deuterobizantina a Ravenna," *Ricordi di Ravenna medioevale per il VI centenario della morte di Dante* [Ravenna, 1921], pp. 15–112, esp. 82–83). The attempt on the part of some scholars (see for example S. Bettini, "Il Battistero della Cattedrale," *FR*, *52* [1950], 43) to derive a date from the bronze cross of Bishop Theodorus (677–88), which was discussed above, pp. 19–20, is quite arbitrary. Frequently this seventh century date is given as one of two alternatives: see G. Bovini, *Chiese di Ravenna* (Novara, 1957), p. 46; and C. C. van Essen, "Verslag van wetenschappelijke Onderzoekingen gedurende 1949 in Noord-Italië verricht," *Mededeelingen van het Nederlands historisch Instituut te Rome,* series 3, 7 (1953), 83. (The article by van Essen was very kindly translated for me by Dr. E. Haverkamp-Begemann.)

42. G. Galassi, *L'Architettura protoromanica nell'Esarcato* (*FR* Supplement, *3;* Ravenna, 1928), 86–87.

43. Ibid., p. 74. Similar windows at the upper part of Theodoric's tomb were opened, according to Galassi, in the later Middle Ages, when the tomb

served as the church of Santa Maria del Faro (ibid., p. 86 n. 39). Another such window, on the facade of Sant'Apollinare Nuovo, dates from a ninth-century reconstruction: see G. Gerola, "La facciata di S. Apollinare Nuovo," *FR* Supplement, *2,* fasc. 1 (1916).

44. Besides the works already cited, see: G. Tura (pseudonym of Gerola), "Deuterobizantino o protoromanico?" *FR*, *33* (1929), 11–20; Gerola, "Per la datazione dell'architettura deuterobizantina a Ravenna," *FR*, *34* (1930), 3–16; idem, "Le chiese deuterobizantine del Ravennate," *Art Studies* (1931), pp. 215–21. Also Galassi, "Ravenna e Milano, formatrici del Romanico," *Studi romagnoli,* *3* (1952), 69–78.

45. *L'Architettura protoromanica,* p. 75. As early as 1917 A. Kingsley Porter posited that "an examination of the masonry leaves no possible room for doubt that the arched corbel-tables were added after the year 1000. In fact, there is documentary evidence that the apse of the Cathedral was reconstructed in 1112, and the character of the bricks is a sufficient indication that the cornice of the Baptistery was remade a century earlier" *Lombard Architecture* (New Haven, 1915–17), *I,* 224.

46. M. Mazzotti, "La cripta della Basilica Ursiana di Ravenna," *FR, 55* (1951), 44 ff.

another pavement at a depth of 1.75 meters. Pointing out that the original pavement of the campanile (ninth to eleventh century) at the northwest corner of the cathedral (*Figs.* 9, 10) is 2.05 meters below the present ground level, Mazzotti maintained that the raising of the antique floor at the Baptistery must have taken place about 1000, and that the exterior too may have been adjusted on that occasion. Such a renovation would fall into the period when the campanile was being built and the cathedral repaired. Unhappily, this argument creates as many questions as it attempts to solve. The intermediate floor, for one thing, has to be taken on faith. Neither Lanciani's report nor his unpublished drawings contain a record of it. Ricci is the only person who speaks of it (briefly, in his article of 1888).[47] If it existed, there is still no reason why the approximate correspondence of the *actual* pavement of the medieval campanile and the *raised* pavement of the Baptistery should indicate a correspondence in date. Besides, the broad margin of about two centuries for the construction of the campanile is of no more assistance in determining a precise date for the Baptistery frieze than is already suggested by an analysis of its architectural style.

The elevation of the exterior wall, whenever it may have been undertaken, had primarily an aesthetic rather than a structural concern. It has been assumed that the stepped extension of the new wall toward the interior, which begins only 0.18 meter above the terminal point of the old masonry, was designed to meet some of the thrust of the cupola (*Fig.* 36).[48] This extension, however, never actually touches the cupola; and besides, the thrust of the tubular vaulting is almost certainly insufficient to require extra buttressing. The function of this stepped extension, the top width of which is half a meter, was most likely that of a service ledge around the extrados. Aesthetically, the advantage of the medieval alteration is evident. It corrected, to some extent, the effect of the rising ground which, by the tenth century, had buried the lower parts of the building, destroying the initial proportions. In covering the deep fifth-century arcade over the windows with slender Lombard bands, the Ravennates were not only enhancing the outer form of their Baptistery, they were also bringing its architecture up to date.

Externally, the Orthodox Baptistery has retained this basic appearance to the present day. One important change, however, was the raising of the floor inside. Whether this occurred twice, which we have to assume if the alleged pavement 1.75 meters below the present ground level indeed exists, or only once, bringing it up from the original level to the height at which the present columns sit (*Fig.* 8), it had the effect of altering irremediably the graceful proportions between the superposed arcades of the two zones and the whole of the building. I am inclined to believe that there was only one raising of the pavement, and that it took place no later than the

---

47. "S. Giovanni," p. 282. Recently Mazzotti has noted the slimness of the evidence for this intermediary pavement: "Dagli appunti e dai disegni del Lanciani esso [the pavement] non appare mai, ma può darsi che Corrado Ricci, pur non lasciando ne traccia nei suoi manoscritti, abbia visto tale pavimento" (*Corsi* [1961], p. 262).

48. Gerola, "L'alzamento e la cupola del Battistero Neoniano," *Atti del reale instituto veneto* . . . , 16 (1916–17), 320.

twelfth century, perhaps even coevally with the building of the exterior arcade. Gerola, in analyzing the walls which support the present columns of Zone I, discovered that the mortar used contained gravel, a practice that disappears in Ravenna after the twelfth century.[49] The renovation brought two further changes in its wake. The tall columns of Zone I, several pedestals of which were disclosed by Lanciani's excavations (*Fig.* 21), could not be retained. They were replaced by the present shorter shafts, unmatched and unattractive. Also, the arches of Zone I were lessened in rise, perhaps in an attempt to reduce the obvious disproportion caused by the new pavement or else to help accommodate the height of the stray shafts that were pressed into service.[50] The operation is evident from the fact that the pattern of the mosaic on the arch imposts has been disturbed (*Figs.* 103, 107). Another proof is perhaps provided by the carving of the pulvins, not inconsistent with the style of the fifth century, which is very similar to the carving on the impost blocks from which the four niche arches spring (*Fig.* 104). If, as is probable, the pulvins were once at the same level as these blocks, and not higher as they are today, the present position may well be due to the medieval shortening of the arch imposts of Zone I.[51]

ANALYSIS OF THE ARCHITECTURE

Much will remain unknown concerning the precise form of the Orthodox Baptistery which was built to complement the Basilica Ursiana in the early fifth century. But enough of its essential character has emerged from the foregoing discussion to warrant further comment within the framework of contemporary Early Christian architecture. The historical circumstances of the monument—its date and its situation—themselves suggest the pertinent questions that have to be raised. In Ravenna, unlike Rome and Milan, there was no substantial tradition of Christian architecture when Ursus began the new cathedral complex. Almost nothing of consequence is known of Roman building in this Adriatic city prior to its rise as the imperial capital of Honorius, or of the fourth-century Christian structures at Classis like the Basilica Probi and its baptistery. The Orthodox Baptistery stands in fact as one of the earliest surviving monuments of the new Ravenna, and as such assumes considerable histori-

---

49. Ibid., p. 317. The common belief that the pavement on which the present columns rest dates from the sixteenth century is a misconception first started by Sangiorgi (*Battistero*, p. 19), who supported this claim by citing a document from 1573, *aptetur pavimentum dictae ecclesiae*. He was, however, misquoting; the sentence should continue with the words *apud Sacrarium* (see our Document 2), that is, Niche D. Cf. above, p. 21. A general impression of the interior of the Orthodox Baptistery before the raising of the pavement may be obtained by looking at a view of the interior of the baptistery at Albenga (Verzone, *L'Architettura religiosa dell'alto medio evo*, Pl. 16).

50. That this medieval raising of the floor and shortening of the arches of Zone I were coeval is proven by the fact that the filling between the pulvins and the capitals uses the same graveled mortar as do the walls which support the floor of the present columns.

51. The question of pulvins and blocks was first considered by Gerola, but he warned against taking them together as a continuous frieze because their thicknesses are different and because the decorative leaves are not exactly similar (n. 48 above; p. 318). One need not suppose, however, that the pulvins and the blocks belonged to the same frieze. It is rather a question of a single base line for both the main arches of Zone I and the four niche arches.

cal importance for our knowledge of the course that was followed by the architects active in the city during the fifth century. To what extent could their work be said to be original? What aspects of their practice were traditional and what were derived from other centers of Early Christian architecture? How does the Baptistery of Ravenna compare with contemporary buildings of similar designation elsewhere in the Empire? And finally, what are its singular qualities as an *individual* work of art, which were the direct outcome of its own discrete program and which distinguish it from other monuments of the same general class?

To begin with the last question, it is fundamental that the general form of the Baptistery, excluding medieval and later alterations, resulted from the combination of two designs within fifty years or less of each other. The pre-Neonian Baptistery was clearly a simple, trabeated structure that presented no special problem of statics: thin, self-supporting walls of brick and a timber roof which rested upon them. The space enclosed within this small sacramental receptacle could be predicted from the exterior view. It was a finite space compressed by eight flat planes and extended only by means of the shallow niches of the lower half of the building, themselves clearly legible on the outside. The presence of the niches can only be justified within a spatial, and probably iconographic, context; they serve no structural purpose. When two of them were subsequently destroyed, the building remained statically intact (*Fig.* 26). In the fifth-century octagonal baptistery of S. Eufemia at Grado, such niches, with the exception of the apse, are omitted altogether (*Fig.* 128).[52]

The thinness of the four niches of the Baptistery of Ravenna and their independence from the main mass of the building should be underlined. Originally they would not have been neatly packed within a single unbroken outline, as is the case today (cf. *Figs.* 7, 14). That they started farther in from the corners would have stressed their separateness, and would not have interrupted the sharp edges of the octagon, which, at the top of the exterior, were prismatically articulated by means of the arcade sunk into the wall plane. Thus, because of their modest size, the niches, the only potentially plastic adjuncts of the exterior, could not alter the basically planar character of the composition defined by the broad, flat walls of the octagon. Only the arcade above the windows, whatever its specific identity, modulated the surface of the walls, which was probably made smoother by the veneer of painted stucco. Such a spare and prismatic exterior is consonant with what can be deduced from other fifth-century Ravennate buildings, like the Basilica Ursiana itself and the church of San Giovanni Evangelista; these too are characterized by clear, linear plans and simple, sharp wall planes which affect even the disposition of the apse. The Ursiana is in fact the earliest known Christian basilica to have had an externally polygonal apse.

With Neon's renovation, the external appearance of the Baptistery ceased to be accurately informative about the arrangement of the interior. The cupola and its

52. For this baptistery see P. Zovatto, "Il battistero di Grado," *RACrist*, *23-24* (1947-48), 231-51.

supporting arcades were not reflected by the pre-existing shape of the exterior, since they formed an essentially disparate structure fitted into the octagonal shell. A visual incongruity was thus created between the exterior and the interior, which still exists today. Neon's design within attempted to reconcile the flat planes of the original shell and his own baldacchino (*Figs.* 8, 39). The most striking characteristic of this design is the light, ephemeral quality of the system of the superposed arcades. The eye moves horizontally from arch to arch at the same time that it is drawn vertically toward the cupola by the columns of Zones I and II. The stucco cornice between the two zones divides the horizontal movement of the respective arcades but does not impede the soaring ascent from the floor to the cupola. Formally, the columns play two parts: they are at once springboards for the circumferential *perpetuum mobile* of the arcades and vertical accents that carry this circular motion up toward the cupola. The arches also have a dual formal role: they unite the separate panels of the octagon into one continuous circuit, and they reflect the rhythm of the cupola, in two dimensions, on every side of the octagon. In this way, Neon's system combines visually the polygonal ambient of the containing wall, which he inherited, with the circular form of the new cupola. The corner columns delineate the angles of the polygon but, as lines, they inevitably lead up to the cupola, a visual and tactile force which in one way is the negation of this polygon. The arches, as two-dimensional architectural members, reflect the flatness of the eight sides of the bounding wall, but at the same time their semicircular form echoes the curvature of the surmounting cupola. The whole interior scheme, then, illustrates the harmonious wedding of curved and straight lines and of horizontal and vertical dynamics.

The system of the superposed arcades is not only a visual scheme, it must be remembered, but also a load-bearing mechanism. For, unlike the mausoleum of Diocletian at Spalato as an instance, the corner columns in the Baptistery, although similarly placed in front of the interior walls, are here assigned a role in the statics of the building and could not be removed without endangering the structure, as they could be at the mausoleum. A closer comparison would be with such Early Christian centralized buildings as Santa Costanza and the Sistine baptistery of the Lateran in Rome (*Fig.* 129).[53] In these buildings also, domes are placed on a framework of columns and arches, but this framework does not make up the whole interior; it is surrounded, as a central feature, by a barrel-vaulted ambulatory, which acts as an expanded, bounding space and a continuous buttress for the dome. In the Baptistery of Ravenna, because of Neon's personal choice of design, the bounding walls and the baldacchino of the cupola are contiguous. The size of the domes over the Roman buildings might require the additional buttressing provided by the ambulatory. But, as a result, Santa Costanza and the Lateran Baptistery present quite a different solu-

---

53. For the architecture of Santa Costanza, see especially F. W. Deichmann, "Die Lage der constantinischen Basilika der Heiligen Agnes an der Via Nomentana," *RACrist,* 22 (1946), 213 ff., and illustrations in Deichmann, *Frühchristliche Kirchen in Rom* (Basel, 1948), Pls. 5–20. For the Lateran Baptistery see G. B. Giovenale, *Il Battistero lateranense,* Studi di antichità cristiana, *1* (Rome, 1929); and E. Sjöqvist, "L'origine del battistero constantiniano romano," *Opuscula archaeologica,* *4* (Lund, 1946), 135 ff.

tion from the Baptistery of Ravenna, for they lack the lightness and the oneness of purpose which are the dominant themes of the Ravennate monument. Their interiors are divided into two individual units—the dome and the ambulatory—each with its own space and its own physical boundaries. In the Orthodox Baptistery the space and the physical boundary are totally interdependent.

In a broad Roman imperial context, the octagonal plan of the Baptistery with its corner niches has ample precedent. It is frequently found in the architectural systems of palaces, villas, and baths.[54] Since, however, these octagonal chambers are most often small units within a larger architectural complex, and since their external appearance is consequently masked by other adjacent units, a more apt historical category for the Baptistery is that of free-standing centralized niched buildings of Roman imperial architecture, not necessarily octagonal in plan, in which the niches stand out from the bounding walls as independent masses and the lighting comes from windows in the drum; a late antique example is the so-called Temple of Minerva Medica, actually a Roman nymphaeum dating from A.D. 320.[55] It should be noted that brick, a basic building material of Roman architecture, is not wedded to concrete in typical Roman fashion in the Baptistery. That is to say that, whereas in pagan buildings like the "Temple of Minerva Medica" brick was often applied as facing for the concrete which was the main sustaining element of the structure, in the Baptistery the brick itself *is* the structure. As a consequence, the Ravennate monument lacks the fluid, monolithic shapes of Roman concrete architecture, and is composed instead of separate members—the niches, the walls, and the cupola—in a process that might be called additive. The cupola itself is further distinguished from the other parts of the building by the fact that different materials are employed in its structure.

In a narrower Christian context, Ravenna's Baptistery belongs to a close family of octagonal niched buildings of similar function, geographically and chronologically allied, which are found in the north of Italy and, by extension, in the southern region of France (*Fig.* 128). It is almost certain that the idea of an octagonal baptistery originated in this area, most probably in Milan, some time in the late fourth century, whence it spread to the east and west of the Mediterranean basin. This type of Early Christian baptistery is only one of several; before its appearance, baptisteries were frequently small rectangular rooms, with or without an apse, or else circular, as was the Constantinian baptistery of the Lateran.[56] The earliest octagonal niched baptistery in the Christian world, to our present knowledge, is that of S. Tecla, the five-

54. For a discussion of the genealogy of octagonal buildings see G. De Angelis d'Ossat, "Sugli edifici ottagonali a cupola nell'antichità e nel medioevo," *Atti del I convegno nazionale di storia dell'architettura, 1936* (Florence, 1938), pp. 13–24.

55. This category is distinguished from centralized Roman buildings in which the niches are carved into the thickness of the bounding wall and in which the source of light is an oculus (e.g. the Pantheon), and buildings in which the niches are within the bounding wall but the lighting comes from a row of windows pierced in the drum (e.g. St. George in Thessaloniki, originally the mausoleum of Emperor Galerius). For this classification see R. Krautheimer, "Santo Stefano Rotondo e la chiesa del Santo Sepolchro a Gerusalemme," *RA-Crist, 12* (1935) 79.

56. A recent compilation of plans of Early Christian baptisteries by A. Khatchatrian, *Les Baptistères paléochrétiens* (Paris, 1962), is the most convenient reference work on the subject.

aisled cathedral of Milan, built, according to the results of new excavations in 1961–62, some time about 378–86.[57] At least three subsequent octagonal structures in Milan, all possessing alternately semicircular and rectangular niches—S. Aquilino and S. Sisto, attached to the church of S. Lorenzo Maggiore; and the martyrial chapel of S. Gregorio, adjacent to S. Vittorio al Corpo and destroyed in the sixteenth century —underline the popularity of this form in the region during the episcopate of St. Ambrose and afterward.[58] Typologically, the form need not be derived from any specific Roman building (or group of buildings) such as the mausoleum of Diocletian at Spalato, as was proposed by Monneret de Villard.[59] The large number of inter-related late antique buildings within the same generic morphology obviates attempts to plot precise origins. Nor is it necessary to espouse the old view, that the form is a result of the transformation of the square, wherein the niches substitute for the corners in order to facilitate the placement and support of the cupola,[60] for it is doubtful that the popularity of the octagonal design in Roman and Early Christian architecture can be pinned down simply to a problem of technology. Milan's baptistery was a matter of choice—and the choice, doubtless, was inspired by other than merely formal concerns.

An inscription which once belonged to the baptistery of S. Tecla and is preserved in a ninth-century codex is of prime relevance here.[61] Often attributed to St. Ambrose himself, the inscription begins as follows:

> Eight-niched soars this church destined for sacred rites,
> eight corners has its font, the which befits its gift.
> Meet it was thus to build this fair baptismal hall
> about this sacred eight: here is our race reborn.[62]

F. Dölger, who was the first to study these verses, gave an excellent exposition of the importance of the number eight for Christian thought in general and for the

---

57. M. Mirabella Roberti, "La Cattedrale antica di Milano e il suo battistero," *Arte lombarda, 8* (1963), 77–98, and bibliography.

58. For the octagonal structures of S. Lorenzo see A. Calderini, G. Chierici, and C. Cecchelli, *La Basilica di S. Lorenzo Maggiore in Milano* (Milan, 1951); for S. Gregorio see Verzone, *L'Architettura religiosa dell'alto medio evo*, pp. 67–69, and now also A. Calderini, "I mausolei imperiali di Milano," *Arte del primo millenio (Atti del II convegno per lo studio dell'arte dell'alto medio evo* [Pavia, 1950]), pp. 42–55, and idem, "Un recinto fortificato di età imperiale scoperto recentemente nel suburbio milanese," *Beiträge zur älteren europäischen Kulturgeschichte (Festschrift für Rudolf Egger*, Klagenfurt, 1952), *1*, 236–41.

59. U. Monneret de Villard, "Nota di archeologia lombarda," *Archivio storico lombardo*, series 5, *41*, part 1 (1914), 11 ff.

60. Ibid., p. 10. The problem was studied earlier

by A. Choisy *L'Art de bâtir chez les byzantins* (Paris, 1883), pp. 80–81.

61. The inscription is preserved in the so-called Sylloge Laureshamensis, Codex Palatinus, 833, at the Vatican Library; for the full text of eight distychs, see de Rossi, *Inscriptiones christianae urbis Romae, 2*, 161.

62. "Octachorum sanctos templum surrexit in usus—octagonus fons est numere dignus eo—hoc numero decuit sacri baptismalis aulam—surgere quo populus vera salus rediit." The translation quoted here is from F. van der Meer and Chr. Mohrmann, *Atlas of the Early Christian World* (London, 1958), p. 129. For full bibliography of this inscription, see *DOP, 5* (1950) 81 n. 153; and now also O. Perler, "L'inscription du baptistère de Sainte-Thècle à Milan et le 'De sacramentis' de Saint Ambrose," *RA-Crist, 27* (1951), 147–66, where the authorship of St. Ambrose is supported and the inscription is dated to 389.

philosophy of baptism in particular.[63] In the writings of the early church fathers the number eight is often associated with regeneration and resurrection. The eighth day, Sunday, is the day of Christ's resurrection.[64] In the Gregorian Sacramentary, six is said to stand for the present age, seven for the age of rest, and eight for the age marked by resurrection.[65] St. Augustine had similar views on the symbolism of these three numbers in the passage from the present age to immortality.[66]

The interrelation of baptism with immortality is also amply documented in the writings of the fathers. The basis for this literature is in a passage of the Gospel according to St. John (3:5): "Except a man be born of water and of the Spirit, he cannot enter into the kingdom of God." St. Paul in the Epistle to the Romans (6:3-4) makes this point of doctrine quite clear:

> Know ye not, that so many of us as were baptized into Jesus Christ were baptized into his death? Therefore we are buried with Him by baptism into death: that like as Christ was raised up from the dead by the glory of the Father, even so we also should walk in newness of life.

It is not necessary here to cite the numerous passages in Early Christian literature where the belief of baptism as second birth is expounded. The font is at once a tomb and a womb; immersion is synonymous with death; from it one rises cleansed and sinless, to start the second life. In choosing the octagon as a new form for the Christian baptistery, the church of Milan was doing so consciously, with the intent to use it as a symbol of the meanings of the sacrament. This particular form, furthermore, reminiscent as it was of late Roman mausolea like the one at Spalato, could evoke in the celebrant, because of his familiarity with traditional typology, meaningful associations between the rite of baptism and the fact of death.[67]

---

63. "Zur Symbolik des altchristlichen Taufhauses," *Antike und Christentum, 4* (1933-34), 153-87.

64. See, for example, St. Ambrose, *Epist. Classis* I.44: "qui autem octavo die generationis sortitur mysteria, consecratur per gratiam, et ad haereditatem regni coelestis vocatur . . . ideoque octavo die soluta paradiso reddidit Spiritus . . ." (Migne, *PL, 16,* col. 1135).

65. For this and similar citations see P. Underwood in *DOP, 5* (1950), 82-84.

66. *De civitate Dei* xxii.30, 4-6 (Migne, PL, *41,* cols. 803-04); *Epistola LV, ad inquisitiones Januarii* (Migne, *PL, 33,* col. 204).

67. The association of baptisteries with Roman imperial mausolea was first seriously proposed by P. Styger, "Nymphäen, Mausoleen, Baptisterien. Probleme der Architekturgeschichte," *Architectura: Jahrbuch für Geschichte der Baukunst, 1* (Berlin, 1933), 50-55. This article is not free from erroneous or questionable comments, and must be read with caution. Styger, in opposing vehemently Ricci's earlier theory that Christian baptisteries derived from the architecture of Roman baths, went to equal extremes to substantiate his own derivation of them from mausolea. The Baptistery of Ravenna, for example, is cited as proof of this new theory because it was "originally surrounded by a cemetery," and because the four niches were meant to contain sarcophagi; both these claims are unfounded. More recently a study by R. Krautheimer, "Introduction to an 'Iconography of Medieval Architecture,'" *Journal of the Warburg and Courtauld Institutes, 5* (1942), 1-33, clearly set forth the grounds for objecting to the bath theory as proposed by Ricci and others (e.g. V. Golzio, *Architetture bizantina e romanica* [Milan, 1939], p. 47. See also E. H. Swift, *Roman Sources of Christian Art* [New York, 1951], p. 40, who in a typically categorical fashion claims: "few scholars doubt that the Christian baptistery derives from the pagan Roman bath, more specifically from a certain characteristic element of those complex structures . . . the *frigidarium*"). Krautheimer concluded that "evidently the round baptisteries form part of a large interrelated group of late antique buildings, and while the central rooms

It was not accident, therefore, that prompted the generic similarity between the designs of the Orthodox Baptistery and of the baptistery of S. Tecla, any more than it was accident that the Basilica Ursiana should emulate the Milanese cathedral two or three decades after its construction by St. Ambrose. The symbolic appropriateness of the octagonal form, and the illustrious precedent of the city which but recently had been the imperial capital, insinuated a formal choice to the Ravennate designers, as indeed to the designers of the baptisteries at Aquileia, Albenga, Novara, Fréjus, and others, all of which followed the prestigious example of S. Tecla in Milan. It is quite probable that Sixtus III was conscious of this general trend in North Italy when he chose to alter the round form of the Lateran Baptistery as built by Constantine the Great into an octagonal form, and to furnish it furthermore with an octagonal font covered by a ciborium on eight columns (*Fig.* 129). In ultimate inspiration, then, the plan of the Orthodox Baptistery may well have been due to the influence of St. Ambrose, as Neon's later renovation of the interior may have been inspired by this elaborate ciborium of Sixtus.

The word inspiration should be stressed. The pre-Neonian Baptistery was not an exact copy, as we would understand the term, of the Milanese baptistery of S. Tecla, nor was Neon's design a copy of the Sistine renovation in the baptistery of the Lateran. Copies in the Middle Ages, as was cogently demonstrated by R. Krautheimer with respect to the continual imitation in the West of the Holy Sepulchre at Jerusalem, derived their relevance from the symbolism attached to the form of the prototype, or to parts of it like the number of columns or a basic measurement or two, and not from the *structural* accuracy in the process of replication.[68] This distinction is vital and should be kept in the foreground when one considers the question of influence between one center of architecture and another or between buildings of the same general form. What relates the pre-Neonian Baptistery of Ravenna to the baptistery of S. Tecla and to those of Albenga, Riva San Vitale, Aquileia, Lomello, Como, Novara, Brescia, Aix, Fréjus, Riez, Nevers, and Marseilles is the *idea* of the symbolic octagon, not the precise architectural expression of this idea in the Milanese prototype. Architecturally, the Orthodox Baptistery shows significant differences from all these symbolic associates, especially the baptistery of S. Tecla (*Fig.* 128).

This nucleus of a dozen or so northern baptisteries of the late fourth and fifth centuries has yet to be studied as a group, a study that should be undertaken only after each of the monuments has been thoroughly investigated.[69] But certain obser-

---

of thermal architecture are among their ancestors, other types may and, indeed, are likely to have exerted a collateral influence" (ibid., p. 23). This collateral influence Krautheimer believes to have come from late Roman mausolea and, in my view, he succeeds in substantiating his hypothesis through the use of both typological and symbolic arguments.

68. Ibid., p. 1 ff.

69. The best reference work for the North Italian

baptisteries is still Verzone's *L'Architettura religiosa dell'alto medio evo nell'Italia settentrionale* (Milan, 1942), although some of them have since received more detailed studies. For excellent plans and sections of the baptisteries at Riva San Vitale, Como, and Lomello, see also F. Reggiori, *Dieci Battisteri lombardi minori, dal secolo V al secolo XII (I monumenti italiani. Rilievi raccolti dalla R. Accademia d'Italia,* fasc. 4; Rome, 1925). A. De Capitani d'Arzago, *Architetture dei secoli quarto e quinto in*

vations can readily be made. No two of the baptisteries are of equal scale or of exactly equal proportions, and they differ among themselves in interior organization, external massing, and the number and disposition of the niches. Compared with the Milanese prototype, which unfortunately survives only in plan, and with the baptisteries closest to it like those at Albenga, Brescia, and Fréjus, the Orthodox Baptistery stands apart by having only four semicircular niches visible on the outside, instead of eight, alternately semicircular and rectangular, buried deeply into the perimetric wall. The baptisteries of Novara, Lomello, Como, and Nevers are like the Orthodox Baptistery in exposing the niches beyond the octagonal perimeter, but unlike it in having eight of them, as have the previously mentioned group. In plan at least, the Ravennate monument comes closest to the baptisteries of Marseilles, Riva San Vitale, and Aquileia. Even here the right angles of the containing wall which transform the internal octagon into a perfect rectangle diverge from the design of the Orthodox Baptistery.

Most of these northern baptismal halls do not antedate the original Baptistery at Ravenna. The one certain, and most pertinent, predecessor is the baptistery of S. Tecla in Milan, a city with which, as we have indicated more than once, Ravenna had immediate historical and cultural associations. The comparison of the plans of the Ravennate and Milanese baptisteries is therefore especially to the point in determining the debt of Honorius' new capital to the city of St. Ambrose (*Fig.* 128). The massive perimetric wall of the S. Tecla baptistery, the deep niches carved into its thickness and not apparent from the outside, and the identical projection of all eight corners of the exterior body, contrast notably with the Baptistery of Ravenna, where the wall thickness and its plastic animation are minimal. Such comparative distinctions do not end with these two buildings. In the last twenty years the excellent work on the Early Christian monuments of Milan by E. Arslan, De Capitani d'Arzago, M. Mirabella Roberti, and others have made it abundantly clear that one cannot explain the architectural interrelation of the two cities as a simple carry-over from the older capital to the new.[70] Identifiable preferences insistently point to native building traditions. For Milan such preferences included single-aisled basilicas, transepts, the predilection toward massive construction, and definite, corporeal space uninterrupted for the most part by illusory screens of columns. Ravenna, which

---

alta Italia (Milan, 1944), is also useful. For the baptisteries of Southern France see J. Hubert, *L'Art pré-roman* (Paris, 1938), passim. The baptistery at Fréjus has been repeatedly considered by G. De Angelis d'Ossat, principally in "L'importanza architettonica del battistero di Fréjus," *Bulletino della commissione archeologica communale di Roma, 63* (1935), 39–51. The most recent study of the baptistery at Albenga is C. M. Casalone's in *Arte lombarda, 8* (1963), 103–10. An unpublished thesis for the degree of Master of Arts, presented by Mr. William Johnston to New York University in 1964, deals with the interrelations among the most impor-

tant baptisteries in this group, including the Baptistery of Ravenna. Cf. also bibliographical references given for each baptistery by Khatchatrian (above, n. 56).

70. The monographs are too numerous to list here. For general appraisal see, among others, A. De Capitani d'Arzago, "L'architettura cristiana in Milano," *Actes du VIe congrés international d'études byzantines, 1948, 2* (Paris, 1951), 67–84; E. Arslan, "Milano e Ravenna: Due momenti dell'architettura paleocristiana," *FR, 84* (1961), 5–38, with bibliography.

shared with its neighbor an interest in articulating exterior wall planes by the application of blind arcades, maintained an individuality of architectural style from the earliest Christian buildings that rose on its soil. One might list polygonal apses, linear design of thin wall planes, generous use of columns for visual and illusory effects, and a consistent priority for vaulting by hollow tubes in apses, cupolas, and similar forms.[71]

To these preferences of the Ravennate builders should be added the insertion of pulvin blocks between capitals of columns and arch imposts. The pulvin, although probably deriving from ressauts in late antique buildings like those at Santa Costanza, is not found in Roman architecture in this later form and was apparently first used almost contemporaneously in the Basilica Ursiana and in S. Giorgio Maggiore in Naples.[72] At the Baptistery the arcades of both Zones I and II illustrate this feature. The pulvins of Zone I have been moved upward from their original position during the raising of the pavement in the later medieval renovation. There is no good reason however to doubt their fifth-century origin. The vegetal carving on them agrees with such a date, and the fact that only two of the four corners are punctuated by salient leaves proves that they were always meant to be seen against a wall and not in midspace (*Figs.* 116–21). The pulvins of Zone II are smaller and undecorated. The arcade here does not rest directly on them but rather on brackets protruding from the wall over the corner columns (*Figs.* 75, 76). The cross and foliage on each of these brackets compare favorably with similar fifth-century examples from a church at Stobi, from St. John of the Studion at Istanbul, and others.[73] The combination of pulvin and bracket appears to have been a consequence of necessity. The columns of Zone II, unlike those of Zone I, could not be made to stand out from the walls in order to meet the arcades, for then a much broader ledge would have been required for the columns, disrupting the surface continuity which has been analyzed above (*Fig.* 70). The brackets were designed to meet the arch imposts and bring their weight back onto the pulvin blocks. In this connection, it is instructive to note that in two other baptisteries of the northern group, at Albenga and Novara, pulvins are also used, but these are so deeply immured that the load of the superstructure is transferred through

71. Vaulting in terra-cotta tubes was of course known to the Romans: cf. L. Crema, "Origine e impiego dei fittili cavi nell'architettura romana," *Bolletino del centro di studi di storia dell'architettura* (1952), pp. 6–8. For tubular vaulting in Early Christian architecture, see especially P. Verzone, "Le cupole di tubi fittili del V e VI secolo in alta Italia," *Atti del I convegno nazionale di storia dell'architettura, 1936* (Florence, 1938), pp. 7–11. Among Roman predecessors the closest to the tubular vaulting of Ravenna is a vault in the villa baths in Capo Lilibeo presso Marsala, in the province of Trapani, excavated by Bovio-Marconi (*Le Arti, 2* [*1940*], 55, 389–91). Another example, quite similar to the system of the Orthodox Baptistery, is found in the villa at Piazza Armerina; I owe the reference of this as

yet unpublished vault to the kindness of Professor W. MacDonald. See also G. Bovini, "L'impiego dei tubi fittili nelle volte degli antichi edifici di culto ravennati," *Bolletino economico,* no. 2 (Feb. 1959), reprinted in *Corsi* (1959), fasc. 1, pp. 27–43.

72. G. T. Rivoira, *Roman Architecture* (Oxford, 1925), p. 259. The feature is common in the early basilicas of Ravenna: note S. Agata, S. Giovanni Evangelista, and others (De Angelis d'Ossat, *Studi ravennati,* pp. 7–39, esp. p. 35).

73. See E. Kitzinger, "A Survey of the Early Christian Town of Stobi," *DOP, 3* (1946), Fig. 134; and Kautzsch, *Kapitellstudien,* Pl. 33 no. 540a. Cf. also a similar pulvin used in the crypt of the Basilica Ursiana (*FR, 55* [1951], 22, Fig. 8).

them to the bounding wall, and the presence of the columns therefore becomes largely nonstructural. Only in the baptistery at Fréjus is the use of pulvins comparable to that in the Orthodox Baptistery.[74]

One final feature of the Ravennate Baptistery deserves comment: the motif of the triple arches within the main arcade of Zone II (*Fig.* 71). Now, as an architectural scheme the triple arch with the central compartment higher than the lateral two is, of course, quite frequent in Roman practice. It is met with on triumphal arches, on palace facades, on *scaenae frontes,* and the like. It becomes the dominant facade order for three-aisled Christian basilicas. But its use as subdivision of a larger encompassing arch in the interior of a building is a characteristic of sixth-century Justinianic architecture, for example the bema of San Vitale and the galleries of Hagia Sophia and Sts. Sergius and Bacchus in Istanbul. Here at the Baptistery this major Byzantine motif makes a precocious appearance as early as the mid-fifth century.[75]

It is tempting to read some meaning into these triple arches of Zone II—a reflection perhaps of the symbolism of the triple immersion which was the canonical procedure of baptism at this time and represented the three-day burial of Christ.[76] But more likely is the identification of the three arches embraced by a larger arch with the symbolic representation of the three elements of the Trinity, one and indivisible.[77] This pictorial representation of the central dogma of Christianity, if the suggestion is true, would be an appropriate declaration of faith in the face of such doubting heresies as Arianism which was to sweep over the orthodox city of Ravenna with the advent of Theodoric's Goths a mere twenty years after the death of Bishop Neon.

The position of the Baptistery of Ravenna in close proximity to the Basilica Ursiana prompts one last general observation on planning. Christian baptisteries as independent buildings appear no sooner than the Peace of the Church. Before that time baptism had been administered outdoors, in streams, rivers, or the sea, or a font was placed in a corner of the cult building for an indoor ceremony.[78] With the recognition and the triumph of the church under Constantine, it became customary to dedicate a special edifice to the sacrament of baptism in the imposing Christian programs that rose throughout the Empire. The baptistery was traditionally adjacent to the cathedral of the city, although its exact relation to it was not prescribed. The baptistery could be situated in the cathedral atrium, as at Parenzo;[79] behind the apse,

74. See De Angelis d'Ossat (n. 69 above), Fig. 4 and p. 50.

75. The arrangement of the upper story in the interior of the baptisteries at Albenga and Fréjus should not be considered as a parallel usage: there the arches are all of equal height and are not bracketed into groups.

76. See Leo, *Ep.* XVI.3 (Migne, *PL, 54,* cols. 698–99); Cyril of Jerusalem, *Catechesis* XX, *Mystagogica* III. 4 (Migne, *PL, 33,* col. 1080 B).

77. A Syriac hymn, probably from the seventh century, which describes a church at Edessa, speaks of the three windows of the choir as being equal to the Trinity; see A. Grabar in *Cahiers,* 2 (1947), 41 ff.

78. The classic work on the subject is J. Corblet, *Histoire dogmatique, liturgique et archéologique du sacrament de baptême* (2 vols. Paris, 1881–82). A good recent bibliography and a list of early baptisteries will be found in T. Klauser, *Reallexikon für Antike und Christentum, 1* (Stuttgart, 1950), cols. 1157–67.

79. Verzone (n. 69 above), Fig. 21 and p. 52.

as in some churches in Tripolitania;[80] or north of the cathedral, as in Grado and Ravenna. The visual role of the baptismal hall in the planning of the cathedral site is noteworthy, especially with centralized baptisteries like the North Italian group which has been discussed above. These buildings, with their vertical mass, helped to moderate the horizontal disposition of the basilical cathedrals; in this respect they anticipated the visual role of the bell towers. An architectural complex composed of one central and one basilical structure was hardly an unknown system of planning in the Roman world. Imperial mausolea were sometimes erected adjacent to a longitudinal building,[81] as in Spalato, and it is this tradition which seems to have been carried on into Christian planning when mausolea or martyrial halls were erected in close proximity to churches. The two round mausolea, S. Andrea and S. Petronilla, to the south of Old St. Peter's, are good examples.[82] Generally speaking, the arrangement at the Holy Sepulchre follows the same tendency; there too a congregational church is juxtaposed with a centralized sepulchral structure, the rotunda of the Anastasis. In this context, though the parallel should not be carried too far, the Christian baptistery may be said to complement a congregational church in the same way, visually and symbolically, that a mausoleum or a martyrium did.[83] Again, the death symbolism in the sacrament of baptism would tend to make this parallel more credible.

---

80. J. B. Ward Perkins and R. G. Goodchild, "The Christian Antiquities of Tripolitania," *Archaeologia, 95* (1953), 67–70.

81. Cf. F. W. Deichmann, *RACrist, 22* (1946), 213 ff.; and *JDAI, 72* (1957), 44–110.

82. See H. Koethe, "Zur Mausoleum der weströmischen Dynastie bei Alt-Sankt-Peter," *RM, 46* (1931), 9–26.

83. Grabar has found instances of martyria being used as baptisteries at Nisibis and in Africa (*Martyrium* [Paris, 1946], *1*, 79, 446). Severus of Antioch is known to have been baptized in the martyrium of St. Leontius (J. Lassus, *Sanctuaires chrétiens de Syrie* [Paris, 1947], p. 228). Evidence of entombment within baptisteries also exists. Indeed the practice must have been prevalent for it was prohibited by the Council of Auxerre in 578 (F. W. Unger in *Bonner Jahrbücher, 41* [1866], 38).

THE DECORATIVE PROGRAM
Description and Iconography

Had the Baptistery of Ravenna succumbed to the centuries, it is upon Agnellus'
description, of tantalizing brevity, that we would be obliged to base the reconstruction of its interior scheme: "With mosaics and golden tesserae he [Neon] fashioned
the images and the names of the Apostles around the vault, and covered the walls with
various stones;"[1] a description that could easily apply to scores of other Early Christian churches. Yet the decorative ensemble of the Baptistery is like that of no other
monument of the Middle Ages. Its general appearance is quite unmatched, and this
uniqueness is one of character rather than substance. For the materials that make up
the decoration—stucco, mosaic, and colored marbles—had been in use for several
centuries before the time of Neon, and the themes of which it is composed were
common enough in Early Christian iconography. Its individuality depends upon the
disposition and interplay of these conventional elements and less upon invented
novelties. The issue then lies not so much with components but with composition
itself, not with materials but with "style." In the next two chapters this decorative
ensemble of the Baptistery is studied, first by a thorough description and considerations of iconography, then through questions of style and attempts to define the distinctive visual and formal principles operative in the interior scheme.

Zone I

Opus Sectile

It has already been pointed out that the present arrangement of the incrustation
of colored marbles within the flat spans of the arcade is not authentic. A good portion
of the design as it now stands dates no farther back than the restoration of the 1890s.[2]

---

1. *Codex*, pp. 77–78; and above, pp. 11 ff.
2. Sangiorgi maintained that by the mid-eight-
eenth century none of the opus sectile was left except for "two discs of porphyry" (*Corriere di Ro-*

magna, April 22, 1898; misdated April 21). This is
an exaggeration. However, he firmly defended the
reconstruction by the Opificio as authentic and true
to the original (*Battistero,* pp. 23–30). Cf. F. Bel-

The placement too is arbitrary. The drawing of the interior as it was in Varneri's time at the end of the eighteenth century shows that the central panel of Side A′ was then missing because of the door leading to the rectory (*Fig.* 37). Side D, which was then flat, lacking the niche later rebuilt by Lanciani, is depicted covered with marbles. Side D′, on the other hand, is shown bare except for the open door. In 1878, the opus sectile was dismounted (*Fig.* 38), and stacked away until the Opificio delle Pietre Dure commenced the work of restoration. There is no reason to doubt, however, that the marble incrustation of the Baptistery was an original feature of the fifth-century design. Agnellus' words "parietes promiscuis lapidibus cinxit" are surely a reference to it. Nor is there reason to doubt that, wherever its initial placement may have been, the basic pattern of the opus sectile was similar to its present arrangement. It is composed of disks of red porphyry alternating with slabs of *lapis lacedaemoniae*, with margins of pink African marbles highlighted by small pieces of majolica. The patterns of Side A′ and C′ correspond precisely: a rectangular slab of green marble is flanked by two disks of porphyry (*Fig.* 107). On Side B′ the pattern is reversed. Here the central element is a large disk of porphyry and the sides are green marble slabs (*Fig.* 108). On Side D′ the door itself forms the central element; otherwise the pattern corresponds to that of Side B′.

Incrustation was a very common means of decoration in the Roman period, and the similarity in the designs of existing examples proves that its arrangement was based on standing conventions. For this reason the dating of such work through formal considerations only is all but impossible. There is in fact little essential difference between the incrustation style of some Hellenistic houses in South Russia on the one hand and that of Early Christian buildings like the Sistine baptistery of the Lateran, the cathedral of Parenzo, San Vitale, Hagia Sophia, and the Baptistery of Ravenna itself on the other.[3] Even the flamelike arabesques around the disks of porphyry in the Baptistery find their parallel in the Lateran Baptistery, and are connected with such decorative patterns in other media as the fifth-century mosaic pavement of the synagogue at El Hammeh or the wall painting from the narthex of the sixth-century episcopal church in Stobi.[4]

Mosaic Inscriptions

The monograms set in the middle of the scriptural inscriptions on the four niche arches were discussed above (pp. 18 ff.); the inscriptions themselves can now be considered. They were first recorded by Ciampini, in the late seventeenth century, and then again by G. Bard in 1844.[5] During the course of Lanciani's work they were re-

trami, *Il Forestiere instruito delle cose notabili della città di Ravenna e suburbane della medesima* (Ravenna, 1783), p. 34: "[Of the sectile work] sono rimaste solamente alcune rotonde tavole di porfido e pochi graziosi arabeschi di porfido, serpentino e di altri marmi in varie maniere intarsiati."

3. For a general discussion of the Roman use of opus sectile, see D. Krencker in *Die Trierer Kaiserthermen* (Augsburg, 1929), pp. 306 ff. A summary of Early Christian incrustation is found in E. H. Swift, *Roman Sources of Christian Art* (New York, 1951), pp. 131–34.

4. See E. L. Sukenik, *The Ancient Synagogue of El-Hammeh* (Jerusalem, 1935), Pl. 11; E. Kitzinger, "A Survey of the Early Christian Town of Stobi," *DOP, 3* (1948), Fig. 151.

5. G. Ciampini, *Vetera monimenta* (Rome, 1690–99), pp. 236–37 and Pl. 69 (here reproduced as *Fig.* 26); G. Bard, *Dei Monumenti d'architettura bizantina in Ravenna* (Ravenna, 1844), p. 26.

newed, and missing parts were restored under the direction of Rafaelle Garrucci.[6] The texts are here given in their present state, lower case denoting words, or parts of words, known to have been restored in the nineteenth century.

Niche A (Fig. 106)

īhs AMBULĀS SUPER MARE PETRO MERGENTI MANum
capit et iubenTE DOMNO ventus cessavit

The text is a paraphrase of Matthew 14:29–32, "And when Peter was come down out of the ship, he walked on the water, to go to Jesus . . . And immediately Jesus stretched forth his hand, and caught him . . . And when they were come into the ship, the wind ceased." Ciampini does not reproduce this particular inscription (*Fig. 26*), and it may be that because it was poorly preserved it proved impossible to decipher. It is also omitted by Bard. Garrucci completed the second line to read: "porrigit iubente Domno continuo ventus cessavit," and it is in this form that Ricci reports it in 1889.[7] The choice of the word "porrigit" was suggested to Garrucci by an inscription from Tours, which included the lines: "Dominus super mare pedibus ambulat / et Sancto Petro mergenti manum porrigit."[8] In the face of serious criticism however, the second line was apparently soon changed to the present reading.[9]

The pertinence of the text to baptism is evident. Several incidents from the Old and New Testaments in which water plays a part, like the ark of Noah, the crossing of the Red Sea, and the Samaritan woman at the well, were regularly interpreted by the church fathers as allegories of baptism. Here also walking on the sea refers symbolically to the sacrament through which one attains to Christ. Barbier de Montault elaborates the parallel and sees in this text a reference to the first effect of baptism, that is, the calming of the tempest of incredulity in man's heart. The boat would represent the church, and the sea the world where unbelievers are wrecked. Through baptism one enters the boat whose pilot is Christ himself.[10]

Niche B (Fig. 103)

BEATI QUORUM REMISSAE SUNT INIQUITATES
ET QUORUM TECTA SUNT PECCATA
BEATUS VIR CUI NON IMPUTAVIT DOMINUS PECCATUM

The text is Psalms 32:1, 2, "Blessed is he whose transgression is forgiven, whose sin is covered. Blessed is the man unto whom the Lord imputeth not iniquity." The

---

6. *Storia della arte cristiana nei primi otto secoli della chiesa, 4* (Prato, 1872–81), 37.

7. "S. Giovanni," p. 299.

8. Garrucci (see n. 6) *4*, 38. The complete Tours inscription is in E. F. Le Blant, *Nouveau Recueil des inscriptions chrétiennes de la Gaule anterieures au VIIIe siècle, I* (Paris, 1892), 236.

9. The present reading is cited by J. P. Richter in 1878 (*Die Mosaiken von Ravenna* [Vienna, 1878],

p. 21). Could it be then that the original inscription read "capit et iubente Domno," and that Garrucci altered it without cause after 1878? Ricci's anger seems to imply such a procedure ("S. Giovanni," p. 300). In any case, by 1900 the inscription was given its present reading (*Battistero*, p. 101).

10. X. Barbier de Montault, "Baptistère de la Cathédrale," *RAC* (1896), p. 76.

inscription seems not to have been tampered with by Garrucci; Ciampini's transcription was identical with the present reading (*Fig.* 26).[11] Again the connection with baptism is clear. The remission of sins is one of the most essential effects of the sacrament. The baptized was not only cleansed of his ordinary sins but was also liberated from the original sin which he inherited at birth.[12] It is this dual purification which is set forth in the Sistine inscription on the epistyle of the Lateran Baptistery:

> MERGERE PECCATOR SACRO PURGANDE FLUENTO
> QUEM VETEREM ACCIPIET PROFERET UNDE NOVUM
> INSONS ESSE VOLENS ISTO MUNDARE LAVACRO
> SEU PATRIO PREMERIS CRIMINE SEU PROPRIO[13]

Niche C (*Fig. 104*)

> UBI DEPOSUIT I̅H̅S̅ VESTIMENTA SUA ET MISit aquam
> in PELVEM ET LABIT PEDES DISCIPULORum suorum

The text is John 13:4, 5, "He riseth from supper and laid aside his garments; and took a towel, and girded himself. After that he poureth water into a bason, and began to wash the disciples' feet." Ciampini transcribed the second line as "in pelvim coepit lavare pedes discipulorum suorum" (*Fig.* 26). Bard's version of the line is even shorter: "coepit lavare pedes discipulorum." The present reading is that of Garrucci, apparently not too accurate except for the suggestions of remaining portions of letters.[14] Two centuries before him the inscription would have been better preserved, and hence it is reasonable to assume that Ciampini's rendering is closer to the original. Parallels between this passage and the sacrament of baptism exist on several levels. The neophyte, like Christ, takes off his garments in preparation for the ritual. The washing of the disciples' feet was early associated with baptism, for example by Aphraates of Syria about the year 340: "our Saviour washed . . . the feet of His disciples, which is the Sacrament of Baptism."[15] In the Eastern churches the *lavatio pedum* was believed to have preceded the Last Supper in the same way that baptism preceded the eucharist. The lavatio pedum was often accepted by the fathers as the act through which Christ had baptized his own apostles, for there is no other evidence in the Gospels of their proper baptism.[16] In Milan, contrary to the church of Rome, the washing of the neophytes' feet by the bishop was an actual part of the baptismal

11. Curiously, both Bard (see n. 5), p. 26, and Garrucci (see n. 6), *4*, 38, omit the third line of the inscription.

12. According to St. Ambrose, baptism itself absolved the neophyte of his actual sins, but the original sin of Adam could be obliterated only by the washing of the neophytes' feet (*De sacr.* III.i.7; *De myst.* VI.32). See also below, n. 17.

13. For the full text of the Sistine inscription see G. B. Giovenale, *Il Battistero lateranense* (Rome, 1929), p. 8.

14. Garrucci wrote: "Il supplemento *LABIT* mi è stato suggerito dagli avanzi delle lettere frammentate L A B T, Il Cav. Lanciani trovò le vestigia del B T sul posto e gli avanzi L A ai piedi dell'arco scavando il pavimento." (Quoted by Sangiorgi, *Battistero,* pp. 105–06; see also figure on p. 106.)

15. Homily xii: see *Texte und Untersuchungen zur Geschichte der altchristlichen Literatur, III.*3–4 (Leipzig, 1888), 191.

16. The question is ably discussed (and richly annotated) by E. H. Kantorowicz, "The Baptism of the Apostles," *DOP, 9–10* (1956), 203–51.

rite,[17] and it is not improbable that Ravenna followed its neighbor on this point.

Niche D (Fig. 105)

IN LOCUM PASCUAE IBI ME CONLOCAVIT
SUPER AQUA REFECTIONIS EDOCAVIT ME

The text is Psalms 23:2, "He maketh me to lie down in green pastures: he leadeth me beside the still waters." This inscription, like that of Niche B, seems to have retained its original form; it was identically transcribed by Ciampini (*Fig.* 26) and by Bard. The association of the psalm with the rite of baptism has been explored by J. Quasten.[18] Interpreted by several of the fathers as a prefiguring description of the effects of baptism, the psalm is in fact a word picture of the theme of the Good Shepherd, common alike in sepulchral art and in the art of baptisteries. The sheep are the neophytes seeking baptism. A vivid proof of this symbolism was seen in the act of branding the neophyte with a *sphragis* during the ritual, as a sign that he was saved by Christ—in the same way that a shepherd would brand the sheep in his possession. The portion of the psalm here quoted in the inscription probably alludes to the leading of the newly baptized Christians to the altar for confirmation by the eucharist.

Whether the four inscriptions had any further role than the exposition of some of the baptismal symbolism is not easily determined. It has been suggested that they referred specifically to pictorial compositions in mosaic which once sheathed the interior surface of the niches.[19] Thus Niche A might show the scene of Peter's salvation from the waves; Niche B, a scene alluding to the remission of sin, like the paralytic or the adulteress before Christ; Niche C might depict the washing of the feet of the apostles; and Niche D, the Good Shepherd with his flock, a scene similar to the one of the "Mausoleum of Galla Placidia." There is unfortunately no substantiating evidence that the niches were indeed decorated. It is unlikely that no vestige whatever should survive of them if such pictorial compositions existed.[20] Agnellus makes no

---

17. See St. Ambrose, *De sacr.* III.i.4–7; and *De myst.* VI.31–33. Note especially: "We are not ignorant that the Roman church has not this custom. Her type and form we follow in all things; however, she has not this custom of washing the feet . . . *Unless I wash thy feet, thou wilt have no part of me*" (*De sacr.* III.i.5, trans. by T. Thompson in J. H. Srawley [ed.], *St. Ambrose. On the Sacraments and On the Mysteries* [London, 1950], p. 73).

18. See J. Quasten, "Das Bild des Guten Hirten in den altchristlichen Baptisterien und in den Taufliturgien des Ostens und Westens," *Pisciculi F. J. Dölger dargeboten* (Münster i.W., 1939), pp. 220–44. For the use of this psalm in the liturgy of baptism, see idem, "Der Psalm vom Guten Hirten in altchristlicher Kultmystik und Taufliturgie," *Liturgischen Leben* (1934), pp. 132–41. Cf. Th. Bogler, "Der Gute Hirt in liturgischer Textüberlieferung des Morgen und Abendlandes," *Liturgische Zeitschrift,*

3 (1931), 174–83; and P. de Puniet, "Pastor ovium. Le symbol du Pasteur dans la liturgie," *Ephemerides Liturgicae, 53* (1939), 273–90.

19. Barbier de Montault (see n. 10), p. 76; and Sangiorgi, *Battistero*, pp. 33–36.

20. Lanciani uncovered a cross and part of a palm tree in mosaic on the arch soffit of Niche D (Sangiorgi, *Battistero*, p. 31), but this does not prove that the mosaic continued upon the intrados. The arch soffit is now entirely covered with gold-ground mosaic, showing two blue crosses with a pair of palm trees on either side, the work of Felice Kibel in the 1860s (Ricci, *Tavole, 2*, Pl. 14). These hypothetical scenes in the niches are still taken for granted; see H. Giess, *Die Darstellung Fusswaschung Christi* (Rome, 1962), p. 97, who lists a scene of this subject in mosaic in the apse of the Baptistery, and pronounces it "zestört."

mention of them, nor does any other writer after him. The question therefore remains unsettled.

The possibility that the inscription in each niche stood for a specific act in the ritual which took place within that niche must also be rejected. The text of Niche C might suggest that the neophytes' feet were washed there; but the assignment of the other niches is not evident. The inscription of Niche D in fact, which seems to have eucharistic implications, did not contain the altar itself, which was in the eastern Niche B. It is wiser ultimately to accept the inscriptions for what they are: commentary on the sacrament of baptism and texts quite familiar to the neophyte who entered into the Baptistery only after a long period of instruction.

Prophets and Rinceaux

The space above the Zone I arcade is sheathed with a continuous mosaic design which consists of eight figures over the columns, about 0.90 meter high, in oval medallions of gold ground with blue-green edges, connected by a pattern of *rinceaux (Figs.* 113–15). The figures are clad in white tunic, white pallium, and black sandals. The outlines of the garments, as well as the *clavi* of the tunics and the as yet undeciphered letters "I" on the edges of the pallia, are also black.[21] Four of the figures are old, bearded men; the other faces are youthful. Each clutches an open book or a roll in his hand. They have been variously identified as apostles,[22] prophets of the New Testament, prophets of the Old Testament who foretold the coming of Christ,[23] or four prophets of the Old Testament (those with rolls) and four of the New (those with books).[24] The first of these interpretations is the least satisfactory. None of the faces can be reconciled with the traditional portraiture of the apostles, all twelve of whom are depicted in fact on a higher zone. The distinction between Old and New Testament prophets is also hard to make, for if the rolls indeed represent the more ancient Scriptures, they should appropriately be held by the older figures. This is not the case, however, nor is there a consistent alternation of roll and book or of old men and youths. The conventional portraiture, the philosopher's costume, and the gesture of "benediction," which is the Roman gesture denoting the act of speech, permit of no more precise identification of these eight personages than that of prophets or fathers of the church.

Before the arch imposts were raised to counteract the elevation of the pavement

---

21. Most of the figures have been restored in part, and the figure at corner C'–D (no. 7 in our diagram on *Fig.* 41) in its entirety, by F. Kibel; those at corners A'–B and B'–C (nos. 3 and 5) are the best preserved. See Ricci, *Tavole,* 2, Pls. 14–19, for these restorations. The fullest illustration of the figures is in ibid., Pls. N, O, and Q; see also F. W. Deichmann, *Frühchristliche Bauten und Mosaiken von Ravenna* (Baden-Baden, 1958), Pls. 88–93. An excellent color plate of prophet no. 5 appears in G. Bovini, *Ravenna Mosaics* (New York Graphic So-ciety, 1956), Pl. 12; here reproduced in black and white as *Fig.* 115.

22. J. Kurth, *Die Wandmosaiken von Ravenna* (2d ed. Munich, 1912), p. 68, where the figure at corner B'–C (no. 5) is identified as St. Peter, that at D'–A (no. 1) as St. Paul, and that at A–A' (no. 2) as St. Andrew.

23. Sangiorgi, *Battistero,* pp. 95–96.

24. J. Ficker, "Der Bilderschmuck des Baptisterium Ursianum in Ravenna," *Byzantinisch-neugriechische Jahrbuch,* 2 (1921), 320–21.

(p. 46), it is obvious that the lower spandrels were decorated with acanthus clusters from which the pattern of rinceaux branched off, as is the case with the scrolls of the arch soffits at the "Mausoleum of Galla Placidia."[25] These lower spandrels are covered today with a very unsatisfactory modern design. Each of the oval medallions containing a prophet is formed by two main branches of acanthus, and other branches shoot off from here to the right and left in richly convoluted gold-green scrolls on a ground of indigo. The leaves that protrude into the gold ground of the medallions produce the same kind of flame-like outline that was noted around some of the panels of the opus sectile (*Fig.* 107). The rinceaux are of a type quite common in the Early Christian art of Ravenna and Rome: slim branches are formed by elongated leaves arranged in a generalized pattern quite unlike the richly naturalistic classical scrolls of the Ara Pacis or the scrolls of later Roman sculpture, which are composed of a succession of interlocking calices.[26] Only the branches immediately surrounding the medallions of the prophets are original. The intermediate sections were restored by Felice Kibel in the 1860s.

Other Ornamental Motifs

The decorative bands that sheathe the eight arch soffits have been heavily restored, but in every case enough of the original survived to enable an accurate reconstruction.[27] The patterns are of four different types. The first, seen on the arch soffits of Sides A and C, is a handsome "twisted ribbon" motif with a heart-shaped leaf rising on a curved stem in each of the volutes (*Figs.* 106, 113). This is a late transformation of the common "twisted ribbon" motif in simple waves, frequently found on Roman pavements.[28] The close partners of the motif as it appears at the Baptistery are in S. Aquilino in Milan (*Fig.* 141), and in Ravenna at the Mausoleum of Galla Placidia, Sant'Apollinare Nuovo, the Archiepiscopal Chapel, and San Vitale.[29] The second motif, used only on the arch soffit of Side D, is an overall pattern of diamonds, alternately blue and green, with a star of eight white rays set in each of the diamonds (*Fig.* 105). This too is derived from the traditional Roman repertory.[30] On four soffits, of Sides A', B', C', and D', a vegetal motif is employed in the form of a garland of green-yellow leaves on a blue ground (*Figs.* 113, 114). A richer variety of the same ornament can be seen at the Mausoleum of Galla Placidia. Finally, a simple pattern of inter-

---

25. Deichmann (see n. 21), Pls. 16, 17.

26. A good discussion of rinceaux, with drawings, is found in K. A. C. Creswell, *Early Muslim Architecture* (Oxford, 1940), pp. 173–81.

27. See Ricci, *Tavole*, 2, Pls. 14–18.

28. See D. Levi, *Antioch Mosaic Pavements, 1* (Princeton 1947), 377 ff., 392 ff., esp. 454 ff. The chapter entitled "Ornamental Style" in this book (375 ff.) contains, in my opinion, the best analysis of late antique decorative patterns to date. A series of three articles by M. Blake should also be consulted: "The Pavements of the Roman Buildings

of the Republic and Early Empire," *MAAR, 8* (1930), 7–159; "Roman Mosaics of the Second Century in Italy," *MAAR, 13* (1936), 67–214; "Mosaics of the Late Empire in Rome and Vicinity," *MAAR, 17* (1940), 81–130.

29. For the "Mausoleum of Galla Placidia": Ricci, *Tavole, 1*, Pls. 2 ff.; for S. Apollinare Nuovo: ibid., *4*, Pl. 30; for the chapel: Deichmann (see n. 21), Pl. 217; for San Vitale: Ricci, *Tavole, 6*, Pl. 60.

30. Cf. Levi (see n. 28), *2*, Pls. 104c, 108d, 126b, 126d.

woven horizontal and vertical lines in black, yellow, green, and blue covers the arch soffit of Side B (*Fig.* 114) and is exactly paralleled again in the Mausoleum of Galla Placidia.[31]

Three other decorative bands, restored in their entirety by Kibel, form a base motif for the inscriptions of Niches A, C, and D; the inscription of Niche B, being longer than the rest, leaves no space for an ornamental base. Two of the bands match. They are composed of a pattern of interlaced circles (*Fig.* 106), a theme which in simpler form is found in Roman art at least from the first century A.D. onward.[32] The circles are alternately light and dark blue with small white leaves set inside them. The third band consists of confronted S-shaped elements, again alternately light and dark blue (*Fig.* 105). This pattern, uncommon in Roman art, is used in the Early Christian mosaics of S. Prisco at Capua Vetere and of the baptistery of S. Restituta in Naples (*Fig.* 139), both probably of the early fifth century.[33]

ZONE II

This zone forms an intermediary passage between the architectural and decorative complexities of the ground story and the relative uniformity of the mosaic sheath of the cupola. Each bay has an identical framework in which the various elements of the decoration are set: a triplet of arches resting on the impost blocks of four columns is embraced by a single high arch resting on brackets over the corner columns (*Fig.* 71). The middle arch of each triplet is pierced by a window. Within the side arches are placed aedicules in stucco with alternately semicircular and triangular pediments. The aedicules contain single figures in high relief; each pediment is filled with a shell. Between the upper limits of the pediments and the small side arches are found either pairs of confronted animals or religious scenes. Finally, the tympana of the large arcade which embraces the triplets are covered with decorative patterns of animal and vegetable motifs.

Prophets

The aedicules contain sixteen personages, two to each side of the octagon, and they have been numbered in counterclockwise sequence beginning at the door. Like the prophets of Zone I, these standing figures are clad in tunic and pallium and are holding books or rolls in their hands. Numbers 1, 3, 6, 9, 11, and 13 are supporting open books with the left hand; the right hand is raised in the gesture of address (*Figs.* 83, 86, 90, 96, 98). Numbers 2, 5, 8, 10, 14, and 16 clasp a closed roll with both hands (*Figs.* 85, 89, 93, 95, 99, 102). The remaining personages are holding with outstretched arms an opened roll spread widely across their bodies (*Figs.* 87, 91, 97, 101). On their pallia appear letters in the form of a Latin Z. Their garments fly out as though caught

31. Deichmann (see n. 21), Pl. 19. Also found as borders in Santa Costanza: W. F. Volbach, *Frühchristliche Kunst* (Munich, 1958), Pl. 33.

32. Levi (see n. 28), pp. 374 ff. A form closer to the motif as it appears in the Baptistery is seen in

the mosaics of Santa Costanza (Volbach [n. 31 above], Pl. 32).

33. J. Wilpert, *Die römischen Mosaiken und Malereien der kirchlichen Bauten von IV. bis zum XIII. Jahrhundert, 3* (Freiburg, 1916), Pls. 76, 33.1.

in the wind. None of the figures is bearded; they have youthful faces and rather long hair with a ring of locks falling onto the brow. The most distinctive features of the faces are the upturned, convex mouths and the staring, terrified look produced by the deeply drilled eyes.

The books and rolls indicate that these personages are also to be identified as prophets. The figures of the two zones might indeed be complementary, making a total of twenty-four, which, by some early counts, was considered the correct number of prophets.[34]

Animal Pairs

The pairs of heraldic animals over most of the aedicules of the prophets, flanking central elements such as vases or baskets of fruit, are, according to the order of the aedicules: 1, goats (*Fig. 78*); 2, doves (?) (*Fig. 73*); 3, deer (*Fig. 73*); 4, seahorses; 5, eagles; 6, lions; 7, sheep; 8, roebucks; 9, peacocks; 10, hares (*Fig. 39, right*); 11, cocks (*Fig. 71, right*); 16, pheasants. To the same decorative class belong also the stuccoes of the tympana of the eight main arches, destroyed in the nineteenth century (p. 27) and retaining their design only in modern fresco painting (*Fig. 71*). They feature the same general pattern of rinceaux as Zone I. In some, simple scrolls rise from vases or acanthus roots set within the two spandrels of the triplets of arches. Others have vine leaves attached to the scrolls and a pair of animals entwined by the branches: confronted harts on Side A, a species of winged quadrupeds on Side A', and on Side C a pair of peacocks.

There is no commoner ornamental theme in Early Christian art than that of confronted animals. The long history of antithetical compositions and its correlation with the "animal style" of the so-called barbaric cultures is familiar through the work of numerous scholars.[35] In the art of the church many of the animal motifs, widely used by earlier cultures, especially by Roman artists, were often infused with connotations of Christian symbolism. It is not necessary to specify the symbolism of each animal. Sangiorgi has already sketched some of the implications of the confronted pairs of Zone II.[36] I believe it would be more accurate, from the viewpoint of the neophyte who would enter the Baptistery only once in his life, to see in this part of the decorative scheme a general atmosphere of associations more than any illustration of precise elements of Christian ideology. The only emphasized animals are the hart and the peacock, which are repeated in the lunettes and in the small arches over two of the aedicules and can be more precisely referred to Christian symbolism, specifically to baptism. Despite the scarcity of Early Christian texts on the meaning of the peacock,

---

34. See Th. Schermann, *Propheten- und Apostellegenden nebst jünger Katalogen der Dorotheus und verwandter Texte,* Texte und Untersuchungen zur Geschichte der altchristlichen Literatur, *31* (Leipzig, 1907), passim, esp. p. 24.

35. A. Riegl has pointed out long ago that symmetrical composition was "ein dem Menschen ein-

geborenes, immanentes Postulat alles dekorativen Kuntschaffens von Anbeginn" (*Stilfragen. Grundlegungen zu einer Geschichte der Ornamentik* [Berlin, 1893], p. 40). Cf. A. Jolles, "Die antithetische Gruppe," *JDAI, 19* (1904), 27–55.

36. *Battistero,* pp. 54–57.

its use as a symbol of immortality, resurrection, incorruptibility, and eternal beati-
tude is well established.[37] The theme was especially popular in Ravenna where it
occurs on twelve existing sarcophagi. The symbolism of the hart is even more evident.
From earliest times Psalm 42 has been associated by the church fathers with the sacrament of baptism: "As the hart panteth after the water brooks, so panteth my soul
after Thee, O God." The psalm was in fact part of the liturgy preceding the actual
rite. During the vigil of Easter, which the catechumens spent in preparatory prayer,
the first verses of the psalm were chanted after the final *lectio*.[38] The text and the
image are clearly conjoined in the baptistery at Salona where a mosaic panel depicts
two harts drinking from a central vase with the first verse of the psalm inscribed above
them: SICUT CERVUS DESIDERAT AD FONTES AQUARUM ITA DESIDERAT ANIMA MEA AD TE
DEUS.[39]

Scenes of Faith and Dogma

Above four of the aedicules of Zone II, nos. 12 to 15, there are reliefs of religious
subjects instead of confronted animal pairs (*Figs. 75, 76*). In composition, however,
they represent the same heraldic antithesis of two elements flanking a central motif,
and in this respect the rhythm of this feature of the decoration is not disrupted. The
scenes are as follows.

Side C', over aedicule 12; Jonah and the whale (Fig. 79). Jonah is shown as a naked
child reclining horizontally over the aedicule pediment, with his hands in the mouth
of one whale and one foot caught in the teeth of a second. The presence of two whales
is due solely to considerations of symmetry. Such antithetic duplication is common in
Early Christian art, as in the case of St. Menas between two kneeling camels, or Lazarus between two dogs.[40] The whales are here delightfully represented as dragonlike
creatures with long convoluted and spiked tails, somewhat like monstrous seahorses
and not dissimilar in fact to the seahorses above aedicule 4 (*Fig. 40*, right). The Early
Christian artist often resorted to this class of generalized sea monsters for the narra-

37. See Cabrol-Leclercq, *Dictionnaire d'archéologie chrétienne*, under "paon"; H. Lother, *Der
Pfau in der altchristlichen Kunst*, Studien über
christliche Denkmäler, *18* (Leipzig, 1929), among
others. St. Augustine refers to the peacock's flesh
as "incorruptible" (*De civ. Dei*, 21.4). In Roman
art and literature the peacock was the symbol of
the apotheoses of empresses, as the eagle was of
emperors. It was the bird of Juno, and was used as
the symbol of immortality by Bacchic cults. As a
decorative motif it is not infrequent in Roman art,
at least since the first century B.C.; the most recently uncovered example is a painting in the tomb
at Montefiore, of the Second Style (see A. Laidlaw
in *Archaeology*, *17* [1964], 33–42). For a Christian
example in another baptistery see L. M. Ugolini,
"Ill battistero di Butrinto," *RACrist*, *11* (1934),

273. A common variation of the theme on Ravennate
sarcophagi is to show the peacocks flanking the
monogram or cross of Christ.

38. "Le cerf et le serpent: Note sur le symbolisme de la mosaïque découverte au baptistère de
l'Henchir Messaouda," *Cahiers*, *4* (1949), 17–60, esp.
39–41, 44–45; and P. Underwood in *DOP*, *5* (1950),
50 ff. See also H. A. Wilson, *The Gelasian Sacramentary* (Oxford, 1894), pp. 82–84; and idem, *The
Gregorian Sacramentary* (London, 1915), pp. 55,
75–76, 157–59.

39. E. Dyggve, "Salona cristiana," *Atti del III
congresso internazionale di archeologia*, Studi di
antichità cristiana, *8* (Rome, 1934), 237 ff.

40. See L. Réau, *Iconographie de l'art chrétien*,
1 (Paris, 1955), 295 ff.

tion of the Jonah story, availing himself of prototypes in classical marine subjects like the Nereids or the triumph of Poseidon and Amphitrite.[41]

The theme is one of the best loved in Early Christian art. It was repeatedly represented in the paintings of the catacombs, on sarcophagi, and on objects of the minor arts, and symbolized the burial and resurrection of Christ. It is in fact the Early Christian theme par excellence, for it all but disappears very rapidly after the fifth century. In the Baptistery version the story has already been stripped of narrative detail and transformed into a symmetrical ornament adjusted to fit a certain available space.[42] Within another half century every trace of symbolism and form will be obliterated from the traditional type. Jonah then will take his place on the wall of Sant'-Apollinare Nuovo as just another prophet of the Scriptures.

Side C', over aedicule 13. The scene represents Christ treading on the heads of two creatures, with an open book in his left hand and his right hand supporting the cross that is laid on his shoulder (*Fig.* 80). The pertinent texts are Psalms 91:13, "Thou shalt tread upon the lion and adder: the young lion and the dragon shalt thou trample under feet"; and Luke 10:19, "Behold, I give unto you power to tread on serpents and scorpions, and over all the power of the enemy." The theme is uncommon in the Early Christian repertory. The closest parallel to the Baptistery version is the mosaic panel in the Archiepiscopal Chapel in Ravenna where Christ is shown similarly treading on the lion and adder with the cross on his shoulder and the book open to EGO SUM VIA VERITAS ET VITA (*Fig.* 133).[43] The similarity between the two renderings is striking, the latter being much richer in naturalistic detail. In both versions Christ has long hair covering part of his forehead and cascading onto his shoulders. It is the usual type in Ravenna, a youthful attractive Christ, distinct alike from the childish innocence of the Christ of the Junius Bassus sarcophagus or of the S. Aquilino apse mosaic (*Fig.* 141), and the aged severity of the Christ of the "city-gate" sarcophagi or of the S. Pudenziana apse mosaic in Rome. He is shown here in the costume of a Roman general: armor, a mantle thrown across the shoulders, and military boots. The position of the beasts is reversed in the chapel, and Christ is shown full front rather than in three-quarter view as at the Baptistery. A third version in Ravenna, on the right gateway of Theodoric's palace in the mosaic panel of Sant'Apollinare Nuovo, has Christ flanked by two other figures.[44] And Agnellus wrote of a fourth,

41. See O. Mitius, *Jonas auf den Denkmälern des christlichen Altertums* (Freiburg, 1897), p. 33; a catalogue of these scenes appears on pp. 104–14. See also Leclercq in Cabrol-Leclercq, *Dictionnaire d'archéologie chrétienne,* under "Jonas." The symbolism of the story is discussed for example by A. Feuillet, "Le sens du Livre de Jonas," *Revue biblique, 54* (1947), 160–86. Also of value is the recent article by E. Stommel, "Zum Problem der frühchristlichen Jonasdarstellungen," *Jahrbuch für Antike und Christentum, 1* (1958), 112–18.

42. There is a similar unsophisticated ornamental rendition of the scene in a relief on the south side of San Marco in Venice near the entrance to the Doge's Palace, at the base of two of the four porphyry tetrarchs: see F. Leiss, *Venise* (Milan, 1953), Pl. 38.

43. This mosaic panel has been much restored and must be considered with caution. See Wilpert, *Römischen Mosaiken und Malereien, 3* (Freiburg, 1916), Pl. 89; cf. Pls. 128, 129 in H. Peirce and R. Taylor, *L'Art byzantin, 2* (Paris, 1934).

44. See Ricci, *Tavole, 4,* Pls. 50–53.

now lost, that was in the church of Santa Croce erected by Galla Placidia.[45] Aside from these Ravennate examples, the theme is unknown in Italy. It seems to have originated in the East, probably in Egypt, and to have been introduced into Ravenna in the early fifth century, where it became popular.[46]

The iconography probably derives from imperial art. Grabar has associated the theme with the painting at the vestibule of Constantine's palace at Constantinople, which showed the Emperor, accompanied by his sons, piercing with his spear a serpent which, according to Eusebius, represented Licinius, the enemy of the people.[47] Similarly, on the reverse of some of the imperial coinage of the early fifth century, the emperor is portrayed in military costume, treading on a serpent with a human head.[48] In the Christianized version, the Lord is represented triumphing over demons as Constantine had triumphed over his own enemies. The presence of the scene in the Baptistery is not surprising. The baptismal vow comprised, and still does, the rejection of Satan and the recognition of Christ—the Apotaxis and Syntaxis, to use the terms of St. Cyril of Jerusalem.[49] During the rite, the neophyte faced west for the Apotaxis and then turned himself eastward, facing the altar. "Thou didst enter, therefore," says St. Ambrose, "to look upon thine adversary, whom thou mayest suppose that thou shouldst renounce to his face; thou dost turn to the east. For he who renounces the devil, turns to Christ, looks at him with direct gaze."[50] It is to this meaning of baptism that the scene over aedicule 13 refers, and therefore its placement on a western bay opposite the apse has liturgical validity. Moreover, the scene is a direct allusion to baptism itself, for the water is the seat of the dragon, or Satan, whose head Christ trampled in his own baptism.[51]

Side D, over aedicule 14; Traditio legis (Fig. 81). Christ is seated on a throne holding the cross in his left hand. He looks to his right where St. Peter extends his arms to receive the Law. (This detail is largely effaced, but there is no doubt that it was intended to show a roll.) To the left of Christ, St. Paul raises his hand in the gesture

45. Ed. Holder-Egger, p. 306.

46. See M. Lawrence, *The Sarcophagi of Ravenna*, College Art Association Monographs, 2 (1945), 26 and bibliography cited in n. 130. A simple summary of the medieval iconography of this theme is given by J. de Borchgrave d'Altena, "A propos de l'ivoire de Genoels Elderen et des fonts de Tirlemont," *Bulletin des musées royaux d'art et d'histoire, 18* (1949), 29–49.

47. A. Grabar, *L'Empereur dans l'art byzantin* (Paris, 1936), pp. 43–44. The description of Eusebius is in *Vita Constantini,* III.3; cf. C. Mango, *The Brazen House,* Arkaeologisk-kunsthistoriske Meddedelser, *4.4* (Copenhagen, 1959), 23.

48. J. Sabatier, *Description générale des monnaies byzantines frappées sous les empereurs d'Orient, 1* (Paris, 1862), 124–25, 131, and Pls. 6.7, 20. A similar coin of Constantine the Great shows on the reverse side the labarum, with portraits of himself and his sons surmounted by the monogram of Christ;

the point of the labarum is piercing a serpent (J. Maurice, *Numismatique constantinienne,* 2 [Paris, 1908–12], Pls. 15.7 and pp. 507–08).

49. *Catechesis* XIX, *mystagogica* I.8: ἡ ἀπόταξις τοῦ σατανᾶ and ἡ πρὸς τὸν Χριστὸν σύνταξις; *Constitutiones apostolorum* VII.40: ἡ ἀποταγὴ τοῦ διαβόλου and ἡ συνταγὴ τοῦ Χριστοῦ. See F. X. Luxman, "Das Anblasen des Teufels beim Taufgelöbnis," *Beiträge zur älteren europäischen Kulturgeschichte (Festschrift für Rudolf Egger;* Klagenfurt, 1952), *1,* 343–46. For the words and gestures that accompanied the Apotaxis and the Syntaxis, see F. J. Dölger, "Die Sonne der Gerechtichkeit und der Schwarze," *Liturgiegeschichtliche Forschungen,* 2 (Münster i.W., 1918), 1–24.

50. *De myst.* II.7; trans. by T. Thompson in J. H. Srawley (above, n. 17), pp. 124–25.

51. Psalms 74:13, "Thou didst divide the sea by thy strength: thou brakest the heads of the dragons in the waters."

of acclamation. The portraiture of the youthful Christ is identical with that of the preceding relief. Again the face presents a three-quarter view with deeply drilled eyes and long hair which flows onto the left shoulder. These features and the full, slightly parted mouth find the closest parallel, if origin need be sought, on sarcophagus no. 455 at the National Museum in Rome, from about 325, which has in turn been compared to the head of Eros on a roughly contemporary pagan sarcophagus in the same museum.[52] The costume of Christ is no longer a military uniform but the tunic of civil dress. Sts. Peter and Paul are also dressed in tunic and pallium, and are identifiable from their generic portrait types commonly used by the mid-fifth century (see pp. 83–84).

This theme is probably also derived from imperial iconography. The giving of the Law to St. Peter, known as the *Traditio legis* or the Mission to the Apostles, has been identified as the Christian version of the type of imperial scene best exemplified on the arch of Constantine in Rome, where the emperor extends a scroll of privileges to one senator while another on the opposite side acclaims the emperor's act.[53] In Early Christian art the theme of the Traditio legis seems to have been restricted to sepulchral monuments and to baptisteries.[54] It is usual on the columnar sarcophagi of the later fourth century and need not be considered purely occidental.[55] In most examples of it on Ravennate sarcophagi, a unique iconographical variation is that Christ is shown extending the scroll of the Law to St. Paul and not to St. Peter, as is

---

52. F. Gerke, *Christus in der spätantiken Plastik* (Berlin, 1940), Figs. 16, 17; the book is useful only for its excellent pictures. For a study of the youthful Christ of Ravenna see H. Dütschke, *Ravennatische Studien* (Leipzig, 1909), p. 99 ff. The Christ on the sarcophagi of the Rinaldo workshop, and in the mosaics of the Archiepiscopal Chapel (Christ trampling the lion and adder), the Arian Baptistery, and Sant'Apollinare Nuovo (the Miracle cycle on the north wall of the nave), as well as in the Good Shepherd lunette mosaic of the "Mausoleum of Galla Placidia," is always of this general type. Cf. the young Christ with short, close-cropped hair on the sarcophagus from S. Francesco in Ravenna (Dütschke, ibid., Fig. 62); and the bearded, austere Christ of the Passion cycle on the south nave wall of Sant'Apollinare Nuovo.

53. J. Kollwitz, "Christus als Lehrer und die Gesetzeübergabe an Petrus in der konstantinischen Kunst Roms," *Römische Quartalschrift*, *1* (1936), 44–66.

54. See L. De Bruyne, "La décoration des baptistères paléochrétiens," *Miscellanea liturgica in honorem L. Cuniberti Mohlberg*, *1* (Rome, 1948), 196. For a list of examples in sepulchral art, see J. Sauer, "Das Aufkommen des bärtiger Christustypus in der frühchristlichen Kunst," *Strena Buliciana* (Zagreb-Spalato, 1924), p. 317. See also P. Borella, "La traditio legis nell'archeologia e liturgia am-

brogiana," *Ambrosius*, *30* (1954), 69–78, for more specific liturgical associations with the rite of baptism.

55. For the meaning of the Traditio, see E. Weigand, "Die spätantike Sarkophagskuptur im Lichte neuerer Forschungen," *BZ*, *41* (1941), 108 ff.; also Wilpert (n. 43 above), 2, 841 ff. M. Lawrence demonstrated sometime ago the ultimate eastern provenance of the "city-gate" sarcophagi (*AB, 10* [1927], 1–45). H. von Schoenebeck's later insistence that the theme is an invention of the West, specifically Rome, is however probably justified, although it must have spread quickly throughout the Christian empire (*Der Mailänder Sarkophag und seine Nachfolge* [Vatican, 1935], pp. 10–15). Cf. A. Baumstark, "Eine syrische 'Traditio legis' und ihre Parallelen," *Oriens christianus*, *3* (1903), 173–200, for an unusual variation of the theme in a Syrian manuscript ("Barberini" VII.62) showing Christ between Moses, to whom he extends the Tablets of Law, and St. Peter, who receives the new Law of the Church. The scene combines in one the two separate representations in Santa Costanza, probably no earlier than the fifth century, of the giving of the Law to Moses by God and of the usual Traditio legis to St. Peter by Christ. I fail to see De Bruyne's contention that the Syrian scene "ne peut pas être considerée comme une *Traditio legis*" ([n. 54 above] p. 194 n. 10).

traditional. K. Wessel proposed recently that this peculiarity reflects a subtle statement of the increasing power of the church of Ravenna and of its independence from
papal Rome.[56] The Baptistery version, and two others (one on a fragmentary sarcophagus in the National Museum of Ravenna and a second on the marble reliquary
of SS. Quirico and Giulitta, formerly in the church of S. Giovanni Battista and now
in the Archiepiscopal Museum), are the only examples in the city where the traditional iconography is maintained.[57] Of the three, the Baptistery version is alone in
showing Christ seated and St. Peter to his right; the traditional arrangement has St.
Peter to the left of the standing Christ. Thus the stucco relief in the Baptistery
combines the seated Christ of the unique Ravennate iconography where St. Paul is
entrusted with the Law, and the traditional choice of St. Peter as the bearer of the
Law. Here, moreover, Christ is holding the cross like an imperial scepter, an iconographic detail which, in this general type of the Traditio theme, seems confined to
the Baptistery relief.[58]

The association of the Traditio legis with baptism is perhaps to be seen in relation
to the adjacent relief of Christ trampling the lion and adder. In the latter, he is destroying the old rule of the devil; in this, he is establishing his own law upon which
His church will stand. Both scenes may be considered dogmatic in purpose, and for
good reason: baptism in the fifth century was a momentous rite through which the
neophyte rejected his sinful past for the responsibilities of an ordered future. Facing
the dark west to renounce his chief adversary, the neophyte saw the graphic depiction
of this act in conjunction with the accompanying act, the establishment of the new
and righteous Law. The two small scenes at one corner of this zone performed a significant role in the baptismal rite: they were the two complementary parts of the
covenant which was sealed below with the laving at the font.

Side D, over aedicule 15; Daniel and the lions (Fig. 82). The last of this important
quartet of religious scenes reverts to the Old Testament, showing Daniel *orans* between two lions. Here also the incident has been reduced to formulaic essentials, and
composed in a symmetrical pattern at least as old as the Assyrian reliefs which show
Gilgamesh as killer of lions. Daniel is usually shown nude in Early Christian iconography or, less frequently, in a short classical tunic.[59] Here he wears an oriental costume—tunic, breeches, and the Phrygian cap (the *pileus?*). On his chest is a medallion
which was perhaps meant to have Christ's monogram incised upon it. The lions are
seated on their hind legs, and their tails are curled up symmetrically in semicircular
loops. Their heads are turned toward the viewer, displaying generous manes and

56. "Das Haupt der Kirche. Zur Deutung aus-
gewählter frühchristlicher Bildwerke," *AA* (1950–51),
col. 298 ff.

57. See M. Lawrence, *The Sarcophagi of Ravenna*, Fig. 35 and p. 19; and R. Bartoccini, "Una
capsella marmorea cristiana rinvenuta in Ravenna,"
FR, 35 (1930), 21–23 and Pl. 4.

58. A later instance is in the *Traditio* miniature
in the Etschmiadzin Gospel. Cf. E. Schäfer, "Die

Heiligen mit dem Kreuz in der altchristlichen
Kunst," *Römische Quartalschrift, 44* (1936), 70 n.
22. See also a list of examples where Christ carries
a cross, in *AB, 11* (1929), 5–6 n. 2.

59. For the scene of Daniel and the lions in
Early Christian art, see especially G. Wacker, *Die
Ikonographie des Daniel in der Löwengrube* (Mar-
burg, 1954).

sharp, pointed teeth. The closest iconographic parallel is found again in Ravenna, on a small side of a sarcophagus in the National Museum; here the monogram of Christ is clearly legible on the medallion clasp of Daniel's cloak.[60] Daniel in the Phrygian costume is repeated also in one other Ravennate sarcophagus and on a small side of the reliquary of SS. Quirico and Giulitta.[61] Apart from these, about a dozen other known similar versions outside of Ravenna all seem to have originated in the East.[62]

At the most obvious level the scene is designed to evoke the crucifixion, the direct rendering of which was still unpopular in the fifth century. More deeply however, it is a visual prayer for the salvation of the Christian soul from evil. Le Blant was the first to relate this and similar biblical scenes in catacomb paintings and on early Christian sarcophagi to one of a collection of prayers, known as the *Ordines commendationis animae* which are included in the Rituale Romanum. In its original form it derives from Jewish liturgy and goes back to the third century. "Deliver, O Lord," the prayer reads, "the soul of thy servant as thou hath delivered Noah from the deluge, Daniel from the lion's den . . ."[63] Such scenes of salvation were thus equally appropriate for sepulchral art and for baptisteries. Jonah and the whale belonged to the same category of visual prayer. Significantly, therefore, the two scenes of salvation, that of Daniel and that of Jonah, are employed at the Baptistery as brackets intercepting the two representations of Christian dogma, Christ treading on the lion and adder and the Traditio legis. Excepting the four scriptural inscriptions of Zone I, this group of small reliefs thus provides the most direct preaching in the decorative system of the Ravennate monument, and it is a reflection of the taste and moderation of the patron that the statement of dogma should be relegated to an unobtrusive section of the decoration, being equated with twelve other corresponding elements of contrasted animal pairs.

The Architectural System

The most extraordinary feature of Zone II is the complex architectural framework into which the decorative elements described thus far have been set. The complexity is born of the fact that solid three-dimensional architecture and simulated architecture of two-dimensional relief have here been intricately combined and peopled by the sixteen prophets in a way that makes the proper reading of the zone at once ambiguous and intriguing. This is the least studied part of the interior scheme, and the only suggestion as yet offered has been that it is designed to represent a gallery of the kind that exists over the aisles of some basilical or centrally-planned churches in Early

---

60. Lawrence (n. 57 above), Fig. 37.

61. Ibid., Fig. 17 (the Isaac sarcophagus); and Bartoccini (n. 57 above), Pl. 4.

62. See Lawrence (n. 57 above), p. 28 n. 144 for a list and bibliography.

63. E. F. Le Blant, *Les Sarcophages chrétiens de la Gaule* (Paris, 1886), "Introduction." For an analysis of the collection of prayers, see L. Gougaud, "Étude sur les *Ordines commendationis animae*," *Ephemerides liturgicae, 49* (1935), 3–27; also A. D. Nock's "Postscript" to C. B. Wells, "The Epitaph of Julius Terentius," *Harvard Theological Review, 34* (1941), 103–09.

Christian architecture.[64] I should like to suggest that a careful examination of this ingenious architectural design rather points to the facade compositions of late Roman buildings, and especially to the arrangement of stone *scaenae frontes*.

Setting aside for the present the true architectural members, that is to say the Ionic columns, their impost blocks, and the triplets of arches borne by these blocks, we will concentrate on the feigned architecture of the plane behind. The single aedicules that house the prophets are most prominent (*Figs. 83–102*). Each consists of two pilasters carrying a horizontal lintel which is continued on a straight or inclined vertical at its two ends, forming a rectangular or trapezoidal shape. Over this in each case is a triangular or segmental pediment, in which is set a shell standing upright in the triangular pediments and inverted in the segmental ones. The capitals of the pilasters consist of a triplet of leaves topped by a double band with a rosette in the center (*Fig.* 100). The pilasters stand on high bases, and two deep grooves are carved on each shaft in lieu of fluting.

Single figures in similar aedicules are quite common in Early Christian relief sculpture, as is amply exemplified by the series of ivory consular diptychs from the fifth and sixth centuries.[65] In some Coptic stelae, one even sees the heraldic pair of confronted animals above the pediment.[66] Undoubtedly these aedicules are meant to simulate, in relief, architectural niches for statues, an ever present element in Roman building since Republican times. The shell set within the pediment is nothing more than an abstracted version of the conch with which the niches were roofed.[67] In some of the consular diptychs the shell is in fact placed immediately behind the head of the consul, acting as a kind of aureole.[68] There are also examples of Early Christian art in which the logical placement of the shell within a pediment is abandoned, and it becomes a totally independent element of ornamentation, as in the vault mosaics of Santa Costanza in Rome.[69] Generally speaking, Weigand has shown the upright shell to be predominant in the West Roman Empire, and the inverted shell predominant in the East.[70] In Ravenna, as earlier at Baalbek, the two types are used simultaneously.

---

64. See P. Toesca, *Storia dell'arte italiana. I. Il Medioevo* (Turin, 1927), p. 111; G. Galassi, *Roma o Bisanzio: I musaici di Ravenna e le origini dell'arte italiana* (2d ed. Rome, 1953), p. 34.

65. See R. Delbrück, *Die Consulardiptychen und verwandte Denkmäler* (2 vols. Berlin-Leipzig, 1929).

66. See K. Wessel, *Koptische Kunst* (Recklinghausen, 1963), Figs. 80, 83; and (Brooklyn Museum) *Pagan and Christian Egypt. Egyptian Art from the 1st to the 10th Centuries A.D.* (1941), Pl. 39.

67. I don't consider the presence of shells in such aedicules symbolic; for a contrary view see E. R. Goodenough, *Jewish Symbolism in the Greco-Roman Period*, 7 (New York, 1958), 95–105, esp. 102. See also M. Bratschkova, "Die Muschel in der antiken Kunst," *Bull. de l'inst. archéol. bulgare, 12* (1938), 1–128.

68. For example, the diptychs of Anthemius (515) and Anastasius (517), W. F. Volbach, *Elfenbeinarbeiten der Spätantike und des frühen Mittelalters* (Mainz, 1952), nos. 16 and 21 (Pl. 5). Cf. the famous Archangel relief of the British Museum, where the shell forms an aureole for the cross (ibid., no. 109 and Pl. 32).

69. See F. W. Deichmann, *Frühchristliche Kirchen in Rom* (Basel, 1948), Pl. 15.

70. E. Weigand, "Baalbek und Rom, die römische Reichskunst in ihrer Entwickelung und Differenzierung," *JDAI, 29* (1914), 63 ff. I do not subscribe, however, to the author's contention that the shape of the niche in itself is illustrative of eastern or western influence.

The schematization of the architectural niche into a decorative aedicule is quite standard in Early Christian relief panels.[71] The two pilasters, the lintel, and the pedimental member containing the shell are almost always present. The shape of the capital is also roughly uniform, and the difference often lies only in the degree of naturalism with which the leaves are carved. As in Zone II, the lintel and pediment are frequently decorated with a highly stylized band of egg-and-dart molding. Usually the human figure contained in the aedicule is depicted in such a way that the head will fall within the area of the pediment.[72] It is here that the aedicules of Zone II begin to differ from the great majority of similar reliefs. For not only are the prophets restricted to the area below the lintel, leaving the pediment to the shell motif, but the size of this pediment is also uncommonly large in proportion to the main body of the aedicule. Moreover, the pediment does not rest directly on the lintel or on the capitals but on the ends of seemingly upright elements which are the vertical or raking prolongations of the lintel. At first glance it might seem that the artist is attempting to show, in effect, that the pilasters and the lintel are more deeply seated than the pediment—and, in the process, the pediment is represented without its horizontal cornice. The upright or raking elements would then graphically represent this recession. This arrangement is further clarified by the presence of other pilasters, much taller than those of the aedicules, which hold up an architrave seemingly connecting all the aedicules of Zone II into one continuous frieze. Two readings are then possible. First, each prophet might be seen as standing in a niche defined by the pediment (with a horizontal cornice understood), by the tall pilasters, and by the shell (*Fig.* 74B). In this case, the lintel and its vertical or raking prolongations have to be seen as representing the recession of the niche, and the short pilasters have to be understood as being directly applied onto the niche wall. The second reading is the more probable, and architecturally somewhat more satisfactory. Here three planes must be distinguished (*Figs.* 71, 74A). The first is formed by the true architecture of the Ionic columns, the pulvin blocks, and the triplets of arches. The second plane repeats the pattern of the first, for here too a triple motif is formed by the arch directly over the window flanked by the pediments of the two lateral aedicules. Each triple motif covers one bay of the zone and is joined to the next by a feigned architrave supported on the tall pilasters in shallow relief. Finally, a third plane is formed by the aedicules themselves, each one framed by a pair of shorter pilasters and a pediment, not represented, containing the figure of a prophet.

Both of these readings however remain abstractions lacking architectural logic, since it would be difficult to imagine workable vaulting systems for either one of the arrangements. But on the analogy of a representation, on the Casket of Pola, of the

---

71. I exclude sarcophagi, especially the "columnar" group, because their architecture always tends to have more structural logic and three-dimensional solidity than the aedicules on ivory carvings or on stelai.

72. There are of course exceptions. Cf. for example the ivory relief showing St. Paul, in the Cluny Museum (Volbach [n. 68], no. 150 and Pl. 48; reproduced here as *Fig.* 145).

shrine of St. Peter at Old St. Peter's,[73] one further reading of Zone II is suggested, which is the most cogent architecturally. It involves the reversal of our position in respect to the tall and short pilasters, and the consideration of the latter as being closer to the viewer (*Fig.* 74C). In fact the tall pilasters are thinner and less substantial, and the corner of their capitals is sometimes overlapped by the upright or raking prolongations of the lintels, exactly as on the Casket of Pola. So seen, each aedicule forms a three-dimensional niche defined by four supports: two in the foreground (the short pilasters) carrying the pediment and two at the back (the tall pilasters).

The plan yielded by the reconstructed arrangement of Zone II in three distinct planes compares favorably with plans of late Roman facade dispositions, especially those of stone *scaenae frontes* like the facade of the theater at Ephesos (*Figs.* 74A, 130). In both cases there are three receding rows of columns, corresponding to the three planes. A reconstruction of the *scaena* at Ephesos indeed shows, especially at the ground story, the position of niches with the statues set deep inside the double screen of the front two rows of columns (*Fig.* 131). What is presented in Zone II of the Baptistery is, I believe, a replica of such an arrangement, simplified and schematized into a flat pattern, combining the second and third planes into a single surface and bringing this surface quite close to the first plane.

These associations with late Roman facades, especially with theater design, may shed some light on the intended function of the zone. A frieze of aedicules containing religious personages is of course a familiar pattern on Early Christian sarcophagi, especially of the class known as "columnar" sarcophagi.[74] Indeed, one such example from Gaul is strikingly akin to Zone II, not only in its aedicules with alternating segmental and triangular pediments but also in the figures themselves with their rolls and with their hands raised in the customary gesture of address.[75] It is reasonable to derive both the composition of the movable work of art, the sarcophagus, and the composition of the permanent architectural story of Zone II from a structural prototype, and not to try to explain one in relation to the other. The vocabulary of the Roman scaenae frons is again pertinent. The alternation of niches with triangular and segmental pediments had been known to the stage at least since the stone scaena of the Large Theater at Pompeii.[76] More important still for this discussion is the

73. See J. Toynbee and J. Ward Perkins, *The Shrine of St. Peter and the Vatican Excavations* (New York, 1957), Figs. 20, 21 and pp. 203–04. For Early Christian perspective in general, see the excellent studies by E. Panofsky, "Die Perspektive als 'symbolische Form,'" *Bibliothek Warburg. Vorträge* (1924–25), pp. 258–330; and M. Schild Bunim, *Space in Medieval Painting and the Forerunners of Perspective* (New York, 1940), esp. pp. 38–44. An important contribution to the subject is the as yet unpublished paper by the late Paul Whitman Etter, "Space Organization in the Wall Paintings from Boscoreale" (1957), a copy of which is in my possession.

74. See M. Lawrence, "Columnar Sarcophagi in the Latin West," *AB, 14* (1932), 103–85.

75. E. F. Le Blant (n. 63 above), Pl. 22.1; cf. also Pls. 41.1, 42.1, and p. 127.

76. The standard work on the early history of the *scaenae frons* is still G. von Cube, *Die römische 'scaenae frons' in den pompejanischen Wandbildern 4. Stils,* Beiträge zur Bauwissenschaft, 6 (Berlin, 1906); but now see also A. M. G. Little, "A Roman Sourcebook for the Stage," *AJA,* 60 (1956), 27–33. For general discussions, see E. F. Fiechter, *Die baugeschichtliche Entwickelung des antiken Theaters* (Munich, 1914); and M. Bieber, *The History of the Greek and Roman Theater* (2d ed. Princeton,

existence of niches for statues at a certain height from the ground. A relief recently uncovered at Castel S. Elia, datable to about A.D. 50, provides a revealing relationship with Zone II.[77] The relief is divided into two parts; the lower, representing a chariot race in the circus, does not concern us; the upper part shows a stage where actors, musicians, and dancers are in the midst of a performance (*Fig. 132*). The scaenae frons behind them is in two stories. Tall columns arranged in pairs form the ground story on which rises a frieze of niches containing statues of divinities. Like this facade, the lower two zones of the Baptistery present a superposition of figural niches supported by a row of columns. Like the Castel S. Elia frieze also, the niches are peopled with divine persons—the prophets—whose presence over the center of action where the performance of the sacred rite takes place is not dissimilar to the presence of the pagan gods looking down upon the spectacle enacted by the musicians and players on the Roman stage. And if for the Roman performers the statues of the deities are only one part of their audience, its human counterpart being seated in front of the stage, the prophets in the Baptistery are the sole audience for the mystery that the neophyte is initiated into. His is a private performance: he is at once the actor and the audience, the giver and the receiver, whose covenant with the Christian God is witnessed by the prophets on the lower walls and in their aedicules above. We shall have to return to this point in the final analysis of the interior scheme.

There is no doubt that the aedicules of Zone II were originally painted. What is of special account in the general appreciation of the decorative program is that the true architectural members—that is the Ionic columns, their impost blocks, and the arcade which these support—were also almost certainly included in this color scheme. It is known that initially the columns were coated, obviously for the purpose of painting, with a layer of stucco which would have concealed the fact that they were cut from varying kinds of marbles. The rector Giulio Varneri, in the second half of the eighteenth century, removed this coating in an effort "to clean" the columns (Document 15).[78] The effect of stage scenery, which has just been proposed, would surely have been much enhanced by sheathing with color the structural reality of this intermediary zone of the interior. The present tinting, of the stucco parts only, in blue and red is modern—the result of the experiments that began in the later years of the last

---

1958). The alternation of semicircular and triangular niche pediments is present also in other types of building in Roman architecture, both east and west: e.g. in the hemicycle of the Markets of Trajan in Rome (*Le Antichità romane di Giambattista Piranesi, I*, Pl. 29); in the great courtyard in front of the Temple of Jupiter at Baalbek (Th. Wiegand, *Baalbek* [Berlin-Leipzig, 1921–25], vol. 1 of plates, Pl. 134); and in the "Temple of Diana" at Nîmes (D. S. Robertson, *A Handbook of Greek and Roman Architecture* [2d ed. Cambridge, 1954], Pl.

15)—to mention only three obvious examples. On this subject see also C. R. Morey, "The Sarcophagus of Claudia Antonia Sabina and the Asiatic Sarcophagi," in *Sardis, 5.1*, (Princeton, 1924), 90 ff.

77. C. Anti, "Rilievo teatrale romano da Castel S. Elia," *Beiträge zur älteren europäischen Kulturgeschichte (Festschrift für Rudolf Egger;* Klagenfurt, 1952), *I*, 189–205.

78. Cf. M. Mazzotti, "Il Battistero della Cattedrale di Ravenna," *Corsi* (1961), pp. 271–72.

century (p. 28).[79] How faithful the present color scheme is to that of the fifth century is impossible to determine. A group of eight photographs, dating from about 1900 and kept in the Archivio Arcivescovile, has been in part painted over by some person, presumably to show the remains of color on the stuccoes at that time.[80] The photographs indicate considerable patches of blue and red ground; the pilasters and the insides of the shells are touched with gold. It is also possible, however, that these photographs are no more than sketches in preparation for the modern painting of the stuccoes, since they are in close accord with the coloration suggested by Sangiorgi in 1897.[81] In any case, the light tints now visible on the ground of this zone are at least not offensive to the eye, although they defeat the initial purpose of the artist by overstressing the independence of this part of the decorative sheath in the marked projection of the untinted prophets, animal pairs, and religious scenes.

Other Ornamental Motifs

To complete the description of Zone II, some secondary elements of the decoration, the ornamental bands that appear on the arch soffits, should be mentioned briefly. The first group is to be found on the soffits of the central arches directly above the windows. On Sides A′, B′, C′, and D′ the bands are identical, consisting of simple rosettes on a blank ground (*Fig.* 70). On Sides A and C the soffits feature a stylized vine motif springing from two vases (*Fig.* 73). Finally on Sides B and D the soffits are divided into square compartments, in some of which are charming representations of birds (*Figs.* 76, 77). The birds occupy two compartments directly over each pulvin, leaving the rest of the arch soffit bare.

A second group of ornamental bands is that which sheathes the soffits of the eight main arcades of the zone. These bands are in mosaic, belonging in terms of medium to Zone III above, but they may conveniently be mentioned at this time. They are actually of two types, one for Sides A, B, C, D, and a second for Sides A′, B′, C′, and D′. The first of these (*Figs.* 67, 69) is the same motif of a garland of leaves already noted in four of the arch soffits of Zone I (p. 63). The second is a simple pattern of stylized meanders in yellow on a ground composed of three strips, respectively blue, black, and blue (*Figs.* 65, 69). According to Ricci's survey, this group of bands is entirely the work of Kibel. [82]

ZONE III

The cupola of the Baptistery and its eight pendentives are sheathed with a continuous carpet of mosaic arranged in three concentric circles which we have named

---

79. The colors are applied according to a regular pattern of rhythmic alternation. Thus in one aedicule the ground for the prophet is blue and that of the pediment red; in the next aedicule this system is reversed. The same alternation of blue and red holds for the tympana of the small arches as well as for the lunettes of the eight main arcades.

80. These photographs are numbered B–8 to B–15 consecutively and are mounted on cardboard. Cf.

Ricci, "S. Giovanni," p. 303: "Su questi [stucchi], prima del ristauro fatto ora nel 1889, si scorgevano qua e là traccie di vecchie (non antiche) tinte, che in genere erano di terra rossocupa pel fondo e di terra gialla pei rilievi."

81. *Corriere di Romagna* (Dec. 16, 1897); and again in *Battistero*, pp. 58–64.

82. Ricci, *Tavole*, 2, Pls. 10–13.

Zones III, IV, and V (*Figs.* 40, 42A). The first of these is divided into eight panels by vertical members which begin from rich acanthus clusters within the pendentives, with alternately green-yellow and blue-white foliage, and rise to the red band which separates this zone from the next (*Fig.* 69). The dividers form a combined design of plants and candelabra which appeared earlier in a much more complex pattern in the now lost mosaics of the dome of Santa Costanza.[83] The form of the acanthus clusters is admirably suited to the area provided by the spherical triangles of the pendentives. Beginning with a tight bowl-like curve at the bottom of the triangle, the foliage then branches out to the right and left while from the core of the cluster rises the vertical divider, like a jet of water gushing from an ample source.[84] At the upper corners of the triangles appear lively representations of birds, flying or gently alighting, or walking about in the foliage. These delightful fowl, snipes and doves, parakeets and quail, are hardly visible from below, and their vivid naturalism is proof of the inventiveness and care displayed by the artist in the minutest details of the decoration. The bowl-shaped cluster of acanthus has a long history as a filling motif for exactly this kind of triangular space. An early Roman pavement mosaic now in the Museum of Cividale and the sixth-century dome mosaic of a church at Casanarello may be sufficient to illustrate its continuity.[85]

The eight panels divided by the plant-candelabra represent two distinct program types repeated alternately around the cupola. The architectural framework of both types is identical, and consists of columns in four parallel rows forming a central compartment roofed over by a conch and two side compartments covered by a flat coffered ceiling (*Fig.* 64). The architectural members are worked in different shades of gold, brown, and yellow tesserae. The dissimilarity between the two types of panels lies in the elements found within the architecture. In one type (Panels A', B', C', and D') the central compartment is occupied by an altar placed on a trapezoidal platform (*Figs.* 65, 66). It is composed of four colonettes, standing on a rectangular base, and a slab laid horizontally upon them. The platform is of varying shades of blue, the rectangular base of dark brown, and the architectural elements of the altar in shades of gold, yellow, and brown. The background, probably representing a curtain, is light green but divided into squares by darker lines. On the altar stands an open gospel with white pages and orange edges. Inscriptions in light blue identify the gospels as follows: Panel A', EVANGELIUN SECUN IOANNE; Panel B', EVANGELIUN SECUN MATTHEUN; Panel C', EVANGELIUN SECUN LUCAN; Panel D', EVANGELIUN SECUN MARCUN. It has been suggested that the spellings of these inscriptions denotes the Greek nationality of the artist,[86] but such a claim is exaggerated since the odd spelling need

---

83. See R. Michel, *Die Mosaiken von S. Costanza in Rom* (Leipzig, 1912), Pl. 2.

84. J. Ficker considers these plants to be more than decorative, and he connects them with paradisiacal symbolism. He cites in this respect Cyril of Jerusalem: Ἤδη μακαριότητος ὀσμὴ πρὸς ὑμᾶς· ἤδη τὰ νοητὰ ἄνθη συλλέγετε πρὸς πλοκὴν ἐπουρανίων στεφάνων ... Ἄνθη γὰρ νῦν ἐφάνη τῶν δένδρων· γένοιτο ἵνα καὶ ὁ καρπὸς τέλειος ᾖ ("Der Bilderschmuck des Baptiste-

rium Ursianum in Ravenna," *Byzantinisch-neugriechische Jahrbuch,* 2 [1921], 321).

85. For the Roman mosaic, see M. Blake, "The Pavements of the Roman Buildings of the Republic and Early Empire," *MAAR, 8* (1930), 115 and Pl. 38.1; for Casanarello, see Wilpert, *Römischen Mosaiken und Malereien, 3,* Pl. 108.

86. Garrucci, *Storia della arte cristiana, IV,* 34; cf. Barbier de Montault in *RAC* (1896), p. 78,

imply nothing more than convenient abbreviations. On either side of the central compartment containing the altar is a small throne placed within a niche defined by one visible column and by its own special white conch with blue ribs. The thrones are in shades of brown and white, with brown seats on which rest bejeweled crowns. The green ground for the altars is continued over the small side niches, but the ground for the thrones themselves is blue.

In the alternating panels (Sides A–D) the central compartment is occupied by an imposing throne splendidly draped in a multitude of colors and surmounted by a white cross in a brown aureole; its front supports and footstool are studded with gems (*Fig.* 67). The ground is green for Panels B and D and indigo for Panels A and C. In every case it is striped by black lines forming a plaid pattern like the ground for the altars. The compartments flanking the throne are screened by low parapets in white with touches of light blue, over which trees and long curved boughs are visible against a ground of rich deep blue (*Fig.* 68).[87] The restoration in all of Zone III, distinguished by its raw and unsophisticated colors, is confined to the throne in Panel A, and to the altar with the gospel according to St. Mark and the side compartment to its left in Panel D' (*Fig.* 42B).[88]

It is possible that the ultimate inspiration of Zone III, as well as of the famous architectural representations in St. George, Thessaloniki, with which the zone is often compared (*Fig.* 140), derives from the Roman painting of the first century after Christ, in particular the fantasies of the Third and Fourth Styles. In post-Pompeian decoration also, schemes like those in the lunettes of the tomb of the Pancratii in Rome (mid-second century) are indeed very close to the architectural organization of Zone III.[89] But though these schemes are comparable, one should note that the linear, elongated, and very elegant architectural decoration of the lunettes is far removed from the firm reality of the representations of Zone III. It is more likely therefore that both Zone III and the mosaics at St. George are based on prototypes of solid architecture, namely late Roman facade architecture like that of stone scaenae frontes (*Figs.* 64, 130), or of the rock-cut tombs of Petra, or of palaces like the Septizonium in Rome. In its two-storied complex organization the architectural painting of St. George is much more akin to these Roman predecessors than is Zone III of the Bap-

---

where the spelling is considered to be due to Latin vulgarization. A good illustration in color of the altar with the Gospel of St. John appears in Bovini, *Ravenna Mosaics*, Pl. 9; here reproduced in black and white as *Fig.* 66.

87. For color, see Pl. 10 in ibid., here reproduced in black and white as *Fig.* 68. The designs of the parapets are not uniform. In Panel B the design is in the form of superposed semicircles; this same motif is found earlier, for example, in Antioch (Levi, *Antioch Mosaic Pavements*, 2, Pl. 137b), and later in Chapel "G" at Bevsan (G. M. Fitzgerald,

A Sixth-Century Monastery at Beth-Shan [Philadelphia, 1939], Pl. 15). In Panel C the design is composed of circles, a pattern common in the Roman decorative repertory. In Panels A and D the parapets employ an identical design in the form of an "X"; cf. a similar motif in the South Basilica at Aquileia, *La Basilica di Aquileia a cura del comitato per le cerimonie celebrative del IXo centenario della basilica* (Bologna, 1933), Pl. 26 (top).

88. Ricci, *Tavole*, 2, Pls. 10–13.

89. F. Wirth, *Römische Wandmalerei* (Berlin, 1934), Fig. 42.

tistery.[90] For the latter, similar in plan to Roman facade architecture, has been simplified in elevation, having been brought more closely into the system of a basilical cross section. In this sense Zone III displays a greater resemblance to contemporary reality than does the elaborate architecture of the St. George mosaics, diaphanous as it is and set against a ground of pure gold. A third monument of Early Christian painting, the mosaics of the Church of the Nativity at Bethlehem, is related to Zone III rather than the St. George mosaics, for in the Nativity program also the architectural hieroglyphs which represent the principal councils of the Christian church simulate cross sections of basilicas more than they do the involved facade arrangement of the Thessalonikan examples.[91]

The earliest attempt at resolving the symbolism of Zone III was made by Ciampini in the late seventeenth century. The altars, according to him, stand over tombs of martyrs or confessors, as indeed the parapets with the trees behind them prove, especially the palms, "than which there is no apter symbol for a martyrium."[92] The majestic thrones between the parapets he sees as monuments to bishops;[93] the smaller thrones in the niches represent episcopal seats "which we call *faldistoria*."[94] The idea of the tombs was elaborated later by Garrucci, who proposed that the parapets were designed to defend the burial ground "from the indiscreet devotion of the people," citing the statement by St. Paulinus that the parapets around the tombs of Sts. Nabor and Felix "sanctorum martyrum ab iniuria sepulcra defendebantur."[95] Lan-

---

90. Illustrations of the St. George mosaics in Volbach, *Frühchristliche Kunst*, Pls. 124–27. They were thought to date from the sixth century (E. Weigand, "Die Kalenderfries von Hagios Georgios in Thessaloniki," *BZ*, 39 [1939], 116–45, where they are dated to ca. 515–30). But since the latest restorations (see H. Torp, "Quelques remarques sur les mosaïques de Saint-Georges à Thessalonique," *Acts of the Ninth International Congress of Byzantine Studies. Thessaloniki 1953*, 1 [Athens, 1955], 491; and more recently idem, *Mosaikkene i St. Georgrotunden* [Oslo, 1963]) they are attributed to the reign of Theodosius in the last quarter of the fourth century, under whom the building was transformed into a palatine chapel from the imperial mausoleum of Galerius. E. Dyggve maintains that the architectural mosaics of St. George are "eine Mischung von Formen des christlichen Bema und der scaenae frons der Römerzeit"; and, rather obscurely, that both Zone III and the St. George mosaics combine the theme of "Glorifikationsliturgie" with "der apotheosierenden Funktion des Bogens oder des Säulenpaares." ("Über die freistehende Klerusbank. Beiträge zur Geschichte des Bema," *Beiträge zur älteren europäischen Kulturgeschichte* [*Festschrift für Rudolf Egger*, Klagenfurt, 1952], *1*, 49.)

91. For the nativity mosaics, see most recently H. Stern, "Nouvelles recherches sur les images des conciles dans l'église de la Nativité à Bethléem," *Cahiers*, *3–4* (1948–49), 82–105. The mosaics of St. George find a better parallel in the architectural scenes of the mosaics at the Great Mosque of Damascus, for which see M. van Berchem in K. A. C. Creswell, *Early Muslim Architecture*, *1* (Oxford, 1940), 230–52 and Pls. 43, 44. Cf. also the ninth-century paintings in San Juliano de los Prados at Ovieda with similar architectural motifs (F. de Selgas in *Boletin de la Sociedad Española de Excursiones*, *24* [1916], 28 ff.).

92. Ciampini, *Vetera monimenta*, pp. 178–79: "per quam Martyrium, seu Martyris sepulchrum delineatum est: index est infallibilis palma in medio altaris assurgens qua nullum Martyrii symbolum aptatius." Cf. also ibid., p. 236.

93. Ibid., p. 179. It is clear from the description and from his illustration (Pl. 43.2) that Ciampini does not see these as thrones.

94. Ibid., p. 133: "hinc inde verò sub quadam absidula sedes Episcopalis conspicitur, quam nos *Faldistorium* vocare consuevimus."

95. *Storia della arte cristiana*, *4*, 35; the small thrones he takes to symbolize "la predicazione della dottrina evangelica nella Chiesa" (ibid., p. 36).

ciani disagreed with this view: "they are simply screens or parapets," he wrote, "not altars or sepulchers."[96] Barbier deMontault suggested the interpretation of the Garden of Eden.[97]

The question of the four main thrones, draped and bejeweled and surmounted by the cross, was even more puzzling. For some scholars[98] this was the empty throne of the second coming of Christ, of which Psalm 89 foretells: "Justice and judgement are the habitation of thy throne; mercy and truth shall go before thy face." Others pointed out, rightly, that this conception of the throne of justice, which became common in late Byzantine thought and art as the ἑτοιμασία τοῦ θρόνου or simply ἑτοιμασία, was as yet undeveloped in Early Christian times.[99] The throne should therefore rather symbolize the glorious presence of Christ in much the same way that an empty throne in Roman times, and earlier still in the East, often represented the presence of a specific deity or the emperor.[100] In this sense, the throne is not empty: it is occupied by the Heavenly Person who is invisible to the human eye and representable only symbolically by the cross or by the book. Indeed Cyril of Alexandria wrote Emperor Theodosius II that the Council of Ephesos "congregated under the presidency of Christ our Lord, for on a holy throne lay the venerable gospel."[101] Tarasius, patriarch of Constantinople, wrote of the Second Council of Nicaea to Pope Hadrian in similar terms.[102] But why four such thrones at the Baptistery? According to Barbier de Montault, they were meant to signify the four principal sees of Christendom—Rome, Jerusalem, Alexandria, and Constantinople; the smaller thrones would then stand for eight lesser sees.[103] The four gospels were similarly explained after the practice of

96. ". . . semplicemente plutei, o parapetti quali si vogliano, e non altari o sepolcri." Letter from Lanciani to G. B. de Rossi: see BAC, II.3 (1872), 137–38.

97. RAC (1896), p. 79.

98. Ch. Diehl, Ravenne (Paris, 1907), p. 40; G. Bovini, Chiese di Ravenna (Novara, 1957), p. 60.

99. Cf. Barbier de Montault in RAC (1896), p. 77. The classic work on the Etoimasia is P. Durand's Étude sur l'Etimacia, symbole du Jugement Dernier dans l'iconographie grecque chrétienne (Paris and Chartres, 1867). For its distinction from Early Christian representations of empty thrones, see F. van der Meer, Maiestas Domini: Théophanies de l'Apocalypse dans l'art chrétien, Studi di antichità cristiana, 13 (Vatican, 1938), 220 ff.; and most recently, Th. von Bogyay, "Zur Geschichte der Hetoimasie," Akten des XI. internationalen Byzantinistenkongresses, 1958 (Munich, 1960), pp. 58–61.

100. Cf. J. Auboyer, Le Culte du trône et son symbolisme dans l'Inde ancienne (Paris, 1949); also A. Alföldi in La nouvelle Clio (1950), pp. 537–56; and an excellent article by Ch. Picard, "Le trône vide d'Alexandre dans la cérémonie de Cyinda et le culte du trône vide à travers le monde gréco-romain," Cahiers, 7 (1954), 1–17. The thrones at the

Baptistery should be compared to similar Early Christian representations on the triumphal arch of S. Maria Maggiore in Rome (Wilpert, Römische Mosaiken und Malereien, 3, Pl. 71); in S. Prisco at Capua Vetere (ibid., Pl. 77); and on the Casket of Pola (see A. Soper, "The Italo-Gallic School of Early Christian Art," AB, 20 [1938], Fig. 4, where it is incorrectly identified as Etimasia).

101. Apologeticus ad piissimum imperatorem Theodosium, Migne, PG, 76, col. 472: "Τότε δὴ μόλις ἡ ἁγία σύνοδος συναγήγερτο μὲν 'εν τῇ ἁγίᾳ ἐκκλησίᾳ . . . σύνεδρον δὲ ὥσπερ, καὶ κεφαλὴ ἐποιεῖτο Χριστόν. Ἔκειτο γὰρ 'εν ἁγίῳ θρόνῳ τὸ σεπτὸν Εὐαγγέλιον . . ." Cf. the representation of the Council of Constantinople (381) in the codex of Gregory of Naziansus, Paris, Bibliothèque Nationale, Gr. 510 (von Bogyay [n. 99 above], p. 59 n. 10 and Pl. 4).

102. Epistola II, Migne, PG, 98, col. 1440: "καὶ προκαθεσθέντων ἁπάντων ἡμῶν, κεφαλὴν 'εποιησάμεθα Χριστόν. Ἔκειτο γὰρ ἐν ἁγίῳ θρόνῳ τὸ ἅγιον Εὐαγγέλιον."

103. RAC (1896), p. 79. Cf. the comments of Martigny regarding the use of baptisteries as halls for church councils, in Bulletin de l'art chrétien (1872), p. 144.

church councils, for there is a reference to the fact that the fourth Council of Constantinople commenced with the exhibition of the Gospels and of the wood of the
Holy Cross.[104] In the opinion of Beissel, the representation of the four gospels may
in fact derive from a part in the ancient liturgy of baptism.[105]

The inadequacy of the views above, summarized without comment, arises from the
fact that they are excessively specific in two ways: first, in that they take into account
small details of the zone, disregarding its totality or continuum; and second, in that
they explain the chosen details with the assistance of restricted references which
would probably have been unintelligible to the persons for whom the decoration
was originally intended and which appear somewhat forced to the modern observer.
The more involved or the more esoteric interpretations were probably farthest from
the minds of those responsible for the program. The decorative elements of the Baptistery were designed to be, generally speaking, self-explanatory—which is not to say
that their meaning would be precisely defined. Rather, the decoration, the acts of the
ritual itself, and the words spoken during the ritual had to work in unison to enhance
the dignity and elucidate the deep significance of the sacrament. The iconography
consequently had to suggest a general field of symbolism, it had to create an atmos-
pheric setting for the word and for the ritual. With this in mind, it is proper to see
that the decoration has no independent existence, and neither does a single decorative element exist independent of the entire program. Each of the two types of panels
making up Zone III (*Figs.* 65, 67) has a meaning in relation to the other and in reference to the rest of the interior scheme, and the repetition of these panels is due to
aesthetic considerations and not to iconographic verity.

The first person to associate these panels with the cross section of a Christian
basilica was J. P. Richter, who called them "ideal views of three-aisled churches."[106]
Since then several scholars have repeated this idea with their own additions and modi-
fications. Richter proposed that the small thrones flanking the altar were meant for
the bishop and the emperor, in accordance with the wishes of St. Ambrose that the
ruler should take his place "in front of the bounds of the holy altar." The Austrian
scholar brought to attention the custom, still prevalent in the Jerusalem of his day,
of placing a throne on either side of the altar, the one to the right occupied by the
bishop, the other empty but destined once for the Byzantine emperor.[107] The expla-

104. See Barbier de Montault in *RAC* (1896),
p. 77, citing Cavedoni, *Concil.* xxii, 539.

105. S. Beissel, *Geschichte der Evangelienbücher*
(Freiburg i.B., 1896), p. 6. The four gospels are
also connected with the four rivers of Paradise,
whose relation to baptism is made evident by St.
Cyprian's remark: "Ecclesia, setting forth the likeness of paradise, includes within her walls fruit-
bearing trees [which] she waters with four rivers,
that is with the four gospels wherewith, by a celestial inundation, she bestows the grace of sav-
ing baptism." (*Ep.* 73.10, as cited by P. Underwood
in *DOP, 5* [1950], 73.)

106. *Die Mosaiken von Ravenna* (Vienna, 1878),
p. 14: "Idealansichten dreischiffiger Kirchen in
Querdurchschnitt."

107. Ibid., pp. 14–15. St. Ambrose's dictum is
quoted by Sozomenos, *Hist. eccl.* III.25: "πρὸ τῶν
δρυφάκτων τοῦ ἱερατείου." The crowns on these thrones
would probably be symbols of the respective powers
of the bishop and the emperor. On this topic see
E. Diez, "Die *sella curulis* auf provinzialrömischen
Reliefsteinen der Steiermark," *Österreichisches Jahres-
hefte, 36* (1946), 97 ff.; and E. Stommel, "Die
bischöfliche Kathedra im christlichen Altertum,"
Münchener theologische Zeitschrift, 3 (1952), 17–32.

nations of Diehl, Kurth, and more recently of Grabar are essentially in accordance
with this interpretation.[108] The added merit of Grabar's thought lies in his attempt
to unite this panel with the second type of panel and to see in the whole zone the
eternal *domus Dei,* the celestial Jerusalem, which the privileged Christian will enter
and enjoy upon his death.

To my mind the most plausible interpretation of Zone III is along the lines of
Grabar's suggestion. But it is perhaps possible to develop the point a step further.
It is evident from our description of the two panel types that one is more specifically
related to the immediate vocabulary of the Christian church. The small thrones, the
altar, the open gospel, and the architecture itself all pertain to the visual image of
the house of God on earth. The world of the other panel type is different. Significantly it retains the same architectural framework, but this architecture is now open
in depth to blue skies, and the outdoor atmosphere is completed by trees and greenery. The throne in the center is more magnificent than the smaller thrones of the
previous panel, and moreover it is fully draped and occupied by the symbolic presence of the cross. In contrast to the recognizable identity of the altar panel, this type
seems to be a variation of the same theme, with more distinctly celestial references
to the glorious presence of God and to the paradise of the blessed. The contrast of
the two panels appears to me to be between the church on earth as the symbol of the
domus Dei and the actual referent of this symbol, the domus Dei itself.

The rhythmic alternation of the two types of panels, the earthly and the celestial,
is in character with the function of the rest of the decoration. The scheme of the first
two zones, depicted on flat walls, acted as a theatrical backdrop for the ritual. The
mystery was enacted in this area, which communicated with the outer world by means
of the windows of Zone II. The curved surface of the cupola, however, is no longer
directly involved in the rite as performed on earth. Rather it represents heaven itself
where the celestial prototype of the Christian sacrament is taking place in the presence of the twelve apostles. Between the *scaenae frons* of the lower decoration and
the "dome of heaven" of the uppermost decoration,[109] Zone III serves, I believe, as a
suggestive passage reflecting the character of the two worlds it conjoins by the rhythmic alternation of two panels, each belonging to one of these two worlds.

ZONES IV AND V

The celestial sphere promised by the resplendent thrones of Zone III opens out
with the twelve apostles of Christ marching, in two files of six led by Sts. Peter and
Paul, on a green ground touched with flecks of yellow, which yields to a background
of deep blue (*Figs.* 42A, 45–51). Each is dressed in a long tunic (the *dalmatica*) with
two broad stripes (*clavi*), over which is worn a pallium. Their feet are in sandals and

---

108. Diehl (n. 98 above), p. 39; J. Kurth, *Die
Wandmosaiken von Ravenna,* p. 80; A. Grabar,
Martyrium (Paris, 1946), pp. 111–12.

109. For this concept in antiquity, see the fundamental study by K. Lehmann, "The Dome of
Heaven," *AB,* 27 (1945), 1–27.

with both hands they hold a crown of gold studded with precious green stones. The color scheme of the costumes alternates between a gold tunic and blue-white pallium for one apostle and a blue-white tunic and gold pallium for the next. The names of the apostles are written in gold letters above their shoulders. Beginning with St. Peter and proceeding counterclockwise they are as follows (*Figs.* 41, 42): (a) PETR/US, (b) ANDRE/AS, (c) IACOBU/S ZEBEDEI, (d) IOHAN/NES, (e) FILIP/PUS, (f) BARTO/LO/MEU/S, (g) IUDA/S ZELOTES, (h) SIMON/CANANEUS, (i) IACOBU/S ALFEI, (j) MATT/HEUS, (k) THO/MAS, (l) PAU/LUS. The order derives basically from Matthew 10:2–4, excepting the omission of Thaddaeus and the inclusion of Paul; also Judas Zelotes, probably St. Jude, replaces Judas Iscariot.[110]

Between each pair of apostles is a gold plant-candelabrum touched with red, in the form of an acanthus base from which, as in Zone III, rises a tall vertical member. The apostles have no nimbuses; their heads, very small in proportion to their bodies, are set against tongue-shaped draperies pendent from the rim of the medallion which contains the scene of baptism (Zone V). These tongues are connected by loops of the same blue-white drapery with red and gold stripes. Such pendent draperies are not uncommon in Roman wall paintings.[111] One Christian example is in the Baptistery of S. Restituta at Naples where a rich system of similar draperies in mosaic hangs down from the rim of the central medallion of the vault (*Fig.* 139).[112]

The face of each apostle is distinctly characterized (*Figs.* 52–63), and this raises the question of the extent to which the artist of the Baptistery is responsible for a new portraiture. In the first three centuries of the Christian era no need was felt to distinguish among the apostles. The variation of bearded and beardless generalized portrait types was considered sufficient in usual *collegium* scenes showing the disciples grouped around the figure of Christ.[113] Broadly speaking, from the early fourth century onward, the individuation of some of the apostles became imperative as Christian iconography expanded to include episodes in which this or that one of them played a specific part. St. Peter's was probably the earliest individual portrait as it appeared in scenes like his conversation with Christ (the *confirmatio*), Peter arrested by two soldiers, and Peter striking water from the rock.[114] St. Paul too was early given

---

110. See Th. Schermann, *Propheten- und Apostellegenden* . . . , pp. 198–239, esp. 218. For restorations done in Zone IV, see Ricci, *Tavole,* 2, Pls. 10–13.

111. See N. Ponce, *Descriptions des Bains de Titus où collection des peintures trouvées dans les ruines des thermes de cet empereur* (Paris, 1786), esp. Pl. 37 which shows a now lost painting, probably from the Domus Aurea.

112. See Wilpert, *Römische Mosaiken und Malereien,* Pl. 31.

113. For the portraiture of the apostles, see among others: J. Ficker, *Darstellungen der Apostel in die altchristliche Kunst,* Beiträge zur Kunstgeschichte, 5 (Leipzig, 1887); J. E. Weis-Liebersdorf,

Christus- und Apostelbilder. Einfluss der Apokryphen auf die ältesten Kunsttypen (Freiburg i.B., 1902; his dates should be taken with extreme caution); J. Wilpert, *Römische Mosaiken und Malereien,* 2, 929 ff.; K. Künstle, *Ikonographie der Heiligen* (Freiburg i.B., 1926); and more recently F. Gerke, *Das heilige Antlitz: Köpfe altchristlicher Plastik* (Berlin, 1940). Ficker's claim (above; pp. 58 ff.) that the bearded saint type developed in the early fifth century and that the young unbearded type entirely predominated earlier is, of course, no longer tenable; see Gerke (above), p. 7 ff.

114. For St. Peter's portraiture, in addition to the works cited in the previous note, see G. Stuhlfauth, *Die apokryphen Petrusgeschichten in der alt-*

a recognizable portrait type in scenes, including the Traditio legis, in which he and St. Peter figure on either side of Christ.[115] The two leaders of the apostles appear twice in the decorative scheme of the Baptistery, once in the Traditio legis of Zone II (*Fig.* 81) and again in Zone IV (*Figs.* 52, 63). In both cases their features conform to the portrait types which had become standard for them by the mid-fifth century. It must be remembered that these portrait types were not strictly obeyed individuations but generic faces in which one or two easily identifiable physical characteristics were prominent.[116] The type for St. Peter was of an old man with gray or white hair and a short beard, often, as in Zone IV, showing a striking resemblance to the portraits of Roman patricians of the Republic, e.g. that of the "Capitoline Brutus."[117] St. Paul on the other hand was distinguished by the high forehead due to the balding head, the aquiline nose, elongated face, and dark, pointed beard—not unlike the Roman concept of a Greek philosopher's portrait, especially that of Socrates.[118]

The facial traits of the remaining apostles of Zone IV are not so easily traced to stylized prototypes. The iconography of Early Christian art did not include stories in which these disciples could appear as protagonists, and for many of them physical descriptions in apocryphal writings were entirely lacking. A portrait type has been recognized by A. Haseloff for St. Andrew, characterized by thick and unkempt hair, and a short round beard;[119] but this type, which is vividly portrayed in the Archiepiscopal Chapel and in San Vitale in Ravenna, is not followed in the earlier Baptistery, where the saint has smooth, clean-cut hair, hollow cheeks, and a thin beard (*Fig.* 53).[120] If the artist of the Baptistery were copying earlier portrait types for the other apostles, it is no longer possible to establish the paradigms among existing monuments of Early Christian art. The remarkable thing about these figures is in fact the confidence and originality with which they have been rendered, as though the artist were working from living models. There is St. Thomas, for example, with a narrow brow, large eyes deeply set above high cheekbones, and a small sensuous mouth (*Fig.* 62); or St. Matthew, whose dignified expression, long eyes, and thin long whiskers bear the stamp of authentic portraiture (*Fig.* 61); or again St. Bartholomew, whose

---

christlichen Kunst (Berlin-Leipzig, 1925); E. Dinkler, *Die ersten Petrusdarstellungen* (Marburg a.L., 1939); F. Gerke, "Duces in Militia Christi. Die Anfänge der Petrus-Paulus Ikonographie," *Kunstchronik*, 7 (1954), 95–101. The theory of the last century that the true prosopography of Sts. Peter and Paul was handed down to the Roman church (de Rossi in *BAC* [1864], pp. 84 ff., and [1887], pp. 130 ff.; Weis-Liebersdorf [n. 113 above], pp. 77 ff.) can now only be appreciated as the zealous effort of Catholic scholars to prove the authenticity of the conventional portrait types of the leading apostles in Early Christian art.

115. In addition to the above references, see E. von Dobschütz, *Der Apostel Paulus* (2 vols. Halle, 1926–28), esp. vol. 2, *Seine Stellung in der Kunst.*

116. Cf. Sts. Peter and Paul of Zone IV with other portraits of them in catacombs: G. Wilpert, *Roma sotterranea. Le pitture delle catacombe romane*, 2 (Rome, 1903), Pls. 79, 182, 254; H. Achelis, *Die Katakomben von Neapel* (Leipzig, 1935–36), Pls. 42, 43.

117. Cf. also R. Paribeni, *Il Ritratto nell'arte antica* (Milan, 1934), Pls. 84, 85 (republican portraits) and 233, 253 (emperor portraits).

118. Ibid., Pls. 52, 53. Very close to the head of St. Paul in Zone IV is the Socrates on a mosaic from the basilica at Apamea, *Antiquités classiques*, 10 (1941), Fig. 1.

119. *Codex purpureus Rossanensis. Die Miniaturen der griechischen Evangelienhandschriften in Rossano* (Berlin-Leipzig, 1898), pp. 54 ff.

120. Cf. Deichmann, *Frühchristliche Bauten und Mosaiken von Ravenna*, Pls. 234, 337.

powerful, bony face has rightly been compared to some of the gladiator portraits in mosaic from the Baths of Caracalla, now housed in the Lateran Museum (*Fig. 57*).[121]

It is instructive to set these gripping impersonations of the disciples of Christ against their counterparts in the portrait galleries of the Archiepiscopal Chapel and of San Vitale, where the inscribed names also dispel all doubt of identity. Compare, as one example, the St. Philip of Zone IV with his counterparts in the chapel and in the bema of San Vitale (*Figs. 56, 134*).[122] The three portraits are different in appearance, but the attempt in the later two has been to generalize the features into distinct crystallizations with little flow between them. The momentariness of expression and authenticity of mien in the St. Philip of Zone IV have been sacrificed in these others for permanence and objectivity. The apostles in the Baptistery are viable, palpable individuals; those in the chapel and in San Vitale have already been transformed into lucid and noncommital abstractions.

Zone IV is separated from the medallion of the cupola by an ornamental band which is an interpretation into mosaic of the popular egg-and-dart motif (*Fig. 43*), whose long existence has been marked by a series of subtle permutations.[123] The form used here appears in at least two other late antique mosaics, one from Italica, of the third–fourth century, and the second from Aquileia, of the fifth century.[124] In the Baptistery it assumes added suitability from the fact that it reflects the same rhythmic pattern as the tongues and loops which terminate Zone IV.

Within the medallion, Christ is pictured nude in the Jordan, whose waters come up to a little below his waist. The Precursor stands on a rocky ledge by the river, one foot placed higher than the other, in a pose often encountered in Roman paintings of Perseus rescuing Andromeda, Theseus triumphant over the Minotaur, and other similar scenes. He is wearing the *exomis* made of the skins of beasts and holds in his left hand a vast *crux gemmata*. His right hand clasps a bowl with which he is on the point of pouring water onto the Savior's head,[125] above whom is the dove of the Holy Ghost. In a corner to the right the magnificent figure of the river god half emerges from his waters, with a marsh plant in one hand and a green cloth in the other which he proffers to the Son of God, looking up at him with a reverent expression (*Fig. 44*). His long hair and beard are strands of green and blue; his sun-baked body is master-

---

121. See M. Blake in *MAAR, 17* (1940), Pls. 25, 28, 29. This comparison has been suggested in general about all the apostles of Zone IV by Galassi, *Roma o Bisanzio*, p. 40.

122. For the St. Philip of San Vitale, see Deichmann, *Frühchristliche Bauten und Mosaiken von Ravenna*, Pl. 335.

123. See E. Weigand, "Baalbek," *Jahrbuch für Kunstwissenschaft, 2* (1924), 175 ff.

124. See *La Basilica di Aquileia* (n. 87 above), Pls. 29, 30; and A. C. De Laborde, *Déscription d'un pavé en mosaïque découvert dans l'ancienne ville d'Italica* (Paris, 1806), Pl. 14. The same pattern has been uncovered in the recently cleaned mosaics

of St. George, Thessaloniki (Torp, *Mosaikkene i St. Georg-rotunden*, figures on p. 20).

125. For some curious reason Garrucci imagined that between the *patera* and the head of Christ there were the letters IXIN, which he then proceeded to interpret at great length (*Storia della arte cristiana, 4, 36*). Ricci was the first to point out, with a severity that seems uncalled for, that these letters are nonexistent ("S. Giovanni," pp. 291–93). The iconography of St. John is discussed in R. Plus, *Saint-Jean Baptiste dans l'art* (Paris, 1937); and A. Masseron, *Saint-Jean Baptiste dans l'art* (Paris, 1953).

fully modeled in various shades of brown. His name is inscribed, in bright letters, above his head: IORDAN̄N̄.

The representation of Christ's baptism is not rare in Early Christian art. Baldwin Smith's list of 1918 includes thirty-nine examples, to which several others can now be added.[126] Despite this popularity, and notwithstanding the fact that Smith distinguished seven iconographic types,[127] the many renditions of the scene display a remarkable generic consistency. The Savior is almost always pictured as a young child[128] and the Baptist as a mature bearded prophet—and this contrary to the account according to the Gospel of St. Luke wherein the difference of age between Christ and St. John is said to be no more than six months (1:24–27). The baptizing saint is more often than not to the left of Christ, with the left leg bent and raised on a rock.

Several elements of the baptism scene at the Ravennate monument differ from this general arrangement, chief among them being that Christ appears as a bearded man and the fact that the Baptist is pouring water onto his head from a bowl (*patera*), a detail apparently not encountered in any other Early Christian representation of the theme.[129] These peculiarities are due, most probably, to restoration and not to the original design. It is obvious even from photographs that a large section covering the heads of the Savior and the Baptist, most of the cross, and the dove of the Holy Ghost, belongs to a modern patching (*Figs.* 42A, 43). The date of this alteration is not certain; Ricci suggested the eighth century or later, the initial painted restoration having been affirmed in mosaic by Kibel in the nineteenth century.[130] Gerola saw no reason to attribute the alteration to anyone earlier than Kibel himself, despite the fact that Ciampini's engraving in the late seventeenth century showed the scene very much as it is today.[131] I doubt that the exact date at which the medallion of the bap-

---

126. *Early Christian Iconography and a School of Ivory Carvers in Provence* (Princeton, 1918), Table IV; to which add: ivory fragment in Lyon (Volbach, *Elfenbeinarbeiten*, no. 149); tombstone of Innocent, Museum of Aquileia (F. van der Meer and Ch. Mohrmann, *Atlas of the Early Christian World* [London, 1958], Fig. 397); painting in the Catacomb of Lucina (Wilpert, *Roma sotterranea*, Pl. 29); painting in the Catacomb of Petrus and Marcellinus (ibid., Pls. 58, 73); ampulla from Bobbio (A. Grabar, *Ampoules de Terre Sainte* [Paris, 1958], Pl. 18); and others.

127. Baldwin Smith, (n. 126 above), pp. 71–84. The distinctions made between these groups are not always clear-cut or important. For the iconography of the baptism, see also J. Strzygowski, *Ikonographie der Taufe Christi* (Munich, 1885); and A. Jacoby, *Ein bisher unbeachteter Bericht über die Taufe Jesu* (Strassburg, 1902).

128. The exceptions are: in the Rabula Gospel; in a painting at Chapel 17 of Baouit (J. Clédat, *Le Monastère et la nécropole de Baouit* [Cairo, 1904–

06], Pl. 45); on a painted panel formerly in the Golenisheff Collection (Strzygowski, *Denkschriften der K. Akademie der Wissenschaften* [Vienna, 1906], p. 199).

129. Cf. Strzygowski, *Ikonographie der Taufe Christi*, p. 10. The attempt by C. F. Rogers ("Baptism and Christian Archaeology," *Studia biblica et ecclesiastica*, 5, part 4, 265 ff.) to prove the use of the *patera* in the early Christian centuries is not convincing, for the dating of the two objects on which his argument rests, a spoon from Aquileia and a cross shaft at Kells, is very uncertain.

130. "S. Giovanni," p. 293.

131. Gerola, "La tecnica dei restauri ai mosaici di Ravenna," *Atti per la Romagna*, 4.7 (1917), 164; he tries to establish the unreliability of Ciampini's engraving (*Vetera monimenta*, Pl. 70) by pointing out that on Pl. 23 of his book, which reproduces the cupola mosaic of the Arian Baptistery, St. John is shown again with a *patera*, whereas in actuality this detail is nonexistent.

tism was redone could be ascertained. More important is the attempt to reconstruct the pristine design of this scene, which perhaps could be achieved by making use of circumstantial evidence. Since the patera in the Baptist's hand is unknown previous to the eighth century or thereabout, and since in all earlier representations he merely lays his hand on the Savior's head, this detail should probably be reconstructed accordingly. Christ should very likely be shown as a beardless youth, as in almost all other Early Christian renditions of the theme, a correction which seems to be urged by the curious disharmony between the large mature head of Christ in the present state of the picture and his youthful fragile body. It may also be tenable to replace the crux gemmata in the Baptist's left hand with a more modest shepherd's hook, the *pedum*. All these suggested changes are indeed present in the equivalent scene in the cupola of the Arian Baptistery of about A.D. 500 (*Fig.* 136), and in still another early representation of the baptism in Ravenna, on the ivory throne of Archbishop Maximian (*Fig.* 135).

A feature that remains dissimilar in these three renditions, however, is the depiction of the river god. He is pictured in the Arian Baptistery completely out of the water, seated majestically on a shelf of rock; and on Maximian's throne he is a young male nude struggling to get away from the scene of the baptism, his powerful back turned toward the viewer. In the Orthodox Baptistery, Jordan is neither allowed too much prominence, as in the Arian version, nor is he made to flee. He approaches the Savior with a cloth in his hands, replacing the angels who attend on him in the version on the ivory throne and in many later Byzantine baptisms. The artist, or his adviser, seem to have had in mind these words of Peter Chrysologos, the direct predecessor of Neon on the episcopal seat of Ravenna, who in a sermon asked, "Why is it that Jordan who fled in the presence of the Ark of the Covenant [the reference is to Joshua 3:16–17] did not flee away from the presence of the Holy Trinity? Why? Because he who yields to piety begins not to be afraid."[132] There is a touching dignity in the carriage of this pagan divinity as he surrenders to the newly manifest God, which makes this small half-figure in the Baptistery one of the noblest creations of late antique art.

It has been suggested in the discussion of Zone III that its iconographic function was twofold: that in the rhythmic alternation of two distinct panels it at once marked the limits of the earthly church within which the neophyte was baptized and introduced the heavenly domain of the blessed spirits to which he hoped, through his baptism, to attain. With Zones IV and V we are in the realm of supranatural existence, where the apostles march on the green grass of Paradise around the spot on which

---

132. ". . . quid est quod Jordanis qui fugit ad praesentiam legalis arcae, ad totius Trinitatis praesentiam non refugit? Quid est? Quia qui pietati obsequitur, incipit non esse timori," *Sermo 160* (Migne, *PL, 52,* col. 621–22). C. Nordström first noted the passage (*Ravennastudien: Ideengeschichtliche und ikonographische Untersuchungen über die Mosaiken von Ravenna* [Uppsala, 1953], p. 33), but his deductions from it about the date of Zone V are inadmissible.

the Savior is baptized by St. John. In one respect the baptism does not belong in the Dome of Heaven, for the event is part of Christ's life on earth when he walked among mortals in the semblance of man. But the scene should be understood as being in apposition to the ritual enacted in the font below, as being in fact the heavenly prototype of which the baptism of the neophyte is only a reflection. The distinction is one of contextual hierarchy. Moreover, in the account of the baptism in the Synoptic Gospels, earth and heaven are brought into a correlation which blurs the worldly specificity of the event: "And Jesus, when he was baptized, went up straightway out of the water: and, lo, the heavens were opened unto him, and he saw the Spirit of God descending like a dove . . ." (Matt. 3:16). The medallion of the baptism then may be said to be functioning on two levels; first, as a divine prefiguration of the sacrament which is being administered to the neophyte,[133] and second, as a pneumatic element above, sanctifying the waters of the font in the same way that the dove of the Holy Spirit sanctified the earthly ambient where the Savior himself came to be baptized. The position of this scene in the decorative scheme of the Baptistery, in direct correlation with the font, achieves the same hierarchy of earth and heaven that is implied in the Synoptic description of Christ's baptism in the River Jordan.

The consecration of the waters of the font, or the *benedictio fontis,* was an important part of the baptismal ritual. Its urgency is powerfully attested by St. Ambrose:

> Thou sawest water. But it is not all water that heals, but that water which has the grace of Christ. The element is one thing, the consecration is another. The water is the work, the working is of the Holy Spirit. Water does not heal, unless the Spirit has descended and consecrated that water.[134]

I suggest that the function and meaning of Zone V are implied by these lines. But St. Ambrose is even more explicit:

> As thou hast read that, when our Lord Jesus Christ was giving the pattern of baptism, he came to John . . . Therefore, if baptism is for our sake, a pattern has been established for us, the pattern of our faith has been set forth. Christ descended, John stood by baptizing, and, lo, the *Holy Ghost descended as a dove* . . . The Holy Spirit . . . descended from heaven, not in the reality of a dove, but in the likeness of a dove. Therefore, John saw and believed.[135]

The parallel is lucid and complete, and it applies inevitably and precisely, I believe, to the decoration of the Baptistery.

What the neophyte observed over the font was not the "reality" of Christ's baptism

---

133. F. M. Braun suggests that the reason why Christ is shown as a young boy in most renditions of the Baptism in Early Christian art is the wish to identify the neophyte with the Saviour ("Le baptême d'après le quatrième évangile," *Revue thomiste, 48* [1948], 367). This attractive idea presupposes, however, the tender age of the neophytes, which was by no means always the case; especially in the early centuries of the Christian era baptism at a later age was the rule.

134. *De sacr.* I.5.15, trans. by T. Thompson in J. H. Srawley (above, n. 17), p. 54.

135. *De sacr.* I.5.15–17 (ibid., pp. 54–55); the italics are not mine.

but its "likeness," and therefore he too, like John, "saw and believed." The water of the font was no longer merely the "element," but it was water that could heal because it partook of the grace of Christ. This active participation of the decoration in the ritual through its meaningful location is a significant commentary on the Early Christian conception of art. Art within the church is not merely pleasant ornament: this is easily conceded by students of the period. Its extraornamental qualities, however, are perhaps too often explained as merely instructive or dogmatic, especially after the Peace of the Church, when, to quote Strzygowski, "symbolism was displaced by a didactic tendency, the purpose of which was to teach the faithful by the help of graphic art how the teaching of Christ and the prophets was handed down through the apostles and the evangelists to the Church. This purpose is clearly expressed in fifth-century mosaics such as those of the Mausoleum of Galla Placidia or of the Orthodox Baptistery at Ravenna."[136] This interpretation of the decorative scheme of the Baptistery appears to me to be misrepresenting the intention of the church officials responsible for it. Instruction of the kind described by Strzygowski was received by the catechumen in the weeks prior to administration of the sacrament. The decorative program was not designed to be merely an illustration of catechistical teachings or merely a set of symbols of the concepts discussed during the instruction. Rather, it was meant to be in direct reciprocity with the various parts of the baptismal ritual. It was meant to create an active ambient for the ritual, substituting for the reality of the heavenly world a likeness which was easy to see and believe. This is a step farther from the intended function of theatrical scenery. For not only does the decoration of the Baptistery provide a setting for the ritual drama: it enacts certain scenes without which the drama would be meaningless. Christ and St. John, the apostles and the prophets, are all fixed on the walls like permanent *dei ex machina* without whose active participation the sacrament of baptism would be deprived of all its essential significance, and the ministers of the church of their assumed authority.

It remains to consider the relationship of the gallery of apostles with the medallion of the baptism and with the rest of the decoration. The main difficulty in understanding the arrangement of Zone IV is that the apostles are shown bearing crowns, but that the destination of the crowns is not included in the same zone. Now the similar iconographic theme of crown-bearing saints at the Arian Baptistery, undoubtedly inspired by the earlier Orthodox Baptistery, has been freed from this ambiguity by the addition of a throne of Christ in the midst of the row of apostles (*Fig.* 136). "Before the resplendent throne of Thy majesty, O Lord," it is said in the Liturgy of the Blessed Apostles, "and the exalted and sublime throne of Thy glory, and on the awful seat of the strength of Thy love and the propitiatory altar which Thy will hath established, in the region of Thy pasture ... we draw near, adore, thank, and glorify Thee."[137]

It has therefore been generally held that the crowns of the Orthodox Baptistery

136. J. Strzygowski, *Origins of Christian Church Art* (trans. by O. M. Dalton and H. J. Braunholtz, Oxford, 1923), p. 163.

137. *Ante-Nicene Fathers*, 7 (New York, 1896), 561.

are also destined for the throne of Christ, which in this case is in a lower zone,[138] and it has been suggested that the reason for this disunified arrangement was due either to the unsuccessful imitation of an earlier model,[139] or to the inability of the artist to divide Zone IV into thirteen compartments.[140] These negative explanations seem to me to underestimate the great talent of the artist of the Orthodox Baptistery and furthermore to raise the question of why it should be necessary to have four thrones of Christ in Zone III when only one would have been appropriate. A small group of scholars held instead that the crowns of the apostles were destined for Christ himself, and that therefore Zone IV belonged, properly speaking, with the medallion of the baptism.[141] Still a third interpretation was offered by S. Bettini;[142] in an attempt to unite all three zones of the cupola, he proposed to read them as one continuous theme disposed in accordance with the inverted perspective, which Grabar had explained earlier in terms of Plotinian philosophy, exemplified by the composition in superposed tiers on the base of the Theodosian obelisk in Istanbul.[143] Thus the apostles must be understood to be marching *in front of* Zone III and *around* the scene of Christ's baptism (*Fig.* 42A). Bettini compared this reconstruction with the mosaics of St. George in Thessaloniki where saints are indeed shown standing in front of the architecture (*Fig.* 140), or again with the "city-gate" sarcophagi on which Christ is shown flanked by saints and in front of an architectural frieze representing the celestial Jerusalem.

A criticism of this hypothesis was provided by. C.-O. Nordström in a recent important contribution to Ravennate iconography.[144] Nordström pointed out that Bettini's proposals left the problem of the destination of the crowns unsolved, and also that the parallel with the perspective used at the base of the Theodosian obelisk was unsatisfactory since in the Baptistery the central figure of Christ is not the largest in size and the apostles the smallest, which inverted perspective would have required, but that the reverse is true. In turn Nordström proposed an ingenious hypothesis of his own, according to which the cupola scheme of the Baptistery represents a Christian version of the imperial theme of the *aurum coronarium* or *aurum oblaticium,* the custom of proffering golden wreaths to the Roman emperor at his coronation as a token of his investiture. Nordström considers the baptism of Christ to be the moment of his coronation as the Son of God, and cites texts to substantiate the parallel custom of presenting the neophytes with crowns after their baptism.[145]

138. Grabar, *L'Empereur dans l'art byzantin,* p. 232; Wessel in *AA, 65–66* (1950–51), 112; H. P. L'Orange and P. J. Nordhagen, *Mosaikk fra Antikk til Middelalder* (Oslo, 1958), pp. 34–35 (not accessible to me).

139. Wilpert, *Römische Mosaiken und Malereien, I,* 70 ff.

140. A. C. Soper in *AB, 20* (1938), 157.

141. O. M. Dalton, *Byzantine Art and Archae-* ology (Oxford, 1911), p. 346; O. Wulff, *Altchristliche und byzantinische Kunst* (Potsdam, 1936), p. 343; Galassi, *Roma o Bisanzio,* p. 41.

142. "Il battistero della Cattedrale," *FR, 52* (1950), 41–59.

143. A. Grabar, "Plotin et les origines de l'esthétique médiévale," *Cahiers, 1* (1951), 15–34.

144. *Ravennastudien,* pp. 41–43.

145. Ibid., pp. 44–46.

Nordström's hypothesis has been received with varying degrees of enthusiasm. Grabar, for one, considers it "certain";[146] F. W. Deichmann finds it in the main a "fruitful and happy" solution.[147] It appears to this writer, however, that the new interpretation raises more questions than it answers. The formidable dogmatic complications which arise with the acceptance of the baptism as Christ's investiture have been considered at length by K. Wessel, and need not be repeated here.[148] More important still is the realization that numerous other Early Christian scenes represent saints bearing crowns to Christ without the least reference to his baptism; in fact the crowns are sometimes offered simply to an empty throne or to the *crux invicta*.[149] I would therefore regard Nordström's reading of the cupola decoration as forced and too specific. The crown as a gift of submission and recognition of power is known in Christian art in such representations as the Magi before the Christ child or the Elders before the throne of justice. When borne by saints, however, the crown denotes Christ's reward to them in recognition of their martyrdom.[150] "Be thou faithful unto death, and I will give thee a crown of life," it is promised in the revelation of St. John the Divine (Rev. 2:10). "Know ye not," says St. Paul, " that they which run in a race run all, but one receiveth the prize? So run that ye may obtain . . . Now they do it to obtain a corruptible crown; but we an incorruptible." (I Cor. 9:24, 25). And again: "I have fought a good fight, I have finished my course, I have kept the faith: Henceforth there is laid up for me a crown of righteousness, which the Lord, the righteous judge, shall give me at that day." (II Tim. 4:7,8). Frequently Christ is depicted handing out such crowns of glory to the victorious martyr. In the apse mosaic of San Vitale the enthroned Christ is proffering a crown to the martyr St. Vitalis who is being presented to him by an angel.[151] Equally commonly, however, the saints are shown returning to Christ the crowns they have won, since in him all martyrdom is realized. This dual relationship of the martyr to the Savior is vividly expressed by St. Cyprian: "Dominus . . . ipse in certamine et coronat pariter et coronatur."[152] Consequently, in some instances, as in the Baptistery of S. Restituta at Naples, saints

146. "Mosaïques à Ravenne," review of Nordström's book in *Cahiers, 8* (1956), 250: "Cette exégèse est certaine."

147. Review of Nordström's book in *BZ, 48* (1955), 412: "[The theory] erscheint in der Hauptsache fruchtbar und glücklich."

148. "Zur Interpretation der Kuppelmosaiken des Baptisterium der Ortodozen," *Corsi* (1957), fasc. 1, 77–81. It appears to me, however, that the arguments raised by Wessel are in themselves often farfetched or debatable. Other dissenters from Nordström's hypothesis are: L. de Bruyne in *RACrist, 31* (1955), 111–12; C. Cecchelli in *FR, 71* (1955), 49–52; G. de Francovich in *FR, 79* (1959), 147–49; and from the methodology of the book in general, E. Schäfer in *Zeitschrift für Kirchengeschichte, 66*

(1954–55), 172–75. For the idea of *aurum coronarium* in Roman and Early Christian iconography, see also Th. Klauser in *RM, 59* (1944), 129–53, esp. 150–53.

149. For these different types of crown-bearing, see K. Wessel, "Kranzgold und Lebenskrönen," *AA, 65–66* (1950–51), 103–04.

150. See among others, K. Baus, *Die Kranz in Antike und Christentum* (Bern, 1940); E. Goodenough, "The Crown of Victory in Judaism," *AB, 28* (1946), 139–59; O. von Simson, *Sacred Fortress, Byzantine Art and Statecraft in Ravenna* (Chicago [1948]), pp. 99 ff.

151. Deichmann, *Frühchristliche Bauten und Mosaiken von Ravenna*, Pls. 351–53.

152. *Epistola 8* (Oxford ed.), 10; Migne, *PL, 4*, col. 255.

are represented holding crowns in their hands with no apparent destination for them (*Fig.* 139).[153]

This very ambivalence of generic symbolism is also characteristic of the decoration of the Orthodox Baptistery. For not only is it in accordance with the essentially non-dogmatic nature of the decorative program but also it assists in the unification of the various segments of the program into a coherent *atmosphere* of meanings. It has already been noted that the repetition of the theme of prophets in Zones I and II helped to merge these two zones, breaking up the artificial dividing line between them; and that the juxtaposition and rhythmic repetition of two motifs with different referential frames in Zone III succeeded in providing a passage from the lower part of the decoration to the Dome of Heaven itself. Once more now in the iconography of Zone IV we are confronted with a similar ambivalence of symbolism which forces the mind to connect the procession of the crown-bearing apostles with both the architectural zone below and the medallion of the baptism above. Such a consistent flexibility of meaning is certainly not the result of accident or of incompetence on the part of the artist; rather, it must be a conscious principle of the collaboration between patron and artist and proof of the remarkable subtlety of their creation. To deny this flexibility or to explain it away is, I think, to do injustice to the intent of the monument. Had the patron and artist sought to be explicit, they would have adopted a system similar to the one used by the cupola mosaics of the Arian Baptistery (*Fig.* 136). There, the twelve apostles approach a central throne of Christ, bearing their crowns and other attributes. The axis of this procession is to the east, exactly over the apse. The scene of the baptism, however, has an opposite axis, to the west. Thus the two zones are clearly separate, both in regard to meaning and to visual arrangement. The essentially pragmatic theology of the Arians, which could not, or would not, comprehend the subtleties of the indivisible triple nature of the Holy Trinity, is reflected in this simplified, single-minded organization of the decorative scheme in their Baptistery.[154]

Now consider again the system of the earlier Neonian monument (*Fig.* 42A). The disciples are marching in two semicircular processions which meet directly under the feet of Christ in the medallion of the baptism. The axis of Zone IV corresponds therefore with that of Zone V and, when continued vertically, this axis leads to one of the four thrones and falls exactly over the niche containing the altar (*Fig.* 41). Visually, all five zones of the decoration are thus united by a common vertical axis corresponding to the east–west axis of the building itself. Iconographically, the barriers of the

---

153. For the mosaics of this baptistery, see G. Stuhlfauth, "Das Baptisterium S. Giovanni in Fonte zu Neapel und seine Mosaiken," *Reinhold-Seeberg Festschrift*, 2 (Leipzig, 1929), 181–212; Wilpert, *Römische Mosaiken und Malereien*, *1*, 214–46; and G. Bovini, "I mosaici del Battistero di S. Giovanni in Fonte a Napoli," *Corsi* (1959), fasc. 1, 5–26 with bibliography.

154. The division of labor in the mosaics, proposed recently by G. Bovini (*FR*, *75* [1957], 22–24), does not invalidate this discussion since Bovini agrees that the baptism, the throne, Sts. Peter and Paul, and the apostle next to Paul are all of one period.

superposed zones of decoration are also obliterated by the demand to complete the meaning of one zone with the assistance of the others. The resulting harmony, to be elaborated in the coming chapter, appears to me to be one of the happiest solutions among monumental programs of Early Christian art.

It must be observed in conclusion that the ambiguity of Zone IV leads to no error in the iconographic aptness of the theme. The presence of the apostles is highly appropriate in the hierarchy beginning with the baptism of Christ and ending in the baptism of the neophyte. St. John and the Savior are the protagonists of the heavenly baptism. Next in importance come the apostles to whom Christ assigned the task of propagating the true faith by means of the sacrament of baptism: "Go ye therefore, and teach all nations, baptizing them in the name of the Father, and of the Son, and of the Holy Ghost: teaching them to observe all things whatsoever I have commanded you," (Matt. 28:19, 20).[155] In this context there is no more suitable intermediary than the apostles between the archetypal baptism of the Lord and its reflection around the font of the earthly church. Their mission is fulfilled and their crowns of glory earned.[156] The crowns of the neophytes are as yet to be earned, but their presence in this building signifies that they have taken the major step in the path which leads to the realm of the crowned immortals, the realm whose likeness is above the font, in the multicolored forms of the Dome of Heaven.

---

155. This relation is so evident that it is hard to agree with Miss Casalone's contention ("Ricerche," pp. 238–40) that the medallion has no connection with Zone IV, and that it was forcibly inserted there. The baptism of the apostles themselves seems to have troubled many early church fathers. Tertullian held that they were never baptized, but they were saved by being close to Christ (De baptismo 12). St. Augustine and others considered the washing of the feet of the disciples at the Last Supper as taking the place of baptism (see above, p. 60 and nn. 16, 17). Clement of Alexandria maintained that Christ baptized St. Peter alone; and Peter, Andrew; and Andrew, James and John; and they, the rest (in a lost passage preserved in the Pratum spirituale of John Moschus). See H. A. Echle, "The Baptism of the Apostles," Traditio, 3 (1945), 365 ff.

156. The martyrdom of the apostles is not doubted by the church fathers. Cf. Hippolytus, On the Twelve Apostles (Ante-Nicene Fathers, 5 [New York, 1899], 254–55) where the different martyrdom of each apostle is described. Cf. also Tertullian, Scorpiace 15 (Ante-Nicene Fathers, 3, 648): "that the apostles endured such sufferings, we know; the teaching is clear."

THE DECORATIVE PROGRAM
Analysis

The chief aim of the previous chapter was expository rather than analytical, but questions of a more formal nature were at times touched upon. If the convenient, but essentially false, division between iconography and style cannot be kept more rigid, it is because the monument itself so dictates; its integrity is such that, as in any significant work of art, the content is inextricably identified with the form. And this ultimately is the more urgent and meaningful task in the study of the Orthodox Baptistery: to understand how the thematic familiarity of Christian content, which the artist could assume in his audience, has been so employed and transcended by him that his creation has become a specific and individual work of art within the general frame of period uniformity. The following pages will concentrate on the definition of the style of the sculpture and of the mosaic, and on the study of visual principles active in the total scheme of the decoration.

SCULPTURE OF ZONE II

Previous estimation of this part of the decorative scheme (*Figs.* 77–102) has been generally cursory and unsympathetic. The execution has been thought gross and unsophisticated, especially in comparison with the relative refinement of the mosaics;[1] consequently, the contemporaneity of these reliefs with the rest of the decoration has been seriously doubted.[2] It has even been suggested that they might have replaced at some later date an initial program of mosaic.[3] What is often overlooked, however, in these negative appraisals is that it is incorrect to judge the work of Zone

---

1. Cf. J. R. Rahn, *Ravenna: Eine kunstgeschichtliche Studie* (Leipzig, 1869), p. 7, where the prophets are said to be "von grösster Roheit"; Ch. Diehl, *Ravenne* (Paris, 1907), p. 34; E. Lavagnino, *L'Arte medioevale* (Turin, 1949), p. 102.

2. Diehl (above), p. 34; A. Haseloff, *Pre-Romanesque Sculpture in Italy* (New York, n.d. [ca. 1930]), pp. 31–32.

3. J. A. Crowe and G. B. Cavalcaselle, *Storia della pittura in Italia*, *1* (Florence, 1885), 28.

II as a finished product of sculpture, since what survives today constitutes only the rough core which, from the beginning, was designed to be complemented by color. Stucco decoration in antiquity was considered more as a durable variation of painting than an independent branch of sculpture. The more obvious blemishes in the apparently careless execution of the Baptistery reliefs would have been adjusted by the overlay of paint and gilding. It is also incorrect to evaluate the sculpture of this zone, as has in fact been done, in terms of other Early Christian monuments of sculpture in marble and ivory.[4] It was inevitable that the inexpensive and comparatively rapid production of stucco ornament should have an effect on its execution, as it was inevitable that more precious materials should have been treated with finer attention. Moreover, the modeling of marble or ivory, being more laborious and allowing little latitude for correction, acquires a careful finality of design lacking in stucco relief which is more a product of the hand than of the tool. Its working is apt to reflect a quality of sketchiness, of extemporaneity, that is quite unlike the finished surfaces in marble or ivory. Thus to compare Zone II with the sarcophagus of Liberius or the Casket of Pola is to put the Baptistery stuccoes at a disadvantage hardly pertinent to the understanding of their value as works of art.

Unfortunately, not many significant examples of Early Christian stucco work have come down with which the reliefs of the Baptistery could be usefully associated. This is an accident of survival, for stucco as a decorative medium was of wide currency in the Christian world, as it had been with the Romans. In Ravenna its use in the fifth century is attested by Agnellus, who records that the Basilica Ursiana featured "diverse allegorical panels in stucco with human figures and animals";[5] and that in the Arian palatine church of St. Martin, later Sant'Apollinare Nuovo, there were similar reliefs, apparently gilded.[6] A third reference to "gipsea metala" appears in his description of the church of S. Croce built by the Empress Galla Placidia.[7] It can therefore be inferred that the method of stucco ornament and its coexistence with other forms of wall decoration was not a novel experiment at the Baptistery; and that, most likely, a local school of *stuccatori* had been at work here since some time before the refurbishing of the Neonian monument. The uninhibited execution and naiveté of spirit evident in the reliefs of Zone II should reasonably be attributed to local craftsmen working under the supervision of a master artist who inspired the entire decorative scheme.

Studied on their own terms, these reliefs reveal a unity of purpose and expression which is not devoid of power and fascination for the modern viewer. The plaster has

---

4. G. Galassi, "Scultura romana e bizantina," *L'Arte*, *17* (1915), 40.

5. *Codex*, p. 67: "et hinc atque illinc gipseis metalis diversa hominum animaliumque et quadrupedum enigmata inciserunt et valde optime composuerunt."

6. *Codex*, p. 218: "suffixa vero metalla gipsea auro superimfixit." These reliefs came between the

nave arcades and the processions of saints and martyrs in mosaic; they disappeared apparently in the sixteenth century because of the raising of the pavement.

7. *Codex*, p. 119: "Galla vero augusta haedificavit eclesiam sancte Crucis preciosissimis lapidibus structa et gipsea metala sculta."

been worked vigorously in molding the general shape of the prophets, which follows a precise contour on the blank ground of the aedicules, and the details of drapery were then engraved on the surface more often with a delight for pattern than the desire for plastic accuracy. This is most true of the loose ends of the pallia, which are treated with an enticing persistence of stylization as though they were purely ornamental or even vegetal motifs (*Figs.* 85, 93, 94, 96, 97). The prototypes of such folds are to be found in classical reliefs of maenads and victories, where flying drapery is appropriate for the spirited movement of the figures. The practice is not uncommon in Early Christian art; there too windblown folds are a logical requisite of the subject, as for example in scenes of the resurrection, or of the approaching Magi, or of alighting angels, the direct descendants of classical victories.[8] Since the prophets of Zone II are obviously intended to be at rest, the choice of the motif cannot itself be justified on contextual grounds, and the odd treatment of the motif isolates it even further from a functional existence. In Prophet 9, for instance, the flying folds are represented in a manner so divorced from intention that the sculptor feels free to insert in one of them the delightful simulation of a human mask (*Fig.* 94).

The articulation of bodies beneath these energetically designed curtains of drapery has little organic logic. A convex curve, on one side of the figures only, renders schematically the idea of a hip-shot pose. The head, hands, and feet which protrude from within the drapery are modeled in very high relief, accentuating the decorative flatness of the clothed bodies. The feet are grossly webbed, and their crudity cannot be justified by the limitations of the medium alone. The fingers are fashioned from thick lumps of plaster with a disregard for anatomy that makes grotesqueries of the classical gestures of address (Prophet 13, *Fig.* 98) or of acclamation (Prophet 11, *Fig.* 96). Yet through their confidence and consistency these same distortions of the draped figure of antiquity transform the prophets into fantastic presences, something on the order of the sculpted creatures of the Romanesque period, carrying the impact of the terrible or the apotropaeic. This expressionism is concentrated on, and projected by, the heads: they are full but soft and the features have been gouged impetuously. The mouth is an upturned crescent, deeply cut into the plaster; the thick eyebrows are brought out with the negative modeling of sharp lines above and below. Two punctured holes, very probably intended to be filled with inserts for pupils, turn the glance into a transfixed and awesome stare; so might prophets look who are divinely inspired by visions of dreadful apocalypse.

This same concern with expressive evocation by decorative means, at the expense of thematic verity, is also seen in the four religious scenes above aedicules 12 to 15,

---

8. Cf. for example the Christ on the Munich ivory panel of the resurrection (W. F. Volbach, *Elfenbeinarbeiten der Spätantike und des frühen Mittelalters* [Mainz, 1952], no. 110, Pl. 33); the Magi on the Isaac sarcophagus in San Vitale (M. Lawrence, *The Sarcophagi of Ravenna*, College Art Association Monographs, 2 [1945], Fig. 12); and the angels on a silver plate at the Hermitage (W. F. Volbach, *Frühchristliche Kunst* [Munich, 1958], Pl. 245). A characteristic example of the flying fold in Ravenna is in the mosaic figure of St. Lawrence at the "Mausoleum of Galla Placidia" (F. W. Deichmann, *Frühchristliche Bauten und Mosaiken von Ravenna* [Baden-Baden, 1958], Pl. 7).

as was pointed out during the discussion of their iconography (*Figs.* 79–82). Thus in the reliefs of Jonah and Daniel the beasts are by far the more fetching elements, and the composition is so arranged as to give them equal prominence with the Biblical figures (*Figs.* 79, 82). Lions, sea monsters, adders—animals with which the sculptor had no personal acquaintance—are treated with that gusto for the fantastic seen in the bestiaries of the later Middle Ages. The sculptor is more at home with common animals and fowl, and even though here too his prime interest has been in the duplication of a single design to form an antithetical composition, the understanding of the physical structure of the beasts he depicts is not negligible (*Fig.* 78). The skill should not be hard to appreciate in a city where sarcophagi, altar screens, ambones, and capitals were covered with every variety of quadruped and fowl.

These general remarks should not be understood to denote a single authorship for the entire stucco program. Recently, and for the first time, Carla Casalone attempted to define distinct stylistic personalities in an article on the Baptistery already referred to in previous chapters.[9] Loyal to her hypothesis that Zone II is for the most part an addition to the monument by Archbishop Maximian in the sixth century (cf. Chapter 3, n. 30), Miss Casalone devotes some effort to substantiate this date for the general style of the reliefs. She then distinguishes four major style groups within the zone. The master artist, according to Casalone, is the author of Prophet 11 (*Fig.* 96) and is also responsible for the heraldic compositions above the aedicules. His work shows strong affinity with the mosaic style of Zone IV. Closely associated with the master's schemes, but lacking the spirit of his work, is a second group including Prophets 1–6 and 15 (*Figs.* 83–90, 101); the execution is rigid and the modeling indistinct. To an inexpert assistant, characterized by Casalone as displaying "an absolute inability to model," are assigned Prophets 7, 10, and 13 (*Figs.* 91, 92, 95, and 98), excepting the heads which are attributed to the experienced hand of the master. Most of the remaining prophets—nos. 8, 9, 12, 14, 16 (*Figs.* 93, 94, 97, 99, 100, 102)— are from a fourth hand, whose work is judged by Casalone to be most widely divergent from that of the master. It indulges in greater stylization and has little talent for composition and perspective.

Casalone's pioneering exposition is, in the main, acceptable. My individual disagreements, however, are too numerous to be profitably argued. A fresh and detailed analysis of the reliefs and a more complete illustration of them than has been hitherto available allows me to propose a modified grouping, based chiefly on the prophets, since the architectural elements and the animal pairs are, in my opinion, too conventional to reveal formal discretions.

Group A. Six prophets—nos. 1, 8, 9, 12, 14, 16 (*Figs.* 83, 84, 93, 94, 97, 99, 100, 102) —are clearly affiliated and should be assigned to one stylistic class. The heads are characterized by a slight upward tilt, large ears, and relatively short hair which is arranged in parallel strands on the skull and comes down behind the ears. The brows

9. "Ricerche," pp. 246–53.

are contracted into worried frowns. The figures are made to stand with one leg frontally placed, part of the foot protruding from the base frame of the aedicule; the other leg is turned sideways, with the foot parallel to the base frame. Drapery is rendered with deeply incised lines, firm and predominantly straight. The form of the pallium is distinct. With the sole exception of Prophet 16 (*Fig.* 102), its spread across the body is from left to right. The borders are stressed with a ropelike pattern which at the hem separates the pallium from the tunic below in a precise outline, often angular. The flying folds are obsessively carved. They begin at the level of the elbows in narrow strips which widen toward the bottom in generous, sinuous outlines repeating the curvature of the bodies. On each fold there is a large letter Z, of unknown implication; it is incised with no regard to the flow of the drapery. The preference for simple broad curves is once more evident in the rendition of the open book held by Prophets 1 and 9 (*Figs.* 83, 94; compare the books of Prophets 3 and 11, *Figs.* 86, 96) and of the scroll widely spread out by Prophet 12 (*Fig.* 97).

Group B. Prophets 3 and 11 (*Figs.* 86, 96), although rendered with unequal skill, seem to belong together. The execution is agitated, the line hurried and nervous. A taste for modeling, instead of the unplastic incision of Group A, is evident, especially in the area of the shoulders and in the flying folds. The heads are small in relation to the bodies; they are turned sharply to the right, framed on the opposite side by long hair. Of the two, Prophet 11 is noteworthy for its abrupt contrapposto which endows the figure with unresolved excitement or, better, with intemperate energy (*Fig.* 96). One of the religious scenes, the Traditio legis above aedicule 14, affords this same impression, and I believe is related to the group (*Fig.* 81). Note that Christ's head is similar to that of these two prophets.

Group C. Less ably executed but without doubt closely allied to the previous group are Prophets 2, 4, 5, 6, and 15 (*Figs.* 85, 87–90, 101). The bodies are again elongated, and the pallium, characteristically, is brought over the left shoulder and arm in a broad fold which turns into a cluster of lines, more or less horizontally disposed, at the waist. The line is muted and less decisive than in Group B; like it, however, unobtrusive Zs are lightly incised in the billowing edges of the flying folds (cf. the letters of Group A). All the heads could not be by the same hand. Only those of Prophet 15 (*Fig.* 101) and, possibly, Prophet 2 (*Fig.* 85), resemble the type described in the previous group.

Group D. Prophets 10 and 13 (*Figs.* 95, 98) stand quite apart from all the others considered above, by the calm gravity of their carriage and by the confident manner in which they wear their robes. Their bodies are full and the composition well suited to the shape of the framing architecture. The figures are exactly centered within the aedicules with a comfortable margin on the two sides and above the head. The hanging edges of the pallia do not fly nervously but fall down in vertical folds which reflect the grooves of fluting on the bounding pilasters. The heads face full front and are solidly modeled; they wear tight-fitting caps of hair and sober expressions. The almost classic reserve of these two prophets contrasts notably with the agitated emotion of the prophets in Group B. The ease with which they fit within their ample costumes is distinct from the compressed bodies of the prophets of Group A, framed by bracketing outlines. The head of the last remaining prophet—no. 7 (*Figs.* 91, 92)— one of the best in the entire zone, compares favorably with those of the two figures under discussion; but the body, as Casalone rightly observed,[10] is quite unsuccessful, with stocky proportions which give the impression that the prophet is seated. The heads of Prophets 5 and 6 are also related (*Figs.* 89, 90).

The question of the three remaining religious scenes is not easily settled. It is hard to agree with Casalone's attribution of all these to the author of Prophets 3 and 11 (*Figs.* 86, 96), for it appears unlikely that the scene of Christ treading on the adder and lion (*Fig.* 80), except for the head, and the scene of Daniel and the lions (*Fig.* 82) could have been executed by as fluid and energetic a hand as that of the two prophets and of the Traditio legis. The first two scenes belong to a more heavy-handed and insistent style, unlike that of any of the groups discussed above. It is possible that the author of these two scenes is the same as that of the animal pairs and different from all the rest.

Whatever the specific division of workmanship may be, there is no convincing evidence to doubt the contemporaneity of the stucco reliefs with the mosaic decoration. On the contrary, Zone II is such an integral part of the decorative system that it is impossible to imagine the interior without it. The triplets of arches and the brackets over the corner columns are linked with the pendentives of the cupola in a way that precludes the existence of one without the presence of the others (*Fig.* 76). The impost blocks were made broad enough from the start to include the smaller arches at the eight corners. Visually, the insertion of a band of decoration in a different medium than mosaic, with its own individual texture and mat colors, was a happy solution which avoided any monotony of continued and undifferentiated surfaces. The strong light pouring in through the windows of Zone II would also have made the use of mosaic at this level impracticable. In size, the stucco prophets play their part in the successive enlargement of proportions from the very small figures of the mosaic prophets of Zone I to the attenuated form of the apostles. The relation of the stucco prophets to the apostles is also one of intended rapport. If in their frontal position and in their attributes the prophets in the aedicules pertain to the same family as the figures of Zone I, in certain visual peculiarities they establish association with the apostles of Zone IV. The curvilinear contour of one part of the body, noted in some of the stucco prophets, is also employed, but with greater anatomical logic, in Zone IV, for example in the figures of St. James of Zebedee and St. Thomas (*Figs.* 45, 47). The size of the head, small in proportion to an elongated body, is common both to the apostles and to some of the prophets; compare for instance St. Thomas with Prophet 15 (*Figs.* 45, 101). The general bearing, even the specific gestures, of several prophets in fact almost duplicates those in Zone IV, as in the case of Prophet 6

10. Ibid., p. 252.

and St. Simon (*Figs.* 50, 90), or Prophet 13 and St. Philip (*Figs.* 48, 98). There is no doubt that the master mosaicist was by far the more competent and subtler artist, but that these similarities between the two zones are not accidental is also evident. Indeed it might be supposed that the artist in charge of the entire decoration made the sketches for the prophets, leaving their execution to lesser hands. At the turn of the century Sangiorgi reported the existence of graffito drawings in places where bits of stucco had fallen off.[11] These might well be visible remnants of such master sketches. One scholar carried this association to the point of maintaining that the persons responsible for the execution of the reliefs were identical with those responsible for the mosaics, that one is dealing with sculptor–mosaicists who were better at designing than at modeling.[12] In any case, neither in form nor in organization is the character of Zone II sufficiently alien to the rest of the decoration to warrant the contention that it was inserted at a later date. Nor is it necessary to look for the source of the stucco reliefs as far afield as Gaul or the Orient.[13] The forms of this sculpture belong first and foremost in the ensemble of the interior of the Baptistery and secondarily to the workshops of Ravenna. Any resemblance to monuments elsewhere in the Christian world would be the result of assimilation from common formal trends and not the result of specific influences from distinct geographical areas.

Mosaics of Zones I, III–V

It follows from our discussion of the early building stages of the Baptistery that the mosaics, sheathing precisely those areas of the interior that pertain to the Neonian baldacchino, cannot antedate 451, approximately when Neon's episcopate began. This fact makes it unnecessary to review extensively the long and untidy debate, which has lasted to the present, on the stylistic "evidence" to date the cupola scheme to the reign of Theodosius (379–95) or, at the latest, Honorius (395–423).[14] Indeed, had the consequences of Gerola's discovery forty-five years ago of the stucco cornice above the springing line of the cupola been properly heeded, such hypotheses would

11. *Battistero*, p. 50.

12. E. Tea, "Gli stucchi del Battistero e un passo di Agnello," *FR*, *21* (1916), 939–41. Her arguments are unconvincing, and the interpretation of the passage in Agnellus, referring to the stuccoes in the Basilica Ursiana, is doubtful. Cf. Ricci, *Tavole*, *2*, 6 n. 2.

13. A. Soper contends that the art of the Baptistery is linked to the school which he believes to have flourished in Gaul, Spain, and Dalmatia ("The Italo-Gallic School of Early Christian Art," *AB*, *20* [1938], 145–92). The stylistic traits on which these associations are based in this much-cited article have always appeared tenuous to this writer. It is dubious, for example, that the upward direction in which the eggs and darts of the ovolo moldings point in Zone II and in the ornamental band around Zone V can be seriously taken as evidence

for a relationship between the Baptistery reliefs and mosaics with the Pola casket or the "Provençal" school of carving (ibid., p. 158). Equally unwarranted is the conclusion reached by Miss Casalone that the style of the reliefs seems "allora aver subito più diretti influssi orientali, mediati attraverso opere che non ci sono giunte" ("Ricerche," p. 256).

14. See A. W. Byvanck, "De Mozaieken te Ravenna en het Liber pontificalis ecclesiae Ravennatis," *Mededeelingen van het Nederlandsch historisch Instituut te Rome*, *8* (1928), 61–82, esp. 74 ff. (I am indebted to Dr. Marcel Röthlisberger for assistance in reading this article.) A brief summary of the arguments in *Byzantion*, *5* (1929–30), 829. More recently, S. Bettini, "Il Battistero della Cattedrale," *FR*, *52* (1950), 41–59; briefly summarized in *Fasti archeologici*, *5* (1950), no. 5662.

never have been proposed. Agnellus' association, moreover, of the apostles of Zone IV with the name of Neon ("Musiva et auratis tesselis apostolorum immagines et nomina camera circumfinxit") is explicit.[15] No reasonable doubt can be maintained, then, that the mosaics of the cupola originated in the first or second decade of the second half of the fifth century.

Since the chronicler's description does not mention the prophets of Zone I, their contemporaneity may conceivably be questioned. Byvanck, who was responsible for the pre-Neonian attribution of the cupola program, and Bettini, who accepted his hypothesis, both contended that an obvious divergence of style between the lower and upper mosaics must be accounted for by a considerable interval in their execution.[16] The style of the cupola program was judged by them to be the more plastic and naturalistic and was therefore assigned to the late fourth century; and the prophets of Zone I, because of their "flat" "Byzantine" manner and its similarity to the figural style of the mosaics of the "Mausoleum of Galla Placidia," were considered not to have been executed until the time of this empress (425–54) and of Bishop Neon. The argument fails on archaeological and historical grounds. But it is instructive in underscoring the danger inherent in a methodology that assumes a uniform progression of style in Early Christian art, wherein every monument might be expected to display a further stage of development than its predecessors along the road to a medieval mode. Such a biological growth of form ignores the historical truth that the transformation of the Hellenistic–Roman language of artistic expression into the abstracted, nonworldly images of a medieval style has occurred erratically and not at the same rate in all parts of the Christian empire. A systematic account of this unpredictable course is still wanting for late antique and Early Christian painting.[17] Attempts to date by formal means alone the mosaics of the Baptistery of S. Restituta in Naples, of St. George in Thessaloniki, or of S. Maria Maggiore in Rome, are notorious.

At the Orthodox Baptistery, the dissimilarities between the mosaic programs of the cupola and of Zone I, which do in fact exist, are mostly explicable, it seems to me, by the role intended for these parts within the total decorative scheme. The rinceaux of the lower zone have no comparative counterpart in the cupola; in any case, they are for the most part restored.[18] The prophets themselves could be compared, however, with the figures in the cupola. Generally speaking, the conventions of color remain similar. The same juxtaposition of elements in gold on a blue ground is present in both Zone I and Zone IV. Also common to both are the shades of green and yellow as a base level on which the figures stand. That the robes of the prophets and the apostles are of different colors need denote no more than a concern for variety, for in fact the method of rendering drapery follows related conventions. Tesserae of dark shades outline the garments and pick out the principal folds, which are then

15. *Codex*, pp. 77–78; and above, p. 11.
16. See n. 14 above.
17. Cf. remarks very much to the point on this

subject in D. Levi, *Antioch Mosaic Pavements, 1* (Princeton, 1947), "Introduction."
18. Ricci, *Tavole, 2*, Pls. 14–19.

developed by rows of lighter tesserae disposed according to their direction. In the upper as in the lower mosaics, scattered highlights in red and orange animate the faces. Glances are given direction by the juxtaposition of one or more large white tesserae and a dark one that forms the pupil. When, as in the case of St. Bartholomew (*Fig.* 57), these vivid touches on the face seem multiplied and overstressed, it should be recalled that they were probably designed to take into account the distance of the apostles from the viewer, in the same way that the excessive makeup of an actor onstage is designed to make him appear natural to the audience.

The span between Zones I and IV explains, in my opinion, one of their more notable differences: the elongated proportions of the apostles in contrast to the "normal" height of the prophets (*Figs.* 45, 115). Not only does the elongation meet the inevitable foreshortening caused by the vertical distance to the viewer's eye but, moreover, it compensates for the curved surface on which the apostles are set. Optical corrections of this kind were quite familiar to the later Byzantine artists, as has been brilliantly demonstrated by the studies of Otto Demus.[19] I am not suggesting of course that the process of "staggering" the apostles is calculated to make them seem the same height as the prophets of Zone I. On the contrary, the effect of varying sizes is maintained despite the correction of proportions, and this disparity conforms to the idea of hierarchical arrangement in the decoration, which was noted in another context. The prophets of Zone II are taller than those of Zone I, and the apostles are in turn taller than both. Visually, this progressive enlargement enhances the soaring effect of height; iconographically, it underlines the hierarchical importance of the apostles over the prophets.

Once again, the placement of the mosaics of the cupola and those of the lower arcade explains, I believe, the relatively rich palette of the former, with its infinite gradations of color, which contrasts so evidently with the simplified color scheme of Zone I. Bettini, accepting a priori that the trend in Early Christian painting had been toward a progressively impoverished palette to go along with the steady abstraction of form, again attributed this fact of the Baptistery decoration to a chronological disparity between the upper and the lower mosaics.[20] Actually, the difference is one of variety of hues, not of subtlety in coloring. The garment of Prophet 5 (*Fig.* 115), as an example, is made up of as many gradations of white, brown, and black tesserae as there are of white, blue, and gold in the garments of the apostles. But in the number and intensity of its various hues the cupola is not equaled. And this should not be surprising. The program of the cupola in the fifth century was obviously the most important part of the decoration, as it is today. It was the culmination of the varied visual impressions of the lower zones where painted stucco, opus sectile, and mosaic

19. *Byzantine Mosaic Decoration* (Boston, 1955); also idem, "The Methods of the Byzantine Artist," *The Mint*, 2 (1948), 64–77.

20. *Byzantine Mosaic Decoration*, pp. 51–52. The difference in palettes between Zone I and the cupola was noticed earlier by H. Peirce and R. Tyler, *L'Art*

Byzantin, *1* (Paris, 1932), 85, without however deriving a chronology for the two programs. For the discussion of color in this chapter, the reader is referred once more to the excellent plates in G. Bovini, *Ravenna Mosaics* (New York Graphic Society, 1956), Pls. 6–12.

collaborated in rich harmonies of texture and color. The climax of this scheme, the decoration of the cupola, had nothing but mosaics at its disposal. It therefore compensated for the wealth of variation due to the use of diverse media by a splendor of color which can compare to any other monument of Early Christian painting. And whereas in Zone I the mosaics, being only part of the ornament, could not ignore the plain color tonalities of the opus sectile, the mosaics of the cupola were restricted only by the unfailing taste of the artist. Again, as in the hierarchy of sizes and of programmatic elements, so too in color there exists a mounting crescendo from the bottom to the top, and the most resplendent region of the decoration corresponds, appropriately, to the most exalted realm of images, the Dome of Heaven.

This analysis, which corroborates what is simplest to believe when one stands in the Baptistery—that the entire program of mosaic pertains to one campaign—should not also be interpreted to mean that the style is uniform in all parts. As in Zone II, so also in the mosaics: the various artists who worked on the program show their idiosyncrasies of approach despite their overall adherence to a master design.[21] The mosaicist in charge of the Zone I prophets, so far as can be judged from unrestored sections, had a notable concern for the corporeal solidity of the figure below its robes (*Figs.* 113–15). Much smaller though they are than the apostles of Zone IV, the prophets in fact appear more monumental for this reason; that is, they occupy their oval frames more confidently, and they possess a generosity of proportion and a firm, economical compactness which is more forceful visually than the diffuse forms of the apostles, whose lateral spread, owing to the complicated disposition of the draperies, dissipates the impact of their plasticity. Within the tight contour of each prophet, maximal use is made of drapery as a means of projecting the three-dimensional reality of the body. Characteristic passages are the right leg, which is bent at the knee, and a triangular shading on the lower torso that brings out the swell of the stomach. If corresponding passages are compared in the figures of the apostles, one cannot but wonder at Bettini's claim that the mosaics of Zone I are more "flat" and "Byzantine."

A strong sense of classical proprieties which stem from the Hellenistic–Roman tradition is in fact the sustaining quality of all the mosaic painting in the Baptistery. Direct reminiscences of the pagan past, like the architectural system of Zone III or the Jordan of Zone V, emphasize the identity of this fifth-century program as a descendant of the artistic thought of the Mediterranean under the Romans. The nude torso of the river god is modeled powerfully to convey the material existence of the human body (*Fig.* 44). Chiaroscuro, and an impressionist technique more suitable to the movement of the brush, are imitated painstakingly in tesserae—white ones

---

21. Cf. also Diehl, *Ravenne*, pp. 35–36, where the cupola mosaics are described as "d'une autre époque, du moins d'une autre main et d'un art un peu différent"; J. Kurth, *Die Wandmosaiken von Ravenna* (2d ed. Munich, 1912), pp. 65–81, who recognizes two masters, one responsible for Zone I and designated as the "Meister mit den Goldranken," the other responsible for Zones III to V and designated as the "Meister mit dem gelben Grunde"; and Peirce and Tyler (n. 20 above), pp. 84–86, where the mosaics of Zone I are said to be "d'une bien autre qualité, l'oeuvre, à coup sûr, d'une autre atelier."

bringing out the areas that receive light, and gradually modulating toward darker shades of color which define the thickness of the arms or the torsion of the chest. The same interest in the solidity of things is true of the inanimate images of Zone III (*Fig. 65*). The perspective, though not scientifically accurate, is certainly plausible visually. And this not mainly because of a recession that is drawn but because of a feel of depth created through color. The gold of the architecture stands out from the green and blue ground. A special white color picks out the pilasters that flank the small throne niches in the altar panels. The columns supposed to be farthest back are dark. But neither these nor the columns and their entablatures that are closer to the viewer are blocked in with solid color, as is generally the case with the architectural mosaics of St. George at Thessaloniki, where gold is used indiscriminately for entire columns to distinguish them from others in the background (*Fig. 140*). Here instead, in three or four vertical streaks of gold-yellow which graduate into brown, the artist succeeded in conveying the impression of curved surfaces and of the flicker of light on the prominent parts of the shiny marble presumably represented (*Fig. 66*). In the Thessalonikan mosaics, the use of undifferentiated gold also for the ground further destroys the illusion of reality, rendering the architectural images into diaphanous, unreal abstractions; whereas at the Baptistery, the checkered pattern of green behind the altars and the main thrones and the clear blue above the parapets are enough to suggest an indeterminate recession into depth. Both the material reality of things, then, and the illusion of light upon things are represented. Note that the Ravennate painter is enough of a colorist to forego the clear-cut outlines in black which make boundaries so precise in the St. George panels. In Zone III, as often elsewhere in the Baptistery paintings, boundaries are not defined by lines but by the meeting of two areas of different color, or rather by the merging of the two, for the junctures are not uncommonly blurred by intermediate passages.

Both human figures and inanimate objects in the mosaic program, as images of solid reality which possess mass and are affected by light, cast shadows around themselves. The light source, though not consistently so, lies to the left of each image. Thus, every one of the apostles, regardless of the direction in which he walks, casts a shadow to the right—two dark diagonal strips on the green border of Zone IV (*Figs. 45 ff.*). It is the one detail which Arthur Symons, the English poet, remembered best and "with most of separate pleasure": "the lapis lazuli which makes a sky in the dome of the Baptistery, against which the twelve Apostles walk in gold and white robes, with jewelled crowns in their hands, and the green grass, on which a shadow turns and darkens with their feet, as the circle goes around with the sun."[22]

The artist's keen understanding of color interplay is demonstrated in passages where shadows absorb the chief tonality of the surroundings. Reddish shadow tracing on the left side of the baptized Christ yields to dark blue in parts of the anatomy sub-

22. *Cities of Italy* (1907), p. 182.

merged under the bluish-white waves of the water (*Fig. 43*). And on the parapets of Zone III the white screen is spotted with soft pads of light blue shadow reflected from the clear azure sky above (*Fig. 68*).

Having insisted upon the Hellenistic–Roman heritage of the Baptistery mosaics, we must however now circumscribe it. For we do not have here an uninhibited attunement with classical prototypes, which the roughly contemporary nave mosaics of S. Maria Maggiore in Rome seem to have to an extent that inspired a whole book that tried to prove they must belong to the same period as the relief sculpture on the Column of Marcus Aurelius.[23] Nor do the forms of the Baptistery so consciously and methodically reconstruct the forms of the past as to merit being described within the context of a classical revival or renascence in the mid-fifth century, like the earlier one under Theodosius I. More Roman than the mosaic paintings of St. George, which precede it by half a century at least, the Neonian program is less Roman than the nave panels of S. Maria Maggiore, which are closer to it by several decades. I think that the originality of the formal language of the Baptistery is precisely in its being uncommitted between the classical past and a crystallized medievalism, and that this midway position is dictated by the specific purpose of the program which is neither merely narrative nor merely iconic.

Consider first the nonclassical elements which confound a simple classification of the style. Color, for one, is employed naturalistically and decoratively, as in classical antiquity, at the same time that it is used symbolically. The same color in fact which serves in an active, that is descriptive, capacity is elsewhere laden with purely symbolical associations. Gold illustrates the point. In the garments of the apostles and in the architecture of Zone III it is an active color, graduated and applied in conjunction with other hues to obtain the modeling and the illusory effects described above. But in the baptism of Christ and in the oval medallions of the Zone I prophets (*Figs. 43, 113–15*) its pure and uniform application as a ground is imbued with supranatural implications, for it lacks even the possible naturalistic connotation of the sky which the blue ground of Zone IV, common in the mosaic art of the fifth century, carries with it. In this the Baptistery follows St. George (*Fig. 140*) and the apse of S. Aquilino in Milan (*Fig. 141*) in prefiguring the use of undifferentiated gold ground, which becomes the norm for all religious representations from the early sixth century onward. It is clear, then, although the postantique iconography of color is as yet largely uncharted, that the artist of the Baptistery avails himself, dependent on his intention, both of what Haeberlein has called "observational color" (*Beobachtungsfarbe*), to describe reality, and of "presentational color" (*Vorstellungsfarbe*),

---

23. J. P. Richter and A. C. Taylor, *The Golden Age of Classic Christian Art* (London, 1904), passim. See also S. Scaglia, *I Mosaici antichi di basilica di S. Maria Maggiore in Roma* (Rome, 1910); and J. Wilpert, *Die römischen Mosaiken und Malereien* *der kirchlichen Bauten, 1* (Freiburg, 1916), 473 ff. and *3*, Pls. 8–28. These panels are now known for certain to belong to the pontificate of Sixtus III (432–40) or a few years earlier: see R. Krautheimer in *AJA, 46* (1942), 373 ff.

to imply iconographic meanings which are chiefly extramundane and irreal, that is, beyond description.[24]

In the portraiture of the apostles, opposite formal tendencies again coexist, which reflect opposite attitudes toward the painted figure. The vivid individuality of the head of St. Bartholomew was noted in the preceding chapter. Far from being a stereotyped face, it has every indication of being a particular portrait caught momentarily and for the first time (*Fig.* 57). The technique is a virtuoso performance. As in the draperies, white is used for the areas bathed in light, such as portions of the forehead and the right cheek. But these areas are joined to one another by passages of intense oranges, reds, and yellows arranged in a seemingly haphazard and confused pattern which recalls, inevitably, the method of the French Impressionists. The rendition of this powerful head, turned sideways on its strong, muscular neck, is as far from the iconic images of later Byzantine art as is the concept of the living, acting personality of the apostle from the frontally posed, aloof, and ascetic simulacrum of the typical Byzantine saint.

But this impression of naturalistic portraiture is negated by degrees in several of the other apostles of Zone IV. Consider St. Peter (*Fig.* 52). Here the face is still composed of multicolored tesserae in sharp juxtaposition, but their arrangement is now quite different. There is a general calculated order, as it were, superposed on the features themselves, so that the immediacy of the portrait of St. Bartholomew is here replaced by a sober definitiveness which is impermeable. The head is turned slightly sideways but in the same direction as the body, not counterpoised as that of St. Bartholomew. The glance is fixed. Clear lines of tesserae of the same color designate the features and set up a rhythm which is obeyed by the parallel alignment of the other tesserae. In a third face, that of St. Jude (*Fig.* 58), the transformation of the vigorous realism of the portrait of St. Bartholomew into a frontal rigidity and an impassiveness of expression is complete. The face is composed symmetrically on either side of a vertical axis: brow matches brow, the eyes are staring and blank, and an uninterrupted line extends from the top of the hair in two precisely balanced directions which meet at the tip of the pointed beard. This demagnetized and frigid countenance, at once detached and obsessive, reverts to the haunting images from the East, like the mummy portraits of El Fayyum or the frescoes from the Roman border town of Dura Europos. It also projects to a future art, and that not too far away, wherein emperors and saints, prophets and patriarchs will ruthlessly transfix the viewer from their walls, creating by their piercing gaze an active metaphysical space between him and themselves.

I say "future art" as a generalization. Earlier than the Neonian mosaics, both in the East and West, an abstracted and unworldly frontality had sporadically replaced the concrete, material presence of the images. The saints in the church of St. George at Thessaloniki, their arms opened in the *orans* pose, and figures like Sts. Maternus

---

24. F. Haeberlein, "Grundzüge einer nachantiken Farbenikonographie," *Römisches Jahrbuch für* *Kunstgeschichte, 3* (1939), 75–126 and bibliography in notes.

and Ambrose in the chapel of S. Vittore in Ciel d'Oro at S. Ambrogio in Milan, probably concurrent with the mosaics of the Baptistery,[25] are patent examples (*Figs.* 140, 143). Strict chronology has little to do with the insistence in an Early Christian monument upon such an immaterial approach to the human body. It had become popular in Roman art long before the fifth century, as increasing spiritual tensions within the Empire, caused by the disintegration of the concrete and worldly existence of the classical cosmos, encouraged the adoption of that principle of frontality which was always native to the remote provinces.[26] To quote the happy and concise aphorism of Kitzinger, "classical art became 'medieval' before it became Christian."[27] The importance of this fact, so often overlooked, is that the fifth-century artist had a choice between diverse modes of expression. Behind him, generally speaking, were both the Hellenistic–Roman tradition, with its interest in the specificities of the natural world and in the approximation of that world by pictorial means; and the nonclassical "medieval" tendencies toward abstraction, frontality of figures, and rhythmic composition. Although in the overall picture of the fifth century the progress toward the latter is undeniable in the steady formulation of a medieval style, not all monuments of painting manifest similar classicizing and nonclassicizing tendencies and in the same degree. And the particular stress of individual works is indicative of definite concepts of the function of the painted image within the decorative scheme.

Reviewed from this aspect, the human figure as represented in the Baptistery betrays again the visual–conceptual tensions that have been sketched above in relation to the use of color and the degree of naturalism in the portraiture of the apostles. The tangible body is never completely denied, but it is at times interpreted in a manner that verges on distortion for decorative reasons or for reasons of schematization. In many of the apostles a sinuous line beginning at the neck and ending at the foot is used to depict the side of the body closest to the viewer. This line consists of three convex parts, one for the back, one for the thigh, and a third for the leg which is about to take a step. In the images of Sts. Paul and Peter such a contour is consonant with the stance of the figures (*Fig.* 45). With St. James of Zebedee, however, the curvilinear pattern becomes a governing principle of the design independent of the stance, and is repeated on both sides of the body and also on the flying folds of the pallium (*Fig.* 47). Or again in St. Simon, the pallium is shown as transparent, for one sees through it the two long sinuous *clavi* of the tunic, which echo in parallel waves the contour of the right side of the body (*Fig.* 50). These effects, as well as the abundance of drapery which flanks each apostle in the form of flying folds at the back and folds created by the extended hands holding the crown, tend to confuse the basic

25. For the mosaics of S. Vittore in Ciel d'Oro, see F. Reggiori, *La Basilica ambrosiana: Ricerche e restauri 1929–40* (Milan, 1941), esp. pp. 216 ff.

26. The best summary of the influence of the "sub-antique" style of the provinces on metropolitan art is still E. Kitzinger, *Early Medieval Art in the British Museum* (2d ed. London, 1955), pp. 1–35.

27. Ibid. p. 16.

structure of the bodies. This ambiguity in the corporeal image is contrary to the naturalism of Hellenistic–Roman art and akin to the dematerialized reality of medieval style.

The relationships between the portraits of the apostles and their bodies are themselves ambivalent and even discordant. For one thing, the heads are quite small in proportion to the bodies; ratios of heights range from 1:8 (St. Andrew, *Fig.* 46) to 1:9 (St. Simon, *Fig.* 50), and even 1:10 (St. James of Zebedee, *Fig.* 47) if the curvature of the body is taken into account. As a result of this, the heads do not belong organically to the trunks, but appear to have been attached loosely as separate entities. This incongruity is accentuated by the fact that even though most of the apostles are shown in the act of walking, with the legs and the bodies in at least partial profile, the heads do not obey the dictates of the action but are presented almost *en face*. Not a single head in the whole decoration of the Baptistery[28] is depicted in profile except that of the river god in Zone V (*Fig.* 44). Whereas in the prophets of Zone I and II a frontal face almost always matches a frontally disposed body at rest, in the case of the apostles the torsion of the heads toward the viewer recalls the moment in military processions when troops sharply turn their faces toward the inspecting officer without interrupting their onward march. This point can be demonstrated by comparing the Apostle James to a gladiator in mosaic from the Baths of Caracalla (*Figs.* 47, 142). The gladiator's motion is contained within the space of the mosaic panel, his glance stressing the momentum and direction of his legs. In the figure of St. James there is a spatial tension created by the body moving parallel to the picture space and by the head which projects into the real space of the viewer. The viewer is therefore unavoidably drawn into the world of the decoration, invited as it were to participate in the procession of the apostles. The logic of the composition is consequently unresolved. In the case of the Roman gladiator, the relation of the pictorial image to the viewer is purely an objective one. In the case of the portrait of St. Maternus in S. Vittore in Ciel d'Oro (*Fig.* 143), this relation is purely subjective, that is to say there exists an explicit rapport between the image and the viewer confronting each other across space. With the apostles of Zone IV the affiliation of the pictorial image is dual. The image is bound on the one hand by the logic of the iconography, bearing a crown to the vague destination that resides in Zones III and V; on the other hand, it assumes an extradecorative function by accosting the viewer, who is an external element to the world of the iconography. The viewer is kept out of the pictorial space of the mosaic panel of the gladiator since his presence is ignored by the pictorial image. He is also shut from the space occupied by St. Maternus on the wall of S. Vittore in Ciel d'Oro, but for a different reason: the strictly frontal and austere saint bars the entrance, so to say, forcing us to keep our place. In this sense Zone IV is much less restrictive. The viewer is allowed to feel that he is a part of the pictorial scene, that what is depicted in two dimensions on the wall has a direct bearing on his own actions

---

28. I purposely disregard St. John the Baptist in Zone V, since there is no way of ascertaining if the present restored image is faithful to the original. See above, pp. 86 ff.

and thoughts. The pictorial image is now neither realistically independent in the Hellenistic–Roman sense nor iconic in the Byzantine sense; instead it is empathetic and invitational.

This leads us to the *function* of the decorative scheme as a whole. Compare three more or less contemporary fifth-century programs: the nave panels of S. Maria Maggiore in Rome, the apse mosaic of S. Aquilino in Milan (*Fig.* 141), and the program of the Baptistery of Ravenna. Not only are their forms disparate but also, and relatedly, their intent. In the Sistine mosaics in Rome the interest lies in the lively narration of the stories of Abraham, Jacob, Moses, and Joshua. This Biblical saga unfolds in a richly detailed, multicolored, impressionistic manner which has been likened to the mosaic counterpart of an illustrated scroll or of the Roman program of historical reliefs like the helical friezes of historiated columns.[29] Hundreds of figures, protagonists with repeated appearances, and landscape backgrounds all contribute to a vivid panoramic narration with a pulsating rhythm which is diametrically opposed to the world of the S. Aquilino apse mosaic.[30] There the tempo has slackened, time stands still, and the twelve apostles seat themselves on either side of a young enthroned Christ in a frozen presentational attitude which might be compared to that of a formal group portrait. When Zone IV in the Baptistery is taken into consideration, the intent and consequently the exposition of the program alters once more (*Fig.* 42A). Like the mosaic cycle of S. Maria Maggiore, Zone IV is divided into compartments associated by a thread of meaning. Unlike the Roman example, however, the compartments here are not tied by the continuity of topographical and chronological sequences but are linked by an indefinite place and an indefinite time. The existence of the apostles in their compartments is unspecified and therefore outside the dictates of a recognizable ambience; that is to say, this existence is permanent, in contrast to the momentary and fugitive existence of the figures in the panels of S. Maria Maggiore. The same sense of permanence implied in Zone IV is also present in the apse of S. Aquilino (*Fig.* 141), and here the distinction between the two programs becomes less obvious. In the Milanese *collegium,* however, the lack of a finite, changing space and time transfixes the figures themselves into a permanent state of immobility. The apostles of Zone IV, on the other hand, retain the power of specific action in a nonspecific place and time. They are seen in motion, walking, which is itself a transient state, but neither is the destination of this motion defined nor do the ambience and the time carry the promise of change. In contrast to the momentary existence of the actors of S. Maria Maggiore and the eternal permanence of the figures in the apse of S. Aquilino, the apostles of Zone IV may therefore be said to be in a state of eternal action, or in a state of active permanence.

It might be profitable at this point to draw some tentative conclusions from the

29. See e.g. C. R. Morey, *Early Christian Art* (2d ed. Princeton, 1953), p. 151; F. W. Deichmann, *Frühchristliche Kirchen in Rom* (Basel, 1948), p. 66.

30. For which see A. Calderini, G. Chierici, C. Cecchelli, *La Basilica di S. Lorenzo Maggiore in Milano* (Milan, 1951), pp. 202–17 and Pls. 89, 90; also Wilpert (n. 23 above), *3*, Pls. 40, 41.

foregoing discussion. What emerges from an analysis of the mosaics of the Ravennate
Baptistery has, I believe, some relevance for the methodology of Early Christian
studies in general. The main point is that formal considerations of naturalism, abstraction, frontality, and the like have no absolute value in the construction of a
historical scheme universally applicable to Christian monuments of the formative
centuries. Each work of painting is conditioned on a broad level by its identification
with a provincial or metropolitan milieu. But, much more significantly, the degree
to which it eschews or emulates conventions of the classical language of form depends
upon the special intent of the program, which governs the specific structure of form.
Moreover, to treat a mosaic or fresco panel as a totality is to assume that it was
planned as such. But actually, in the great majority of monumental Christian painting, whether it has survived intact or only fragmentarily, one has to contend with
programs, less or more involved, which are comprised of dependent units. The formal
structure of each unit is conditioned as much by circumstances internal to the program as by contemporary fashion or the prevalent *Zeitgeist*. What matters for the
unit is the following: its *physical location* within the whole design; the *contextual
role* assigned to it in the iconography of the program; and the *function of imagery* it is
to perform in relation to the purpose of its architectural ambience. When comparing
paintings from different programs, or one unit with others in the same program, it
is imperative therefore that the historian recall this circumscriptive information and
that he qualify his inferences by it. The fact that the saints in the cupola drum of
St. George in Thessaloniki are less or more frontal than the apostles of the Ravennate
Baptistery has no *absolute* historical significance. It cannot of itself be accountable
by, or informative of, date; nor of itself can it be interpreted within a scheme of
regional dichotomies, of East versus West. And by the same token, the more pronounced naturalism of one zone in the Baptistery in comparison with another signifies no lapse of time between their respective execution and, possibly, may not even
suggest different artists.

Reconsidered in this context, the apparent inconsistencies of style in the Neonian
program—that is, the collateral presence of discrete modes of form sometimes even
within the same zone—take on new meaning. It is not a question of historical inevita-
bility. They were utilized, by conscious choice, for their expressive possibilities in a
specific and individual content. The prophets of Zone I, as we have seen, are the most
notably "real" among all the standing figures of the program. Their stance and costume recall familiar antique archetypes, and firm, plastic modeling endows them with
the authority of the third dimension (*Fig.* 115). Their movement is curtailed in
depth, however, by the impenetrable gold background, which projects them forward
toward the interior space. It is clear that the "presentational" use of gold here does
two things. It helps identify these figures with a divine order by isolating them within
aureoles of sanctity, and it specifies their function in the Baptistery by allowing their
bodies illusion of movement in one direction only, away from the walls and toward
the font. But what distinguishes them from the comparably placed saints in the in-

terior of S. Vittore in Ciel d'Oro in Milan (*Fig.* 143), say, is the flexibility of their form and its independence from the viewer, which is to say their classicism. The pose is relaxed, their corporeal presence credible under the drapery, and their glance free to communicate with neighboring prophets as well as with celebrants below.

As they move farther from the celebrant, the images grow taller and replace this comfortable ease with an agitation and expressive overstatement more pronouncedly theatrical in nature. Thus the prophets of Zone II, who belong thematically with the lower figures in mosaic, are contained in frames which, by imitating actual architecture, overstep the bounds of pictorial illusion with a "realism" that, for all its emphasis, appears more artificial, more constructed or contrived, than the oval medallions in gold. And, parallel to this magnification of effect in the frames, the stucco prophets contained by them agitate without the justification of being in motion (*Fig.* 96). The folds of their costumes fly when they themselves are intended to be at rest. The gaze becomes insistent. Having lost the confident plasticity of Zone I, the drapery, flatter now and understood less organically, deprives the bodies of some of their material validity.

Movement, free from enclosing frames, which is promised by the restless energy of the stucco prophets, is unleashed in earnest after the architectural interlude of Zone III. As on several other counts examined in preceding pages, on this too the cupola diverges from the zones below in that it permits the images of the apostles a lateral motion upon the curved surface of the vault which, visually, disengages the decoration from the frontality it had maintained in its figural art up to this point. The eye, as it follows the progress of the apostles' march, sets the whole dome revolving (*Fig.* 40). The row of figures, being part of a thematic unity, does not confine itself now to simple communication with the viewer. Taller, more intricate in design but less articulate in structure than the prophets over whom they stand, the Twelve establish a psychological distance from the viewer by their elusive march, to complement the physical distance of their position in the general scheme. Yet they do not become equivalent ciphers in an inexorable rhythmic pattern. Some turn toward the interior space of the Baptistery more than do others, and one, St. Philip, faces out completely (*Fig.* 48). The beat of the march halts for a moment, then recovers. The heads too in the uneven naturalism of their portraiture, now serve the content of the cupola program, now stare out like icons to institute direct contact with the celebrant below. Vivid likenesses like St. Bartholomew's have a physical immediacy to the eye, but they evade it by turning their gaze elsewhere within the program (*Fig.* 57). And masklike hieratic faces like St. Jude's or St. Andrew's (*Figs.* 53, 58), distant in a physical sense, yet captivate the viewer by the magnetic stare which they direct upon him.

With the medallion of the cupola, for the only time in the decorative scheme if we discount the four heraldically disposed reliefs above aedicules 12 to 15 of Zone II, the interest shifts to a narrative episode, one that occurred at a definite moment in the past and in a known place (*Fig.* 43). But the artist's effort, because of the role this baptismal scene was intended to play in relation to the interior of the Neonian monument, has been to make permanent the transiency of the event. To this end, frontality, although at odds with narrative exigency, has been chosen purposely for the figure of Christ. To this end also, the rocks and water which briefly sketch the environment of the baptism are denied complementary atmosphere by the gold sheathing of the remainder of the background. On the throne of Maximian, a whole century later, the same event is described objectively through the appropriate relationships of the main characters to one another (*Fig.* 135). A fleeing Jordan, the two attendant angels, and St. John extending his hand to the childlike Christ who moves to confront him, are connected by the dramatic unities of place, time, and action. Not so at the Baptistery. The river god and the Baptist, involved in the logic of the narrative, do turn toward the Savior. But he, ignoring a dramatically justified move toward the saint who is baptizing him, looks down instead upon us. Without the font below, this dual orientation of the actors would be questionable. With it, it is faultless, final, and deeply eloquent.

VISUAL AND COMPOSITIONAL PRINCIPLES

The System of the Cupola

It follows from the intimate correlation of the images, with each other and with the central space of the interior, that Neon's baldacchino was undertaken less as a structural improvement of the first Baptistery of the Basilica Ursiana than as an armature on which a coherent system of decoration could be disposed to satisfy both liturgical and artistic demands. To ponder whether the architectural construct or the decorative was the prime mover, would be academic. In the case of the dome, the architectural idea was dictated, assuredly, by symbolic needs. From the start the dome was purposed as a receptacle for imagery. It may have been the inadequacy of the perimetric wall to support the dome that prompted the architect to raise the tiered arcades but, if so, they were so adroitly integrated with the more purely decorative features, as we shall note presently, that in the end they seemed inevitable.

Most of the credit for wedding the Neonian implantation to the initial octagon must go to the artist who conceived the decorative program. His task was threefold. For the unbroken hemispherical surface of the dome a web of divisions had to be created which would be consonant with the intended iconography. Below, in the area of the perimetric wall on which the structural framework of the arcades had already been superimposed, the decorative order was to be accommodated to the intricate pattern of blank surfaces effected by this framework. Finally, these two general areas of decoration, the dome and the walls, were to be united in such a manner that the passage from one to the other would be smooth and effortless and that interrelations of meaning would be assisted by visual links. These demands were so ably and harmoniously satisfied by the artist that the interior system of the Orthodox Baptistery ranks as one of the subtlest and most successful monumental compositions in Early

Christian art. Its success is shown by the fact that at no time is the viewer given reason to isolate visually any part of the decorative system or to observe breaks in the integrated armature of this system. Its subtlety becomes clear after one attempts to determine the factors by which such a purposeful integrity was achieved.

To begin with the dome, its decorative organization, considered as a flat design, consists of three concentric circles, forming a central tondo and two encompassing bands of unequal width (*Fig.* 42A). The innermost band (Zone IV) is divided radially into twelve compartments, and the outer band (Zone III) into eight, with exact correspondence to the segmentation of the inner band in only four places. In other words, every other divider of the outermost band is continued upward by every third divider of the inner band. In an attempt to trace the precedent of this organization, C.-O. Nordström suggested the compositional system of the base of the column of Arcadius in Constantinople as it survives in a sixteenth-century drawing.[31] Here the surface of the base is divided into four superposed tiers, of which the lowest shows weapons and spoils of war, the next a file of senators, the third the emperors Arcadius and Honorius flanked by soldiers, and the fourth winged victories. A second proposal, still within the vocabulary of imperial art, was advanced by Cyril Mango, who saw in the mosaic program of the Chalkê, the vestibule of the Great Palace of Constantinople, as described by Procopius, a late parallel of the type of imperial compositions from which the Baptistery might have derived its own cupola system.[32]

Compositional resemblances between the base of Arcadius' Column and the Baptistery cupola are weak. The former presents flat surfaces which can be treated as decorative panels independent of an architectural space. A disposition of decoration in horizontally parallel tiers has been common enough in ancient art at least since Egyptian times. In this respect Mango's suggestion is more plausible, since it proposes to compare two similar systems, that is to say, interior surfaces of cupolas. However, reconstruction of the Chalkê program from Procopius' description is by no means a simple task. There have already been several varying views on the subject, and Mango himself offers two possible reconstructions.[33] In the face of these uncertainties, it is wiser to derive the cupola system of the Baptistery from parallel monuments actually surviving. There is no lack of such analogical material. Closest in context and chronology are examples of vault decoration from the Christian catacombs, in Rome and elsewhere, and several vault systems in mosaic which have come down to our day, like those of the Baptistery of S. Restituta in Naples (*Fig.* 139) and of S. Prisco at Capua

31. *Ravennastudien: Ideengeschichte und ikonographische Untersuchungen über die Mosaiken von Ravenna* (Uppsala, 1953), pp. 42–43. For the column of Arcadius, see E. H. Freshfield, "Notes on a Vellum Album Containing Some Original Sketches of Public Buildings and Monuments Drawn by a German Artist Who Visited Constantinople in 1574," *Archaeologia*, 72 (1922), 87 ff.; and G. Q. Giglioli, *La Colonna di Arcadio* (Naples, 1952).

32. *The Brazen House: A Study of the Vestibule of the Imperial Palace of Constantinople*, Arkaeologisk-kunsthistoriske Meddedelser, *IV*.4 (Copenhagen, 1959), 32–34. Procopius' account of the Chalkê mosaic is in *De aedificiis* I.x.12–15.

33. Mango (n. 32), pp. 32–33; also A. Grabar, *L'Empereur dans l'art byzantin* (Paris, 1936), p. 81.

Vetere. Equally useful, if more distant, is the evidence provided by surviving specimens of Roman radial schemes, usually associated with pictorial calendars.

Concentric celestial maps were known to the Hellenistic world and were used for radial calendars which included the Sun God in the center, the zodiac, and the personifications of the months and the four seasons.[34] Although no specimens of these Hellenistic calendars survive, there are at least six representations of radial calendric systems in Roman art that reflect the general disposition of the Hellenistic prototypes.[35] In two of these, mosaic calendars from Bevsan and Antioch, the radial arrangements are strikingly similar to the cupola of the Ravennate Baptistery.[36] In the mosaic from Bevsan, a central medallion in which are depicted the images of Sol and Luna is encompassed by a circular band that is divided into twelve segments with full-length figures of the twelve months, designated by their proper names (*Fig.* 138). The dividers of these radial schemes are simply straight lines, but another mosaic calendar from the fourth century, found in Carthage and now in the British Museum, illustrates the use of more organic dividers in the form of garlands stemming from vases and surrounded by acanthus scrolls.[37] Decorative filaments composed of vases, plants, and candelabra were quite common in Roman art, so it is unnecessary to derive, as did Strzygowski, the dividers of Zone IV in the Baptistery from the stylized trees employed in the compositions of the East, especially of Persia.[38]

The astrological–astronomical conception of the cosmos was one of the most vital ideas that the pagan antique world passed on to the monotheistic religions of the Mediterranean. It had a deep effect on Judaic thought and on the celestial imagery of Christianity. The number twelve, which was employed in relation to the tribes of Judah (and later in relation to the apostles who stood for these tribes), corresponded to cosmological referents such as the twelve signs of the zodiac, the twelve hours of the day and of the night, and the twelve months of the year.[39] Ezekiel's vision and the Revelation of St. John the Divine are Christian counterparts of the celestial imagery of the antique world which, by extension, goes back to Babylonian times. Not only are these associations fruitful in establishing a late antique and Early Christian vocab-

34. See G. M. A. Hanfmann, *The Season Sarcophagus in Dumbarton Oaks,* Dumbarton Oaks Studies, 2 (1951), p. 99 n. 52, and pp. 264–65.

35. See D. Levi, "The Allegories of the Months in Classical Art," *AB, 23* (1941), 251–91, esp. the drawing on p. 281; also J. C. Webster, *The Labors of the Months* (Princeton, 1938). The continuation of antique cosmic schemes in later medieval thought and art is studied by H. Bober, "The Zodiacal Miniature of the *Très Riches Heures* of the Duke of Berry—Its Sources and Meaning," *Journal of the Warburg and Courtauld Institutes, 11* (1948), 1–34: see also idem, "An Illustrated Medieval Schoolbook of Bede's 'De Natura Rerum,'" *Journal of the Walters Art Gallery, 19–20* (1956–57), 65–97.

36. For the Antioch calendar, see D. Levi, *Antioch Mosaic Pavements, 1,* 36–38, where it is dated

in the Hadrianic period and called "perhaps the earliest calendar of the Roman age"; also *Antioch-on-the-Orontes, 2* (Princeton, 1938), 190 ff. For the mosaic at Bevsan, see G. M. Fitzgerald, *A Sixth-Century Monastery at Beth-Shan* (Philadelphia, 1939); also J. W. Crowfoot, *Early Churches in Palestine* (Oxford, 1941), pp. 134–39 and Pls. 19–21.

37. See R. P. Hinks, *Catalogue of the Greek, Etruscan and Roman Paintings and Mosaics in the British Museum* (London, 1933), pp. 89 ff.

38. J. Strzygowski, *Altai-Iran und Völkerwanderung* (Leipzig, 1917), p. 169.

39. See especially D. Feuchtwang, "Der Tierkreis in der Tradition und im Synagogenritus," *Monatschrift für Geschichte und Wissenschaft des Judentums, 59* (1915), 241 ff.; also *Encyclopedia Judaica, 9* (Berlin, 1932), 779.

ulary of radial schemes but moreover they assist in the understanding of the persistent identification of the cupola and its decoration as a simulacrum of the Dome of Heaven. As the skies were peopled with celestial beings who controlled the destiny of the inhabitants of the earth, so the cupola was that part of a building where the images of divinities and their rotational relationships could be fixed.[40]

Radial schemes of decoration in Roman art were not confined of course to representations of the calendar; other subjects, like the Seven Sages, were equally suitable.[41] The painters of vaults in the Christian catacombs, who continued in the Roman decorative tradition, very often availed themselves of compositional systems in which a central medallion contains an important religious figure like the Good Shepherd, or a group of figures such as the *collegium* of the apostles around Christ. Attached to it by some pattern of linear armature there is frequently a circle of panels, either in the form of semicircular lunettes or of radial segments similar to those of Zone IV, containing further religious scenes.[42] In every case, however, the geometric scheme of the vault does not correspond to any coherent contextual order; that is to say, it is possible for the viewer to consider the geometric scheme as a design independent of any contextual correlation of the subjects contained in its various compartments. The scenes depicted in the compartments, although tied to be sure by a general thread of religious appropriateness, do not constitute a unified program with a precise organic logic. Each one is self-contained and does not exist in a specific correlation with the others and with the central medallion. In a painted vault of the catacomb of Domitilla (*Fig.* 137), for example, ten unequal wedge-shaped compartments alternate between plant-candelabra and scenes such as Noah's ark, Moses striking water from the rock, the multiplication of loaves, and the sacrifice of Isaac; they depend from a central tondo with a scene which is not clearly identifiable. The mosaic program on the vault of the Naples baptistery (*Fig.* 139) falls essentially within this category of decorative system, since narrative scenes are posed between the central tondo, with the monogram of Christ on a star-studded background of blue, and the crown-bearing saints on the wall space between the squinches with the

---

40. The classic study of the subject is K. Lehmann, "The Dome of Heaven," *AB*, 27 (1945), 1–27; it is completed by A. C. Soper's study of Eastern examples, "The 'Dome of Heaven' in Asia," *AB*, 29 (1947), 225–48. See also E. Baldwin Smith, *The Dome, A Study in the History of Ideas* (Princeton, 1950), pp. 61 ff.; and H. P. L'Orange, *Studies on the Iconography of Cosmic Kingship in the Ancient World* (Oslo, 1953), passim.

41. See e.g. a mosaic pavement in Cologne showing Diogenes in the center and the busts of the six other sages disposed radially around him (E. Krüger, "Römische Mosaiken in Deutschland," *AA, 48* [1933], Fig. 16); and a new mosaic from a villa in Baalbek, inadequately published, showing Calliope in the central medallion surrounded by the Seven Sages and by Socrates (briefly described by M. Ché-

hab, "Mosaïques de Beyrouth et de Baalbeck," *Actes du 6ᵉ congrés internationale d'études byzantines, 2* [Paris, 1951], 89 ff.). A good Hellenistic prototype of vault schemes in concentric bands exists in a tomb at Kazanlak in Bulgaria: see V. Micoff, *Le Tombeau antique prés de Kazanlak* (Sofia, 1954); and A. Vassiliev, *Grabmal bei Kazanlak* (Sofia, 1959), with excellent plates.

42. See J. Wilpert, *Roma sotterranea. Le pitture delle catacombe romane* (Rome, 1903), Pls. 9, 55, 75, 96, 217; and H. Achelis, *Die Katakomben von Neapel* (Leipzig, 1935–36), Pl. 2. A fragmentary wall painting in S. Giovanni e Paolo in Rome, dated by Wilpert to ca. 385, shows a radial scheme with figures and animal pairs in the compartments (*Römische Mosaiken und Malereien, 4*, Pl. 128).

symbols of the four Evangelists. One can imagine, in such decorative systems, that the artist *first* conceived a pleasing geometric design for the compartmentation of the vault, and *then* fitted certain suitable subjects into the panels that had thus been created.

Now in the case of the Baptistery cupola, as previously in the Roman radial calendars, the process differs in that the radial scheme is not an independent entity but, rather, a function of content (*Fig. 42A*). Each compartment of Zone IV containing the image of an apostle is exactly commensurate with all the others and stands in the same relationship to the central medallion of the baptism as any other compartment. Consequently, it can be stated that the geometric skeleton of the decoration was conceived by the artist as a direct result of the context; in other words, a causal relationship exists between the form and the content of the decoration. The unity of the cupola is simultaneously evident in the geometry of the scheme and in the meaning of the content.

This basic difference between the decorative programs of the catacomb vaults or the Naples baptistery and the cupola of the Baptistery of Ravenna leads to a further distinction which concerns the relationship of the decorative programs with the actual fabric of the architecture. In the case of the catacombs and, to a lesser extent, of the Naples baptistery, the painted decoration takes into account only the flat surfaces of the architecture. Each scene in its special, delimited compartment acts as a framed picture which adheres to the architectural skeleton, and its axis corresponds to the surface of this skeleton. The entire vault decoration is the sum total of several such picture panels, so that in effect the curvature of the vault has not much bearing on the activation of the painted images. The artist does not avail himself of the spatial possibilities of the vault, but uses its surfaces as he would those of flat walls.

In contrast to this simple *two-dimensional* surface decoration, the arrangement of Zones IV and V in the Baptistery can be said to form a *tridimensional* spherical composition where the images on the surfaces revolve around a common vertical axis that corresponds to the actual space enclosed by the architectural form of the cupola. The artist of the Baptistery uses the cupola both as a curved surface and as a container of space. The two-dimensionality of the surface is recognized by the correspondence of the axis of the baptism scene with the axis of Zone IV, where Sts. Peter and Paul confront each other under the feet of Christ (*Fig. 40*). The possibilities of the cupola as a spatial container, on the other hand, are also recognized in the way in which the images depicted on the surface are allowed to communicate with one another through the actual space enclosed by the cupola. The plant-candelabra of Zone IV are therefore only linear conjunctives that unite the surface of the circle of Zone IV with the surface of the central medallion. The contextual conjunctive of the apostles and the figures of the medallion is the physical space itself. Whereas in the catacomb vaults and in the mosaic program of the Naples baptistery a group of independent decorated planes is united by a geometric skeleton of painted motifs, in the cupola system of the Baptistery the geometric division into compartments is negated by the spatial unity of the content. To resume, the contrast is between surface decoration and spatial decoration. In the one, the painted decoration remains true to the surfaces afforded by the architecture, whether they are flat or curved; in the other, not only the solid framework of the architecture but also the space enclosed by it is activated and enlivened by the pictorial decoration.

Again, as in the hierarchic ranking of its zones, so too in the conception of architectural space as the metaphysical ambience of the painted images, the Orthodox Baptistery establishes affiliation with monuments of the Byzantine world several centuries later.[43] To be sure, its case is not an isolated one in Early Christian times. To an extent, the "Mausoleum of Galla Placidia" nearby sets up in the upper reaches of its mosaic decoration a hierarchy of symbolic and figural images starting with the cross at the crown of the vault in a circular field of stars and progressing downward through the tetramorph to the eight apostles who direct their glances to the heavenly vision and their gestures at one another (Fig. 146).[44] Even closer perhaps was the original mosaic decoration of the cupola of St. George at Thessaloniki. Remains of mosaic, first discovered by E. Dyggve in 1939 and subsequently cleaned by Hjalmar Torp, show that in a central medallion was Christ holding a cross; over his head four flying angels supported a crown; below this was a zone of apostles and prophets (?); and finally, the architectural frieze that can be seen today.[45] These, and other monuments which may have disappeared, form a small minority in the Christian world of the fifth century, but a significant one for the future of medieval art in the Eastern Roman Empire.[46] Properly studied, they will shed light on the formal changes which separate late antique mentality rooted firmly in the Hellenistic–Roman tradition of preceding centuries and the medieval mentality that produced the unique pictorial images of the cosmos in Middle Byzantine decoration.

The System of the Lower Zones

Because he was obliged to conform to the architectural ordering of the walls, the artist's freedom was somewhat restricted in the decorative organization of the two lower zones (Fig. 39). In the case of the cupola, the mosaic carpet simply sheathed the structure from view. Farther down the role of the decoration could not be one of encasement only. Here the artist had to collaborate more intimately with the architect, and therefore the system of Zones I and II reveals more tellingly the relation of structural and ornamental elements in the ensemble of the interior than do the upper zones. But a strict division of labor between architect and decorator cannot

---

43. For these aspects of Byzantine art, see Demus, *Byzantine Mosaic Decoration*, pp. 14–29.

44. Deichmann, *Frühchristliche Bauten und Mosaiken von Ravenna*, Pls. 2–4, 19–27.

45. The cupola mosaics are published in a preliminary report by H. Torp, *Mosaikkene i St. Georgrotunden* (Oslo, 1963); an earlier description can be found in E. Dyggve, "Fouilles et recherches faites en 1939 et en 1952–53 à Thessaloniki. Recherches sur le palais imperiale de Thessalonique: Architecture et mosaïques," *Corsi* (1957), fasc. 2, 83–86. See also above, Chap. 4, n. 89.

46. Cf. also the original decorative program of the Sancta Sanctorum Chapel at the Lateran (Wilpert, *Römische Mosaiken und Malereien, 1,* 176). The cupola mosaics of the Arian Baptistery are not very useful in this context since they imitate Zones IV and V of the Orthodox Baptistery.

be defined since it is not easy to determine precisely where architecture stops and decoration commences. Speaking in visual terms, architecture as structural framework may be said to be nonexistent for the reason that the tiered arcades, which in reality sustain the tubular cupola, fail to preserve their structural raison d'être when all they appear to be carrying is an aerial envelope of color and light. Moreover, those elements that can be rationally isolated as structural—the eight main arches and eight corner columns of each of the two zones—are repeated also, with decorative intent only, in the bays of Zone II, thus obviating a clear statement of architectural logic. In other words, whereas the main arcade of Zone II is continued structurally to the ground by means of its eight corner columns and the corresponding columns of Zone I, the triplets of arches embraced by the main arcade are not themselves grounded but remain suspended in mid-air (since the columns flanking the windows rest simply on the cornice which separates Zones I and II). Or again, from a formal point of view, what conjoins the corner columns of Zone II with those of the ground story are passages of mosaic, themselves unsubstantial, with figural representations of the prophets. Two other considerations further blur the distinction of load-bearing and ornamental members: the painting of all the columns at the level of Zone II (see p. 75) —and perhaps of the lower ones also—and the simulated architecture in two dimensions, whether it is the aedicules in relief that house the stucco prophets, or the mosaic panels of Zone III where the play of flat and curved surfaces echoes the alternation of flat walls and niches in the architecture of the ground story.

The equivocalness of the architectural statement in the interior is proven again by the relation of separate planes. Through an ingenious manipulation of fragmented surfaces, the correspondence of the two nearly parallel planes of the exterior shell and of Neon's baldacchino has been thoroughly disintegrated. This is most clearly illustrated in the bays of Zone II (*Fig.* 71). Beginning at the level of the segmental pendentives, the eye slips to the plane of the lunettes, and once more into a different plane defined by the tympana of the triple arches. But even the continuity of this latter plane is not explicit. For one thing, the tympanum of the central arch of each triplet is bare, in contrast to the carved surfaces of the flanking arches; and second, the window piercing the central compartment destroys the illusion of an extended plane directly behind the Ionic columns. The window, in addition, negates any perspective into depth that might be otherwise created by the successive layers of inscribed arches. The main embracing arch, the central arch of the triplet, and the window arch itself, instead of marking a steady progression into depth, are constantly projected forward by the transparent surface of the window as well as by the pulvins of the columns and the general ambiguity of overlapping forms. What saves this profusion of planes from becoming chaotic is the forceful delineation of the multiple elements in each bay. At an imaginary line that runs through the pulvins, the several planes are fastened together in tightly packed ganglia prominently defined by the Ionic capitals, the trapezoidal blocks upon them, and the arch imposts (*Fig.* 76). The eight brackets at the corners bring forward the fragmented surface of each bay and make the transition to the relatively smooth surface of the cupola.

Similarly, the correspondence of the various planes in Zone II with the planes of Zone I is left indefinite. The surface of the mosaic scrolls, that of the four inscriptions, and that of the opus sectile cannot be visually continued upward to meet any one of the several planes in Zone II which have just been analyzed. The flat walls of opus sectile are interrupted by the corner columns and emerge on the other side only to dip into the spatial pouches formed by the niches (*Fig.* 104). Flat surfaces that retain their continuity from bay to bay, such as the area above the main arcade in Zone I, are disintegrated and desubstantialized by the decoration which, with its pattern of convoluted spirals, nullifies the planar integrity of this spandrel area (*Figs.* 103–08). Where bay meets bay, a straight edge is avoided by the oval medallions of the mosaic prophets. And the disposition of the rinceaux is such that each cluster begins at a spandrel and terminates at the midpoint of the adjacent bay, so that the divisions of the rinceaux do not in fact correspond to the divisions of the architecture.

Our analysis of the lower zones should not give the impression here of *horror vacui*. On the contrary, diverse media of decoration, fragmented planes, and discrete modes of ornament notwithstanding, the arrangement has surprising clarity and almost classic reserve. Every single element of the decoration—stucco prophets, shells, heraldic animal pairs, rinceaux, and the prophets of Zone I—is neatly framed in a distinct compartment, and thus isolated from the others. And within the frames, every decorative element is placed with a sense for uncrowded spacing.[47] To appreciate this point it is enough to contrast a bay of Zone II with a Coptic stele in Boston which employs a similar architectural ordering of arches and aedicules (*Figs.* 73, 144).[48] In the stele, the heraldic pair above the triangular pediment is so oversized for its space that the legs of the birds overlap the architecture, while at the same time a pattern of ornamental carving occupies the ground about their heads and wings. The phoenix fills its aedicule entirely, and the stubby pilasters are covered with carving. In Zone II, the stucco prophets keep within the bounds of the aedicule proper, while the pediments are occupied by shells. Between the pediments and the arches above are placed the heraldic pairs of animals composed uncrowdedly within the bounds of the allotted space. This area is in turn separated from the lunette above, which is on a higher plane and which features a different element of decoration. One more comparison, between any one of the prophets of Zone II in his aedicule and the ivory plaque of St. Paul in the Cluny Museum (probably of the sixth century)[49] may profitably be made to emphasize the clarity of organization in the interior of the Baptistery (*Figs.* 98, 145). The size of the saint being larger than the niche in which he stands, his right elbow and the gospel in his left hand overlap

---

47. It must also be noted that not every available surface provided by the architectural compartmentation is used for decorative purposes. Thus, the pulvins of Zone II are left uncarved, as are the tympana of the central arches just above the windows. On the other hand, though the soffits of these central arches have ornamental bands in stucco, the soffits of the small flanking arches are left free of decoration so as not to confuse the existence of the heraldic animal pairs.

48. Published in *Pagan and Christian Egypt. Egyptian Art from the 1st to the 10th Centuries A.D.* (Brooklyn Museum, 1941), no. 39.

49. Volbach, *Elfenbeinarbeiten der Spätantike*, no. 150.

the two pilasters of the niche. In the background, the ornamental pattern of a curtain fills the space left bare by the position of the figure. In contrast, no part of the prophet of Zone II except the feet touches the architecture of the aedicule. The ground is left empty and would have been simply painted in a flat color. Even the position of the shell in the pediment follows the same principle of uncrowded composition, as opposed to the broader fanning out of the shell in the niche of the Cluny St. Paul.

By the same token, the figural parts of the decoration of the Baptistery are not allowed to intermingle with the strictly ornamental. This point is especially pertinent for Zone I. The idea of figures amid a profusion of vegetal motifs was not unknown in later Roman times, as for example in a mosaic from Sainte-Colombe showing Lycurgus entangled in the Ambrosian vine.[50] Appropriately for the theme, Lycurgus is not isolated in any way from the surrounding scrolls; therefore, contextually, the comparison with Zone I may not be entirely justified. But consider the mosaic decoration of the broad soffits at the "Mausoleum of Galla Placidia" where prophets and rinceau are similarly depicted. The figure in the Mausoleum stands on a branch of acanthus, while another branch grows out of his head and supports the tondo containing Christ's monogram. In Zone I, the prophet is set in a gold medallion which isolates him from the rinceaux but, since this medallion itself is formed of acanthus branches, the merger of figures and scrolls is in fact visually unmarred (*Figs.* 113, 114). Once more, then, the artist of the Baptistery demonstrates that the whole is made up of the sum of independent parts, in the classic tradition, and not of the sum of interdependent parts as with the soffits of the Mausoleum.

The Linking of the Zones

It remains to consider how the artist united the two general areas of decoration, the cupola and the walls, to form a coherent ensemble. The main point to be noted is that the segmental pendentives which joined the octagonal body to the cupola were also employed as decorative links. Zone III has a definite base line exclusive of the pendentives, and the upper limits of Zone II are properly defined by the soffits of the main arcade. By filling the area of the pendentives with acanthus clusters which continue as dividers up into Zone III (*Fig.* 69), the decoration of the bounding walls is connected with that of the cupola, since the motifs within the pendentives belong vertically with Zone III and horizontally with the arcade of Zone II. The extent of these plant-candelabra which separate the eight panels of Zone III is carried upward into the Zone of the apostles and downward to the ground through the two stories of corner columns (*Figs.* 39, 40). Thus the whole interior decoration appears as a swelling, colorful, umbrella-like web held down at eight points by ribs which termi-

---

50. The scene represents Lycurgus, king of the Edones in Thrace, who, having scorned the God Dionysus, is punished by being inextricably bound by the tendrils of a vine, which is in fact no other than the transformed maenad Ambrosia. The mosaic was published by G. Lafaye and A. Blanchet, *Inventaire des mosaïques de la Gaule et de l'Afrique,* *1* (Paris, 1909), no. 236. For similar representations of the myth, see Levi, *Antioch Mosaic Pavements,* *1,* 178 ff. For the use of rinceaux as dividing elements of decoration, see ibid., pp. 509 ff.

nate at the pavement. The visual role of these ribs, like those of Brunelleschi's dome in Florence, is one of fluid conduction. The eye, caught anywhere along their length, is free to follow an upward, surging path to the summit, or a downward, grounding path toward the base; the visual scheme, in other words, can be read equally in either direction.

The superposed bays of Zones I, II, and III, limited by these vertical ribs, are arranged symmetrically on either side of central axes. Each axis passes through the middle of a mosaic panel of Zone III, cuts through the lunette decoration of the arcade of Zone II, and continues down through a window and through one of the inscriptions of the niche arcades of Zone I (or through the central motif of the opus sectile paneling). On either side of this axis the composition of the bays is identical with the heraldic arrangement of the confronted animal pairs in Zone II. Thus, going downward, two parapets flank the throne of Christ, two small arches flank the central arch, two stucco prophets flank the window, two tendrils of acanthus meet at a central leaf, two parts of an inscription meet at a centrally located monogram. In one instance, at Side B, the central axis of the three superposed bays is continued into Zones IV and V, where Sts. Peter and Paul confront each other under the feet of Christ. Consequently, from a point on the floor in front of Niche D, the entire system of decoration is firmly fixed along the wall surface as though it were one single painting above the altar niche. From all other points the viewer's eye is caught in the circumferential flow of the wall surface which, like a whirlpool, is sucked toward the center, the medallion of the baptism. Despite the careful compartmentation of the decorative scheme, which was discussed above, it becomes impossible for the eye to single out one framed element for the reason that every such element is mirrored numerous times on the interior surface, becoming part of an overall field composed of the repetition of an identical motif.

A consistent principle which furthers this relentless rotation is that of rhythmic alternation. The eye is constantly forced to move along the surface, following the regular interchange of two distinct elements: of niches with flat walls, of triangular and segmental aedicule pediments, of thrones and altars, of gold and white pallia. This circular movement has no beginning and no end but, like a multicolored Ferris wheel set in motion, the whole interior of the Baptistery rotates incessantly around a shaft of enclosed space. In the zones closest to the viewer the speed of rotation is slack, but it accelerates as it mounts into the cupola. Looking up from below, the resplendent tourbillion gains momentum as the apostles' procession marches around the central medallion, so that the entire cupola turns with the dizzying regularity of some glowing, ethereal body in a cosmic sky.

The Meaning of the Decoration

And so it must have seemed to the catechumen who stepped into the Neonian Baptistery—a vision of the celestial cosmos revealed to him at the moment of the

Christian mystery. This superb tour de force of decoration was not motivated by the cut-and-dried intentions of a dogmatic didacticism, since the Baptistery was not intended for spreading the faith or preaching doctrine. For this there were the congregational cult buildings, the houses of God. Repeated visits to them strengthened the converts' spiritual convictions, and made converts of the curious and interested. To promote this religious education, precise symbolism and instructive illustration were desirable in the decorative programs of the churches. Through pictorial and sculptural representations the Christian story could be told, the doctrine stated.

Not so in a baptistery. Its prime concern was with neither fact nor parable. It was the stage for the final ratification of the convert's faith through the mystery of the baptismal sacrament. Those who were allowed to enter had accepted the tremendous responsibility incurred by baptism, after which sin was infinitely more heinous than before. As catechumens they had undergone religious instruction by attending the regular services. When they decided to present themselves as candidates for the sacrament, they separated themselves from the many converts who were Christian only in name and who shrank, often until death approached, from the awesome onus of moral living imposed by the baptismal seal. Those few who expressed willingness to make the choice were known as *competentes, electi,* or φωτιζόμενοι, and they received special and concentrated instruction for another period of time, particularly during Holy Week. Then, on Easter day (and also, by the fifth century, at Pentecost) they filed into the baptistery. The person who had come this far did not need to be convinced further on points of dogma. The approaching rite would only sanctify his conviction. What awaited him in the baptistery was not an added lesson but a mystery. It would be the culmination of all his previous instruction, the proof of the splendor and importance of the occasion, the intimation of the reward that would be his. Consequently, and this is essential, the artist's intent could not be direct and straightforward exposition, as it might be in the naves of basilicas. For the small mystery buildings, the baptisteries, his method must lean on poetic implication. He must create an atmosphere of faith wherein the initiate might reciprocate with his God. The forms must have a tentative appeal—they must not state but imply, not proclaim but sing.

This long and detailed analysis of the interior scheme of the Baptistery of Ravenna should not obscure this elemental power of suggestion. Approaching the building, the neophyte saw the plain walls of the exterior. This was still part of that material world to which he himself belonged. As he passed through the door, material reality and the dangers with which it was burdened were left behind. "After this," wrote St. Ambrose in reviewing the rite with the new Christians, "the *Holy of holies* was unbarred to thee, thou didst enter the shrine of regeneration . . . Thou didst renounce the devil and his works, the world and its luxury and pleasures."[51] The door was not so much the entrance to a religious building as the curtain dividing the world

---

51. *De myst.* II.5; trans. by T. Thompson in J. H. Srawley (ed.), *St. Ambrose. On the Sacraments and* *On the Mysteries* (London, 1950), p. 124. The italics are not mine.

of pleasures from one which promised a coming supranatural existence. So too the space behind the door was not simply the interior of a religious building but the likeness of that other world, palpably splendid and overpowering. It was alive and in motion. It glittered, for the neophyte, with the diffractive glory of some celestial vision. Roundabout, it was peopled with activated images of divine presences, prophets and apostles, looking down and beckoning. Directly above, the Lord himself submitted to baptism, his Messiahship was confirmed. Here was a multicolored glimpse at eternity: "The Apostle has taught thee that we must *not look at the things which are seen, but at the things which are not seen; for the things which are seen are temporal, but the things which are not seen are eternal.*"[52] For a brief moment inside the Baptistery the neophyte saw the things which were not seen by most men, and all the powers of the artist had been concentrated on making this momentary image as vivid and brilliant as it was incomprehensible by, and incommensurable with, everyday reality. In this respect the decorative scheme was proper for the occasion: it was, as it had to be, visionary. It was meant to be revealed only once and retained in memory from then on. The greatness of the artist who devised the Neonian interior lies in this—his successful evocation of the eternal by means of the transitory.

52. *De myst.* III.8; ibid., p. 125. The italics are not mine.

THE SIGNIFICANCE
OF THE BAPTISTERY

*The art of Ravenna cannot without absurdity
be called Byzantine*—WALTER LOWRIE[1]

One result of this study has been to establish Ravenna's Baptistery as a monument
primarily of the fifth century, with its initial design dating from the early part and
the interior scheme, as a whole, from the third quarter of that century. Its immediate
context is the renascence of Christian art in the city of Ravenna after it had been
singled out, in 402, to be the western capital of the Roman empire. The Baptistery
is the only monument remaining from the impressive episcopal complex which
Bishop Ursus initiated when the imperial court was transferred from Milan to Ravenna, and which included the five-aisled cathedral of the Anastasis (Basilica Ursiana), the palace called Tricolli, baths for the clergy, and other subsidiary buildings.
The nature of the Baptistery's architectural statement and of its figural program,
taken in conjunction with several other surviving monuments of the fifth century
within the city should be indicative of local practices in building and decoration, and
also of relationships with other cities of the contemporary scene.

But the Baptistery has also a broader historical context. As a notably well-preserved
monument of the fifth century, it is a significant representative of that period of postantique art which links the formative century for the official Christian language of
art and architecture, the fourth, with the culmination of this language in the reign
of Justinian, under whom one final, heroic, and ultimately unsuccessful endeavor was
made to convert the Mediterranean anew into a Roman lake. In the background of the
small but accomplished Baptistery stand more than a hundred years of invention and
adaptation to rehabilitate the forms of pagan antiquity for the exigencies of the

1. *Art in the Early Church* (New York, 1947), p. 157.

Christian present. There is no unity of vision in the art of this period, as there was none under the Roman Empire in earlier centuries, when multiple and concurrent modes of expression were held together in the single bounding frame of reference, Romanitas.[2] After Constantine this general *condition* of art became the Christian way; but the visual environment remained as diversified. It is evident from the monuments which it encompasses that the term Early Christian cannot be one of formal language, like Gothic or Baroque. It denotes, simply, all art, regardless of specific form, which has Christian subject matter or meaning.

Viewed in its broad historical context, this is the background of the Ravennate Baptistery. But ahead, less than a century in the future, lie the fluent monuments of the age of Justinian. San Vitale in Ravenna, and Sts. Sergius and Bacchus and Hagia Sophia in Istanbul, to take only three extraordinary creations of this age, mark the end of Early Christian art, since they state explicitly formal characteristics which, viewed as a whole, indicate a uniformity of vision that might justly be called a new style. These monuments are, in a way, the last flowering of that artistic fervor which accompanied the triumph of the church under Constantine. The death of Justinian ushered in a long artistic interregnum marked by the abrupt subsidence of creative energies in both the East and the West. San Vitale, Sts. Sergius and Bacchus, and Hagia Sophia had precedents but no immediate successors. They were conceptions so fully realized that they left, it seemed, no avenue open for the future but the formidable one of occasional direct copy. The two centuries that followed them saw the consolidation of essential differences between the forms of the East and those of the West, and in art as in the religious and political spheres, the two halves of the Christian world developed henceforth along palpable, idiosyncratic ways.

To take it in its immediate context first, as a *Ravennate* monument, the Baptistery was indebted for its general shape, as we have seen, to the region of North Italy and southern France, and especially to Milan. But the resemblance between it and the baptisteries of this region was a symbolic one. Speaking in general architectural terms, the form of an octagonal niched building was too widespread in previous centuries, both chronologically and geographically, to allow any meaningful specification of an ultimate source. Only so far as it constitutes an early example of this form for the Christian baptistery in particular can the Ravennate monument be traced to a direct antecedent: the Ambrosian baptistery of S. Tecla in Milan. In methods of building and in certain aesthetic preferences, however, the Orthodox Baptistery stood apart both from the general class of Roman niched structures—incorporated in baths and residential complexes, or erected independently as nymphaea, mausolea, and the like—and from the special class of late fourth- and early fifth-century octagonal baptisteries within Milan's field of influence. Thin walls of brick laid independently of poured concrete, blind arcading for the articulation of exterior masonry surfaces; vaulting with hollow tubes; the use of pulvin blocks between capitals and

2. See the excellent study of O. Brendel, "Prolegomena to a Book on Roman Art," *MAAR, 21* (1953), 9–74.

arch imposts—such features, evident in the architecture not only of the Baptistery but in other fifth-century structures of Ravenna as well, speak strongly for the presence of a local tradition of building.

To be sure, no one of these features, with the possible exception of the pulvin block, is an invention of Ravennate architects or unique to their field of activity. Hollow tubes were employed at least as early as the second century in North Africa and in parts of Italy.[3] Blind arcades were common to such distant cities of the empire as Trier, Milan, and Rome. Thin walls of brick, left exposed or coated simply with stucco, characterized the external appearance of some late Roman buildings such as the curia by the Roman Forum, reconstructed by Diocletian, and the "Sedes Justitiae" at Trier. But what describes a local tradition is not so much invention as preference, and the use of certain eclectic elements in concert and consistently. In Early Christian architecture, as the Orthodox Baptistery clearly illustrates, general formal resemblances per se signify little. Speculation of interchange of East with West based on them is often misguided. Most of the Mediterranean basin in the early centuries of the Christian era was a vast reservoir of architectural forms and usage.[4] Choice of one form over another was frequently involved with questions of symbolic meaning; choice of usage, with local materials and the native building tradition. And the character of the architecture in a certain region of the Christian empire depended on these two criteria—appropriateness of symbolism in the forms and harmony in building practice—together with aesthetic predilections in such things as proportions, interpretation of the function of walls, and the relation of space to the solid statement of mass. A good instance of this last is Ravenna's preference for thin planes of wall, in contrast to the deeply articulated masses of Milanese architecture.

Caution should be exercised, similarly, in assessing Ravenna's debt to other cities, as against its own original contribution, on the subject of its figural art. It has been common practice to view works of Early Christian art under two separate headings: iconographic content and visual form or "style." I suggested earlier, and I hope the analysis of the Baptistery has made it abundantly clear, that the statement of such a dichotomy, although useful, is essentially misleading inasmuch as it presupposes that "style" is measurably distinct from content. It assumes that the form of a work of art exists as an insular aspect of its creation; either as a reinforcing constituent, so to speak, which is added on to content or, better, as a mold into which content can be poured. What results from the exclusive application of this approach to Early Christian art is that content is seen most frequently only in terms of bare schemata of iconography, and "style" in terms of measurable characteristics which constitute clear-cut schemata of morphology. The method has the advantage of positivism. It allows the formulation of stylistic progress in time toward a preconceived goal; and the formulation of geographic styles within the Christian world, like "Egyptian,"

3. See Chap. 3, n. 71, above.

4. This idea is admirably presented by J. B. Ward Perkins, "The Italian Element in Late Roman and Early Medieval Architecture," *Proceedings of the British Academy, 33* (1947), 1–32.

"Constantinopolitan," or "Eastern." Inevitably it sacrifices what might be called *quality,* that is, the individual solution of a monument where content and form are inextricable, or rather where form is understood as the structure of content. And yet quality, tentative and basically inimitable, is what reveals the particular meaning of any work of art under consideration and, for that matter, the meaning of an entire period of art in a given geographical region.

In general it is doubtful that, for the fifth century, iconographic schemata can be considered indicative of allegiance to definite areas of influence in the Christian world. The greater part of the Early Christian repertory came into being in the third and fourth centuries. Especially after the Peace of the Church, imperial iconography, translated into Christian terms, provided dogmatic and new narrative content which enlarged the substantially paradisiacal vocabulary of the catacombs and the early sarcophagi. Where each new schema of iconography originated, whether in Rome, Gaul, or some corner of the East, is of interest for these two centuries. But the schemata, once invented, were certainly transmissible. By the mid-fifth century they constituted as much a *koine* over a large part of the Mediterranean world as did architectural forms like the basilica or the octagon. In the Baptistery, certain themes which probably originated in Rome, like the Traditio legis, and others, like Daniel in the Phrygian costume and Christ trampling the lion and adder, which seem to have been current first in parts of the East, coexist without embarrassment. It would be idle, in my opinion, to pursue these regional associations very far. What is of greater importance, and perhaps also of greater historical validity, is to note the personal ways in which these traditional schemata are handled; to decide whether certain iconographic themes are preferred consistently in the existing monuments of Ravenna; and to distinguish themes that might be totally unique for the city.

We have commented in a preceding chapter on the originality of such details as the cross in the hand of the Christ pictured enthroned between Sts. Peter and Paul in the Traditio legis relief; and the beautiful figure of the river god Jordan extending a cloth to the Christ in the baptism mosaic in Zone V. The difference of this last scene from its counterparts in the Arian Baptistery and on the ivory throne of Maximian is sufficient evidence for the inventiveness with which the artists of the city approached identical content. No parallel exists elsewhere in the Christian world for the eloquent interpretation of the popular theme of the Good Shepherd in one of the lunettes of the so-called Mausoleum of Galla Placidia. Fresh and purposeful too are the architectural panels of Zone III in the Baptistery, and the row of crown-bearing apostles above them—despite the currency of their general ideas, and regardless of the places of origin for the pristine formulae of these ideas. Where there was no authoritative imagery to restrain them, as in the portraiture of all the apostles but Peter, Paul, and sometimes Andrew, the artists gave free reign to their imagination. Most of the portraits of Zone IV have a private authority, far removed from the faithful but soulless likeness of the stereotype. On occasion, the city developed a portrait type of its own to which it adhered regularly. Such is the Christ of Ravenna; youthful but not childlike, with sober face and a vivid glance and, more often than not, long hair which cascades to the shoulders. Of the three times when Christ appears in the decorative program of the Baptistery, twice, in the Traditio legis and in the trampling of the lion and adder, he is represented in this manner. The remaining one, in the baptism of Zone V, would probably have conformed to this type if a late restoration had not altered its initial design.

The second and third conditions for a native unity of iconography are also demonstrable in the art of Ravenna. As befits an indigenous tradition, some themes were clearly more popular here than others. A pertinent example is the Traditio legis which is frequent on fifth-century Ravennate sarcophagi. More significantly, the theme of Christ trampling the lion and adder, practically nonexistent elsewhere in Italy and not too frequent in other parts of the Mediterranean, appears to have been well liked in Ravenna. Themes unique to the city are also not lacking. The most notable surviving example is the St. Lawrence mosaic in the "Mausoleum" of Galla Placidia. Miss Lawrence, in her thorough study of the city's sarcophagi, distinguished others, and underlined the singularity of this iconographic repertory within Early Christian art.[5] These summary observations suffice, I think, to illustrate that at least in the iconography of its figural art the Ravenna of the fifth century was far from being merely derivative.

Generalizations about visual form are harder still to indite than about iconography. In our analysis of the decorative program of the Baptistery, it was noted that the use of frontality, blank ground, and rhythmic composition—or of their formal opposites—cannot be localized within the Christian world. Comparisons between the Baptistery and other fifth-century programs like those of St. George in Thessaloniki and S. Vittore in Ciel d'Oro in Milan suggested that the presence of some of these formal means instead of others should not be taken to indicate regional affiliations or chronology. The choice was urged by the purpose of the program in question. This applied not only to the program as a whole but to details as well; their placement within the program, conditioned by the visual and contextual role assigned to them as parts of the whole, frequently affected the degree of naturalism or abstraction with which they were depicted. Once again, as in the architecture and in the iconographic schemata of figural art, we should be willing to recognize concurrent modes of vision, common to all regions of the Mediterranean, which the artist felt free to employ, singly or in conjunction, as the specific assignment at hand required. The so-called Asiatic or Alexandrian styles, as recent studies repeatedly illustrate, have little to do with geography.[6] The art of even one city, within closely circumscribed

5. M. Lawrence, *The Sarcophagi of Ravenna*, College Arts Association Monographs, 2 (1945), esp. 23–28.

6. The late Professor C. R. Morey and his students were chiefly responsible for the concept of an "Asiatic" and an Alexandrian" style, the first characterized by oriental frontality, descriptive isola-tion, and rhythmic composition; the other, by an interest in the individuality of narrative content and in specific setting, and by impressionist technique. This thesis, which has dominated Early Christian studies in this country for the last four decades, is set forth in detail in Morey's *Early Christian Art* (2d ed. Princeton, 1953), esp. Chaps. 1–3 (pp. 3–57).

chronological limits, does not always bear a uniform character that can be discerned and formulated with any degree of meaningful accuracy. To extend the definition of style to broader areas of conformity, to speak in fact of the East as against the West, of Egypt against Rome, is, I believe, quite unprofitable.

This study has therefore eschewed any easy judgment for the art of the Baptistery. Generic similarities could link it, superficially, both with eastern painting as represented by the mosaics of Antioch and of Thessaloniki, and with western painting in Milan, Rome, and Naples. The very abundance of this comparative material has tended to be more of a hindrance than a boon to the student of Ravennate art. Always, the latent danger has been to drown the particular instance in a sea of general associations. For this reason I have chosen to use selective comparisons, only where they might bring into focus the individual achievement of the monument within a picture of generalized period uniformity.

Actually, the most meaningful stylistic affinities between the Baptistery program and the rest of fifth-century art exist in Ravenna itself, as is natural. I refer of course to the mosaic program of the "Mausoleum of Galla Placidia," probably a memorial chapel to St. Lawrence, attached to the palatine church of Santa Croce which the empress sponsored, and rededicated in the ninth century to Sts. Nazarius and Celsus.[7] For the present discussion it is unfortunate that of all the fifth-century painting in Ravenna only these two programs should survive. Both were occasional monuments; that is, they were conceived to create ambiences of special religious designation and of limited use. Had the decoration of other types of building come down to our day, such as the imperial portrait cycle of S. Giovanni Evangelista or the Petrine narrative cycle of the celebrated Neonian refectory in the episcopal palace, the evaluation of Ravennate "style" for this century might well have been considerably more diversified. What one can study, however, strongly suggests the presence of an accomplished school of mosaicists in the city, which was responsible both for the Baptistery and for the chapel. The two programs are united in fact by a similar technique and a similar pictorial character subtly divergent from other programs of mosaic of roughly the same period elsewhere in Italy and in the East.

A number of details could be singled out to demonstrate the congruity of these two programs. Three of the ornamental bands that frame the compartments of the decoration and parts of the acanthus rinceaux are identical. Both programs make use

---

One part of the convenient but untenable dichotomy, the so-called Alexandrian style, has recently been decisively challenged by B. R. Brown, *Ptolemaic Paintings and Mosaics and the Alexandrian Style* (Cambridge, Mass., 1957); see also a review of her book by O. Brendel in *AJA, 65* (1961), 211–14.

7. A. Testi-Rasponi first ("Il 'Monasterium Sancti Laurentii Formosi' di Ravenna," *L'arte, 28* [1925], 71–76) questioned the validity of identifying this small building with a burial monument of Empress Galla Placidia, and equated it instead with the S. Lorenzo Formoso and the S. Lorenzo in Pannonia cited in documents. This view has prevailed: See a summary of arguments in G. Bovini, *Il Cosidetto Mausoleo di Galla Placidia in Ravenna* (Vatican, 1950). Recently M. Mazzotti reopened the discussion ("Ferrettiana. Notizie di storia e architettura ravennate," *FR, 69* [1955], 39) by challenging the identification of the monument with the two cult buildings to St. Lawrence mentioned above, on the evidence of new documents.

of a tall cross either held like a staff of state, as by the Good Shepherd in the chapel and by the Christ of the Traditio legis in the Baptistery, or else laid on the shoulder like the *fasces* of a lictor, as in the case of St. Lawrence and of Christ trampling the lion and adder. Landscape elements are conventional. Serrated rocks and wisps of greenery scattered here and there on the ground characterize both the ledge of land on which the Baptist stands in Zone V and the idyllic surroundings of the Good Shepherd in the entrance lunette of the chapel. Broader branches in the latter, flat and exquisitely highlighted with gold, match the boughs above the thrones of Christ in Zone III. Indeed, the palette of the two programs and their special chromatic harmonies and effects correspond quite closely. Both make generous use of blue ground, of gold as an active color for drapery and accessories, of gold in conjunction with green for rinceaux, and of specks of orange distributed erratically but with inspiriting effects. The color of St. Lawrence's pallium and its forceful modeling are almost duplicated in the small prophets of Zone I; the curious flying folds of drapery unite him with several of the apostles in Zone IV and the majority of the stucco prophets. Standing figures in both programs frequently cast pointed shadows at their feet.

But more telling than these contacts of detail is the overall character of the decorative programs. Since their architectural skeletons and religious purpose are heterogeneous, they do not employ the same method of organization. But they achieve a total impression which is sufficiently similar to suggest that it must arise from related concerns. Prime among them would seem to be the concern to unify the entire scheme of decoration, not only visually but thematically, in such a way that the many compartments of decoration create a cohesive construct of form and meaning. Solid architecture is made to serve this purpose and, in the process, its physical reality is destroyed. The two monuments can be read as buildings only from the outside. Inside, they are no other than weightless and immaterial canopies billowing above the celebrant and shielding him from associations of the real world. The seams of this canopy are mere bands of color. They frame elements of decoration without definitely dividing them. This is because all the images share one ethereal space across which they communicate. The bounds of the space are measureless: they correspond to the dilating color-stuff of the canopy within which the figures stand, bright and substanceless, as if floating in midair. The canopy surges above them, at once palpable and out of reach. In its crown, borne aloft by the patterned seams of color, hangs a vision of heaven more sacred than any imagery below: the cross in a bed of stars, and the apparition of the manifest God in a celestial baptism.

Neither the chapel nor the Baptistery, then, can be considered simply as decorated buildings, since the decoration in them is in no way subsidiary, and the function of the building is in no way merely one of containment. Encrusted with mosaic and colored marbles, the walls inside are hidden from view, with the result that the decorative web appears autonomous, self-supporting. Space enveloped in an immaterial sheath of this kind is not *usable* in the ordinary sense. There is no movement within it that is not governed by the images. The space exists more for them than the user—

it is peopled before he enters. When he does enter, he has stepped into a metaphysical space activated by presences that are not mere pictures on the wall. This is a total world they stand for, which has its own order and its own logic. Looking up at them the viewer cannot admire objectively. The images, being neither didactic nor purely symbolic, engage him directly so that he shares the space with them and attunes his identity to theirs. They, flat shadows in truth, take on the element of his corporeality. He, a being of physical validity, attains through them to the extracorporeal realm their presence represents.

It is this special character of the two Ravennate programs, it appears to me, and not their chronological position, which assures their significance in the broader historical perspective of medieval art. Their *quality*, which isolates them from contemporary monuments outside of Ravenna, allies them at the same time with future trends, much more so than the majority of fifth-century monuments are allied. In compositional principles and in the psychological intention of the images, especially with the interior scheme of the Baptistery, one discovers surprising intimations of properties attributed to later Byzantine programs, as we know these from the monuments of the so-called Second Golden Age which succeeded the arid century of the Iconoclastic Controversy. I refer to the direct reciprocity between the painted image and the viewer, ensured at the Baptistery, above all, by the tensile coexistence of Hellenistic–Roman and nonclassical elements; to the employment of such optical refinements as "staggering," which take into account the distance between the image and the viewer; and to the hierarchy of images arranged from top to bottom according to rank and to religious importance—principles which have been shown by O. Demus to operate, with plainer consistency, in Middle Byzantine decorative art of the ninth century and onward.[8] In all these, the Baptistery foretells, precociously, and inexplicably in terms of an unbroken chain of development, such classic Byzantine programs as that of Hosios Lukas at Stiris and the church at Daphni.

In one final respect within its broad historical perspective, the Orthodox Baptistery might be designated as proto-Byzantine—and for this the Neonian renovation is responsible. It was shown in Chapter 3 that the Ravennate monument as it exists today represents the wedding of two separate buildings: first, the octagonal, timber-roofed structure erected as the initial Baptistery of the Basilica Ursiana; and second, the interior baldacchino-system added by Neon a short time later. Substantially, the first building presented a clear, logical statement of structural relationships. Solid walls rooted in the earth carried the timber roof, and the interior was decorated, so far as can be surmised, with elements—columns, painted stucco, colored marbles—which were applied directly to the structural fabric. The division of labor between structure and ornament was unambiguous. The building was a space-enclosing body with a straightforward expression of flat wall planes on the exterior and a more variegated

8. *Byzantine Mosaic Decoration. Aspects of Monumental Art in Byzantium* (Boston, 1955; earlier British ed. London, 1948). Also idem, "The Methods of the Byzantine Artist," *The Mint*, 2 (1948), 64–77.

appearance in the interior, where ornament was employed to sheath the bare surfaces of the masonry. The bounding walls had therefore two faces, a modest one turned to the outside world and a richer face, multicolored and multitextured, designed for the person to whom entrance was granted. The illusion of the interior was one of surface, not of space, for the interior could easily be read as the negative of the outer mass. The cubic composition of this mass was reflected in the cubic space enclosed within. In all this, the pre-Neonian Baptistery followed the principles of late Roman and Early Christian architecture.

The Neonian renovation looks forward instead to a new conception of architecture which involves the support of vaults by structural skeletons independent of bounding walls. A building so conceived does not grow upward from foundations, but rather reaches down to the ground in a series of tentacles whose visual lightness and deliberately ambiguous presentation renders the vault itself seemingly weightless and immaterial. This dematerialization is not comparable to the mere sheathing of masonry that dissolves the solidity of the interior in such Roman buildings as the Pantheon. Even in the "Mausoleum of Galla Placidia," which was so forward-looking in its use of a construct of decoration associated with later Byzantine solutions, the billowing canopy is achieved through pictorial means only; the walls are dematerialized by an envelope of color underneath which the structure of the building has the traditional arrangement of masonry walls bearing a vault. The Neonian renovation is also unlike the dematerialization of a Gothic cathedral, where matter itself is reduced to the barest possible structural skeleton, so that the building has a minimal volume of solids. In a baldacchino-system such as the one erected by Neon, the walls are not dispensed with or simply enveloped in a color-curtain. Their character is altered, from one of structure to one of solely visual effect. They are no more than screens distended between the ribs of the baldacchino.

The system of the baldacchino in early medieval architecture was investigated at length by H. Sedlmayr in two articles of 1933 and 1935.[9] He distinguished two types of roofed space: in the first the roof is a supplementary element, as in a Greek temple or in Roman buildings like the Pantheon; in the other the roof is a vaulted canopy, the baldacchino, in which the vault is supported by columns or piers rather than walls. Even though the latter type is prefigured aesthetically in Roman imperial architecture, for example in the Piazza d'Oro at Villa Adriana or in the praetorium at Muzmiyeh, it does not become the prevalent architectural system, generally speaking, before the time of Justinian. First in Sts. Sergius and Bacchus, and later in Hagia Sophia, the supports of the baldacchino are drawn back into the wall, becoming parts of it and using the bounding walls as nonstructural, space-defining screens. This system, combined with the further principle of "overlapping forms," that is to say, the

---

9. "Das erste mittelalterliche Architektursystem," *Kunstwissenschaftliche Forschungen, 2* (1933), 25–62; "Zur Geschichte des justinianischen Architektursystems," *BZ, 35* (1935), 38–69. A more elaborate statement of the thesis is the recent work by the same author: *Spätantike Wandsysteme (Bayerische Akademie des Wissenschaft, Phil.-hist. Klasse, Sitzungberichte, 7,* 1958).

formal subdivision of load-bearing arcades by smaller embraced arches which function as mere filling for the larger arcades, constitutes the basic formal definition of Justinianic architecture.

Sedlmayr's thesis, briefly summarized above, is one of importance for the character of sixth-century architecture as opposed to the Early Christian architecture of the previous centuries. It is therefore vital to realize the existence of the overlapping baldacchino system (*übergreifende Baldacchinsystem*) in the Orthodox Baptistery more than a half century before the Justinianic examples. The objections raised by Sedlmayr against the Baptistery as a monument prefiguring sixth-century principles rise from the fact that the structural history of the building was not then clearly understood. The Baptistery was therefore accepted either as the result of an additive process or as all of one period. If the former, elements such as the triple arches in each bay of Zone II could be explained by the assumption that they were later additions to the structure, modeled on the triple arches in the bema of San Vitale.[10] If the latter, wherein the cupola and the bounding walls were taken to be contemporaneous, the structural incongruity of the two tiers of arcades and columns with the walls could not reasonably be explained. The history of the building as it has been reconstructed in this study throws light on the far from ordinary achievements of the Neonian renovation. Since the corner columns, and not the walls, are the chief support of the cupola, Sedlmayr is misguided in assuming that columns are used in the Baptistery for decorative purposes alone, and in comparing them with the columns and arcades of the Porta Aurea of Diocletian's palace at Spalato. His further observation that, unlike Justinianic practice, the columns are still *in front* of the walls as in late Roman architecture is explained by the fact that Neon was obliged to take into account the pre-existing octagonal shell, and that therefore his baldacchino should not be judged as an entirely independent design.[11] With this clarification in mind, the Orthodox Baptistery anticipates the conception of a billowing and visually insubstantial architecture, well suited for the cult buildings to the unseen and immaterial Christian deity.

In Chapter 3 the Neonian system of the Baptistery was compared with Early Christian buildings like Santa Costanza and the Sistine Baptistery of the Lateran in Rome. With them, the vaulted canopy is not the essence of the building but only one part of the total arrangement. It is surrounded by the annular barrel-vaulted ambulatory which has physical boundaries and a compact space of its own. One might consider these two buildings an early step toward the developed system of the sixth century. Their solution consisted in inserting a single baldacchino in a space-enclosing frame to emphasize the focal point of the building, which, in the Lateran Baptistery at least, was the central baptismal font. In the Orthodox Baptistery, the inserted baldacchino was made to serve as the totality of the interior, so that the distinction between a

---

10. This is the explanation of C. Casalone, among others ("Ricerche," pp. 243–44).

11. For Sedlmayr's observations on the Orthodox Baptistery, see the article cited in n. 9 above, *BZ, 35* (1935), 55–56.

central focus and less important surrounding spaces was obliterated. Finally, in the case of San Vitale, where once again the central space was circumscribed by an ambulatory, this was no longer barrel-vaulted but was itself composed of a series of smaller, radiating baldacchini which destroyed the continuity of the exterior wall.

To be sure, comparison of the Baptistery with buildings like Hagia Sophia and San Vitale suffers first from the widely disparate scales and second from the various intentions. The vast size of the Justinianic monuments creates many problems that cannot successfully be related to the Baptistery. The structural complexities of Hagia Sophia or San Vitale, as well as the spatial intricacy of their interiors, find no parallels in the comparatively minute measurements of the Baptistery. Then too it must be stressed that Sts. Sergius and Bacchus, Hagia Sophia, and San Vitale were all designed as congregational churches, but the Neonian Baptistery was a small religious edifice of restricted use, dedicated to a very special cult ceremony. Despite these reservations, the recognition of formal operative principles in the Baptistery which are novel for their time and prophetic of future developments is legitimate and, indeed, vital. The difference between the pre-Neonian octagon and the Neonian baldacchino is the difference between late antique and early medieval architecture. This early medieval period, especially the age of Justinian, deserves to be recognized as a specific formal language and to be designated as such. In itself the designation is not important. The confusion that arises from the use of the term "Byzantine" to characterize sixth-century art and architecture is basically one of semantics and is comparable to the similar usage of "Roman." In both cases the associations of the terms with a primarily historical context tend to jeopardize their service as art-historical denominations. Yet the different stylistic worlds for which they can be made to stand are themselves valid and definable. When the Orthodox Baptistery is therefore designated here as a significant proto-Byzantine monument, the reference is clearly to the anticipation in it of formal characteristics which are to prevail in the future.

Anticipation of Justinianic principles of architecture in the Baptistery do not stop with the "overlapping baldacchino system." Conscious dematerialization of structure and ambiguity in load-support relationships were stressed by W. R. Zaloziecky, in his thorough and penetrating analysis of Hagia Sophia, as the two most important aesthetic principles employed in its composition.[12] Both are decisive factors in the aesthetic effects of the interior of the Baptistery as well. The means are not identical. In Hagia Sophia, the continuous masonry planes are disrupted by puncturing them with arcades and rows of windows. In the Baptistery the same disruption is achieved by the fragmentation of interior surfaces into several indefinite planes in ambiguous relationship to one another. Unlike the restful planes of the tympana under the

---

12. *Die Sophienkirche in Konstantinopel und ihre Stellung in der Geschichte der aberländischen Architektur,* Studi di antichità cristiana, *12* (Rome and Freiburg i.B., 1936). Some of Zaloziecky's arguments were anticipated in embryonic form in an earlier article by G. A. Andreades, "Die Sophien-kathedrale von Konstantinopel," *Kunstwissenschaftliche Forschungen, 1* (1931), 33–94. Summaries of both arguments in E. H. Swift, *Hagia Sophia* (New York, 1940), pp. 36–49.

major north and south arches in Hagia Sophia, the surfaces of the Baptistery flicker with a nervous activity, encouraged by the movement of the eye from plane to plane and emphasized further by the play of colors and of various textures. Designs like acanthus rinceaux, by their sinuous complication, are themselves instrumental in the disintegration of surface continuities. This particular illusionism of the Baptistery interior is concentrated in two dimensions, whereas the illusionism of Hagia Sophia resides in the interplay of fragmentary views caught when looking through the arcades of the nave toward the aisles.

Again, the obscurity in the organic connection of supporting members and their loads is managed in depth at Hagia Sophia, but two-dimensionally in the Baptistery. To mention one instance, the four piers on which the superstructure of Hagia Sophia rests are allowed to protrude only slightly from the nave walls, and the functional members which meet the major thrusts of the superstructure are concealed in the aisles and the galleries. In the Baptistery, the structural mechanism is not hidden from view; it is illusionistically confused with the purely decorative members, so that it becomes impossible to determine where architecture stops and decoration begins. Thus arches and columns may be structural or ornamental; architectural units may be actual or simulated in stucco and mosaic; and the superstructure itself which the arches and columns are designed to carry, sheathed completely in glittering mosaic, may be considered more a hovering envelope of light and color than a mass which has density and weight.

One last aesthetic principle common to the Baptistery and to the architecture of the sixth century should be acknowledged. It is the successful combination of horizontal and vertical axes. In Chapter 3 it was seen that the longitudinal disposition of the lower zones (and also of the decorative bands of the cupola) was skillfully counterbalanced by visual vertical stresses provided by the tiered columns and continued into the cupola by the forms of the plant-candelabra. Similarly, in the discussion of the last chapter, the same principle of the intersection of lateral and vertical axes was noted in the manner in which the apostles of Zone IV marched around the cupola while at the same time their vertiginous motion was pinioned by the perpendicular correspondence of the axes of Zones IV and V at the point where Sts. Peter and Paul meet under the feet of Christ. A like coalition of horizontal and vertical dynamics is present in the interior of Sts. Sergius and Bacchus, where a substantial continuous cornice between aisle and gallery levels carries the eye circumferentially around the building without impeding the soaring effect of the eight piers. In Hagia Sophia, this extraordinary duality becomes the artistic crux of the monument: a longitudinal basilical area closed off at either end by two large hemicycles is pierced by the dominant vertical shaft of space created by the great dome, so that a vibrant interchange is established between axial movement toward the apse and vertical transfixion under the Dome of Heaven.

It would be premature to conclude, from this one study, anything more categorical or elaborate about the Early Christian art of Ravenna. Only when each of its remaining monuments has been subjected to a detailed investigation which focuses on the evidence of the monument itself and not on any prethought master scheme, will we be in a position to assess the true legacy of this Adriatic city. And in the process, we might have to revise parts of the current view of Early Christian art in the fifth and sixth centuries. The analysis of the Orthodox Baptistery alone has suggested that Ravenna had a coherent native tradition, distinctive already by the mid-fifth century in the character of its architecture and in the iconography and formal preferences of its figural art; and that this tradition would seem, in the hindsight of history, to bear on Justinianic and later Byzantine art more plainly and meaningfully than the art of Early Christian Rome, Milan, or Naples. This study has shown, at the same time, that the Baptistery is one of the most individual creations of early medieval Christianity. In the stylistic ambivalence of its mosaic painting; in the equivocalness of the structural statement of its interior architecture; and in the ambiguity of its generic symbolism which is instrumental in conjoining the various zones of decoration—in all these, Neon's monument embodies a unique conception which defies neat classification. The statement of the Baptistery of Ravenna, as with all works of art, remains personal first, and is only secondarily historical.

APPENDICES

APPENDIX 1.

Furniture and Furnishings of the Baptistery

The Font (Fig. 122)

The most prominent piece of furniture in the Baptistery is the central octagonal font, which measures about 3.45 meters wide and 0.84 meter deep. It is composed of slabs of white marble, with average dimensions of 1.20 by 0.79 meters; on Sides A and D′ the outer slabs are of porphyry, belonging, in the opinion of Sangiorgi, to the original incrustation of the flat walls of Zone I (*Battistero,* pp. 70–71). The area between the inner and outer slabs is filled with brick and rubble, which is concealed by horizontal slabs (about 0.35 meter wide) forming the rim of the font. In the outer corners are inserted shafts of small columns, also of marble. Inside the font the slabs are inscribed in Latin and Greek in a blue-green paint, which has faded completely at places. The inscriptions are:

Side A

> ΤΟ ΓΕΓΕΝΝΗΜΕΝΟΝ
>
> ΕΚ ΤΟΥ ΠΝΕΥΜΑΤΟΣ
>
> ΠΝΕΥΜΑ ΕΣΤΙ

(John 3:6, "that which is born of the Spirit is spirit.")

Side A′

> QUICUMQUE IN CHRISTO
>
> BAPTIZATI ESTIS X̅TUM
>
> INDUISTIS

(Gal. 3:27, "For as many of you as have been baptized into Christ have put on Christ.")

Side B has no inscription, and Side B′ is taken up by the pulpit. Side C is inscribed with a seven-branched candelabrum.

Side C′

> BAPTIZETUR UNUS
>
> QUISQ[UE] VESTRUM IN
>
> REMIS[SIONEM] PECCATOR[UM]

(Acts 2:38, "and be baptized every one of you . . . for the remission of sins.")

139

The Greek inscription of Side D is now almost totally obliterated; the only visible letters are ΘΗ and ΑΙ.

Side D′

DVT

D JOHANNI XTI PRECURS[ORI]

ZACHARIE FILIO

[URSU]S RAVEN[NAE] PONTIFEX

D

The marble pulpit on Side B′ is semicircular; on the convex surface which protrudes into the font there is a deeply incised cross, once probably filled with mosaic or colored marble. The cross measures 0.71 meter (long arm) by 0.47 (short arm). At each end of the semicircular pulpit, on the outside of the font, is an engaged column, the capital of which is carved with the same design of foliage as is seen on the pulvins of Zone I; the columns are 0.96 meter high (1.14 including the capital). One ascends the pulpit by two steps, each 0.20 meter high. Here the officiating bishop would stand to administer the sacrament. An exact parallel to the pulpit is found at the font of the baptistery at Lomello (P. Verzone, *L'Architettura religiosa dell'alto medio evo nell'Italia settentrionale* [Milan, 1942], p. 26).

The octagonal font of the Orthodox Baptistery, as we have it today, is probably the work of the later medieval renovation when the pavement was raised to the level on which the columns at present stand (see above, pp. 45–46). It rests on the foundations of the original fifth-century font, as was proved by the excavation of Lanciani (Pl. 21 and p. 36 above); it is possible that some of the slabs belong to this antique font which, however, was internally circular. The pulpit, on the other hand, may very well go back to the fifth century, and indeed the carving of the capitals appears to connect it to the pulvins of Zone I and to the impost blocks of the niche arches (see above, p. 46).

Until quite recently part of the pulpit was concealed by the small font of *pergamo antico,* which Giulio Francesco Varneri had inserted into the larger font in 1775 in order to put an end to the custom of filling the latter with water (Document 15). Varneri's font was detached and removed by Monsignor Mario Mazzotti on October 14, 1960, when the pulpit was cleaned and restored to its original state. It was necessary during this operation to disengage the outer slab of Side B of the font; that slab, which presented a smooth surface on the outside, was found to be carved on the reverse with a handsome relief showing a lamb, a cross, and part of a wreath (*Fig.* 127). This relief must pertain either to a sarcophagus front or to a *pluteo,* perhaps of the sixth century; the design of the lamb and the cross was probably repeated on the other side of the central wreath (*Corsi* [1961], p. 276).

The Altar (Fig. 123)

The present altar of the Baptistery, standing in Niche B, is composed of two separate parts. A marble slab, 0.80 by 1.30 meters, carried on four small marble columns, forms the main part. The front two columns have Corinthian capitals; those at the back, slightly shorter and of a different kind of marble, have capitals of the same type as those of the pulpit. Underneath this table is a smaller altar, 0.96 meter high, 0.74 wide, and 0.55 deep. The front consists of two fluted pilasters with decorative capitals and a lintel across them carved with vine tendrils on either side of a central cross; two birds are pecking at the grapes, an obvious reference to the eucharist and to the celestial joy of the blessed spirits (see C. Rohault de Fleury, *La Messe; études arché-ologiques sur ses monuments* [Paris, 1883–89], p. 134). Inside this is an aedicule, with two spirally fluted columns surmounted by an arch which is carved with a highly stylized egg and dart motif. The area between the arch and the lintel is filled with palm trees, a reference to immortality. The window in the main body of the aedicule (*fenestella confessionis*) is closed by a bronze lid showing the dove of the Holy Spirit in an oval medallion of rays. The carving of this smaller altar is very similar to the relief style of the pulpit of Bishop Agnellus in the Basilica Ursiana, and probably dates like it from the sixth century. The altar is believed to have been brought to the Baptistery from the cathedral (B. Fiandrini, *Annali ravennati* [Ravenna, 1794], p. 265), perhaps on the occasion of the erection of a new altar in the cathedral by Archbishop Roverella (G. Fabri, *Le Sagre Memorie di Ravenna antica* [Venice, 1664], p. 537). The present large marble table above this antique altar was placed there by order of Archbishop della Rovere in April 1573 (Document 2). In 1606, the antique altar was entirely concealed from view (Document 6). It was again on the initiative of Varneri that the encasement was removed in August 1784, the antique altar cleaned, and the present bronze lid placed over the *fenestella confessionis* (Documents 15 and 17).

The Urn (Fig. 124)

In another niche (Side C) of the Baptistery stands an urn which has been included in most modern descriptions of the monument since 1500. It is a large volute krater of Parian marble with a diameter of about 0.85 meter and a depth of about 0.40, resting on an inverted composite capital akin in style to the pulvins of Zone I and the brackets of Zone II. On either face of the krater there is a high relief of two nude winged putti holding a garland between them; the design is completed with bows and arrows and crossed torches. Under each handle is an eagle with outstretched wings. The handles themselves are carved in a scaly pattern. The relief is not without merit, and stylistically it should probably be attributed to the second century A.D. The inventory of 1785 by G. Varneri speaks of a certain Father Lodovico Pattuzzi Scolopio who studied the krater and proved that it was not a funerary urn—that the symbolism of the relief referred to its use for matrimonial purifications. The explanation is rather fanciful. In fact putti holding garlands, the eagle as a symbol of immortality, and the torch are well-known in the iconography of funereal art. There are at least two instances on sarcophagi where bows and quivers represent Apollo and Artemis, the sun and the moon (F. Cumont, *Recherches sur le symbolisme funeraire des romains* [Paris, 1942], pp. 318, 339). The further suggestion of Scolopio that the eagles allude to the fact that the krater once belonged to a temple of Jupiter soon took hold, and often from then on the krater is said, untenably, to have been found in the Temple of Jupiter at the suburb of Caesarea (J. Corblet, "Des lieux de bap-tême," *RAC, 24* [1877], 143). It appears that before Varneri's new font was installed, the krater was employed as a container for baptismal water, and hence it is frequently referred to as the "piccolo Battistero" (e.g. Document 9).

The Bronze Cross

In Niche A, on an Ionic capital, is a bronze cross which until June 1963 sur-mounted the roof of the building. It is 0.63 meter high and 0.48 wide. On it is in-cised the following inscription disposed vertically on the longer arm and continued horizontally on the short arm: DE DONIS DEI ET SCE MARIE FELEX ET STEFANUS OPTU-LERUNT TEMPORIBUS DN THEODORO APOSTOLICUM. It is generally conceded that "Theo-doro" refers to Archbishop Theodorus of Ravenna, whose episcopate came between 677 and 688. Nothing is known about the donors Felex and Stefanus, but in con-trast to the titled Theodorus they were apparently ordinary citizens. The meaning of the inscription has been considered above, pp. 19–20.

On the reverse side of the cross is another inscription incised by the rector Prospero Grossi to commemorate his renovation of the roof: BAPTISTERII HUIS TECTUM EX IN-TEGRO REFECTUM FUIT; and on the horizontal arm the date: ANNO DOMINI MDCCLXV (see Document 11). Later Varneri had a replica of this cross carved on a marble slab which he put on one of the interior walls of the Baptistery. Below it on another slab was the following inscription:

ARCHETYPUM AENEUM ADHUC EXTAT

IN VERTICEM HUIUS ECCLESIAE

POSITUM

VII INCLINANTE SAECULO

THEODORO ARCHIEPISCOPO

I saw both these slabs in October 1960 in a heap of fragments piled in a corner on the floor.

The Relief (Fig. 125)

On the exterior of the Baptistery, in the blind arcade on Side D, there is a relief (0.80 by 0.82 meter) inserted into the brick masonry. The stone is badly weathered. It shows a male figure on a horse, dressed in a long mantle and high boots (?), hold-ing up a crown with his right hand. The poor state of preservation makes it impos-sible to date the relief with any accuracy. The identity of the horseman is also diffi-cult to ascertain. He was likely an imperial personage; the crown, held above the horse's head, may refer to his investiture, as is certainly the case in a third-century relief at Bishapur depicting the investiture of Bahram I. A crown similarly extended by a mounted saint alludes to his martyrdom; for example, in two wall paintings from Chapel 17 at Baouit (*Fig.* 147). The suggestions of S. Busmanti that the person shown on the Baptistery relief is Emperor Constantine and that it belonged to an interior frieze are unwarranted (*Guida breve per Ravenna antica e moderna* [Ravenna, 1883], p. 94). A similar relief of a horseman, even less well preserved, is found in the masonry of the Torre del Comune in Ravenna.

Miscellanea

1. During the reconstruction of the Baptistery by Lanciani in the later nineteenth century, a fragment of a slab with the following inscription (*Fig.* 126) was found buried in the masonry: . . . LI CAESIAE PRI/MIGENIAE UXO / Q. PUB. GENIALI / FRATRI ET PECULIARI MATR. / IUVENALI O LIB. / MODESTI / QUI MORTALE GENUS / STATUIT ANIMAM-QUE / CREAVIT ATTRIBUIT / REDDI CORPORA ELY/SIIS HOC SIMUL UT CREDA / TU MORITURE LEGIS. The fragment was reused in the reconstruction of the walls (see O. Gardella in *L'Atterramento di una parte dell'ardica della Basilica Classense di Ravenna* [Ravenna, 1890], p. 18), and the inscription survives only in a cast, now at the Superintendency of Monuments, made by C. Ricci's father. The epitaph is certainly pagan, and I am privileged to have permission to relate the opinion of the distinguished epigraphist Monsignor A. Ferrua, expressed in a communication to Monsignor Mazzotti, that the inscription pertains very probably to the second half of the first century A.D.

2. In Niche A stood a marble slab on a stone cylinder, which appears to have been used as a secondary altar. It was removed in October 1960.

3. The fragments of a curious frieze carved with some sort of twisted ribbon motif are laid in a corner of the Baptistery. I assume that this is "the architrave of a door" that Varneri uncovered during the course of repairs at the Baptistery (Document 15).

APPENDIX 2.

Transcript of Documents

The following selection, arranged in chronological order, is from the most important documents relating to the history of the Orthodox Baptistery. See above, pp. 9–10, for the archives in which they are at present kept. Some of the documents are unpublished; references are given for those that have been quoted in print. Numbers in brackets next to the date refer to pages in the text where the document is cited; composite numerals refer to notes (3.2, for example, means Chapter 3, note 2). No corrections have been made in the original texts.

Document 1, 1566 [21]

"Acta et decreta visitationis," v. I, p. 25 recto. In the Archivio Arcivescovile.

Visitavit Mansionariam S. Johannis in fonte apud sanctam cathedralem ecclesiam situatam, in qua constitutus est Fons baptisimalis, et omnibus ibi visis et perspectis ordinavit quod per Rectorem dictae Mansionariae fiant et reducantur vascula Sanctorum oleorum pro baptismo in unum tamen, cum lamina argentea intermediante . . . Item instauretur Musaicum capelle et alia devastata.

(Quoted by Giulio Varneri in "Varia," p. 3 recto. Published by Ricci, "S. Giovanni," p. 305.)

Document 2, 1573 [21, 23, 141, 157; 3.49]

"Acta et decreta visitationis," v. I, p. 34 verso. In the Archivio Arcivescovile.

Ordinavit quod fiat tabula marmorea pro altari. Aperiantur duo fenestre, una ab oriente et altera ab occidente, et eis fiant empanate Tele line. Item quod aptetur pavimentum dicte ecclesie apud Sacrarium.

(Quoted by Giulio Varneri in "Varia," p. 3 verso; and in part by Ricci, "S. Giovanni," p. 306, and Sangiorgi, *Battistero,* pp. 19, 43, 79.)

Document 3, 1591 [21, 157; 2.48]

"Libro sacra visitationis diocesis Ravennaten. facte anno 1591 sub Ill.mo ac Rev.mo DD Christofori Boncampagni Archiep. Raven."

In Metropolitane Ecclesia et sic aliis Parochialibus huius Civitatis non inest Fons Baptismatis, sed huiusmodi Baptismi Sanctum ab Antiquissima usque mode continuo fuit ministratum et hodie exercetur tantum in dicta Parochiali Ecclesia S. G.ois in Fonte ...

Que omnia manifeste apparent ex nobili et antiqua structura in forma angulari, et opere, ut vulgo dicitur Musaico et elaborata, et instructa una cum multis figuris picturisque tangentibus, et concernentibus misteria concernentia huius Sacramenti Baptismatis.

Que fabrica et figure respective cum ob earum antiquitatem minaretur ruinam et apparent fere consumpte et in dies collaberentur opere et compensis factis ab eodem Parocho de introitibus dicte Ecclesie et odie ob eandem restitutionem, Ecclesia ipsa stat decenter, tantum remanserunt nonulle reliquie, que adhuc indigent reparatione modo prout actum fuit in locis, et figuris jam resarcitis ac restauratis.

(Transcribed from "Raccolta," pp. 3–4. Unpublished.)

Document 4, 1605 [21, 157]

"Libro decretorum fact. Anno 1605 in occasione S. Visit. is facte sub. Ill.mo ac Rev. mo Card. Aldobrandini Archiep.," Prot. I, p. 5a tergo.

Baptisterium ex pluribus laminis marmoreis forma octangulo constructo, et opperimento plano ligneo non decenti operto, cibborium adhibeatur, quod columellis suffultum sit, que labro summo collocetur queis, vel alia matheria decenti, periti iudicio, conflatis, itta accludantur, et cum usu venerit apperiri queat, in earumque colunellarum sumitate choronis de Architecti consilio adhibeatur, tum totum opus contegatur ticto eiusdem matterie forma orbiculari, aut piramidali, in cuius summa parte statua collocetur S. Jo.is B.tte Christum Dominum Baptizantis, quod opperimentum Ciborium appelletur conopeo albi coloris tegatur, idque impensis Parochorum Civitatis fiat.

(Transcribed from "Raccolta," p. 5. Unpublished.)

Document 5, June 9, 1606 [21, 157; 3.23]

"Acta et decreta Ill.mi et Rev.mi D.ni Petri Card. Aldobrandini Archiep. Rav. in p.a sua ejusdem Ecclesie Visitatione," c. 24 et seq. Feria 2.

Metropolitane Ecclesie modico intervallo Septentrionem coniungitur Baptisterium S. Jo.is in Fonte consecratum non minus ornamentis, quam structuram insigne, forma eius octangularis est tectum exterius coctis lateribus constat, interior autem facies ad congruam altitudinem et solo recta producitur, tum viginti quatuor collumellis e greco marmore succedentibus arcus octo innituntur, unde Templi fastigium informicem flectitur, ac paulatim ejus latitudo in testudinem.

Ornamenta vero quibus undique illustrantur eiusmodi sunt, ut Ecclesie antiquitatem, et nobilitatem facile testentur, quocumque n. aspicitur, et picture musive, et figure Prophetarum e plasti et porphiretici orbes, ac serpentine tabule occurunt miro artificio concinate atopo disposite, nam in summa fornice Xti Domini a Joanne Baptizati [?] musiva eminet, tum subsequuntur duodecim Apostolorum simulacra et aliorum Sanctorum effigies, tum plastis tum coloribus expresse. Ad orientale latus appellit Altare et Divina Misteria perficienda. In huius templi medio Fons aque Baptismalis existit, eadem octangulari figura et amplitudine singulari, ejus latera marmoreis, et porphireticis Tabullis inter se coherentibus constructa s.t. Adheret Sacro Fonti ex ea parte qua aspicitur aditus marmoreum pulpitum . . .

(Transcribed from "Raccolta," pp. 6–7. Unpublished except for the opening words which are quoted by B. Fiandrini, *Annali ravennati . . . , 3* [Ravenna, 1794], 106 *bis;* Ricci, "S. Giovanni," p. 313; Sangiorgi, *Battistero,* p. 137; and Mazzotti in *Corsi* [1961], p. 264; and the last sentence which is quoted by Sangiorgi, *Battistero,* p. 72.)

Document 6, August 16, 1606 [141, 157]

Ibid., Feria 5.

Ill.mus D. Card. Aldobrandinus . . . in ea visitatione sic statuit: Ad Altare S. Jo.is Baptistae claudatur fenestrella que sub altari est, et mensa marmorea extracto ab utroque latere muro firmetur.

(Transcribed from "Raccolta," p. 7. Quoted in an inventory of the rector Giulio Varneri which is transcribed by Sangiorgi, *Battistero,* p. 80.)

Document 7, October 30, 1612 [21, 157; 2.55]

"Acta et decreta Ill.mi ac Rev. D. Petri Card. Aldobrandini Archiep. in tertia suae ejusdem Eccl.e Visitatione," c. 17 et seq. Feria 3.

Templum Divi Jo.is Baptiste Sacrum Metropolitane proximum adiecit forme octangularis et testudine . . . tres habet fenestras vitreas quadratas, tegule lattericus, cooperitur extrinsice, pavimentum laterensis stratum est, sed dextrum Ostii marmorei quadrati collocatum est Vas. marmoreum rotundum aque benedicte. [The font] quod marmoree e porphiretice tabule undique completuntur, ligno operculo contegitur . . .

(Transcribed from "Raccolta," p. 8. Quoted in part by Sangiorgi, *Battistero,* p. 77.)

Document 8, September 1673 [22, 157]

Unsigned letter in "Varia," p. 25 recto.

Io infrascritto faccio fede per verita ricercato [———]. Io mi ricordo, quando l'Ill.mo Card.le Aldobrandini già Arcivescovo di Rav.na fece fundare, e fabricare la capella del SS.mo sacramento del domo, e come in tal occasione fece guastare la casa Parochiale di S. Gio. in Fonte i di cui fundamenti dalla porta d'avanti sulla strada, che correva dietra la muraglia del Domo, dico ricordarmi esser quelli, che al presente si vedono a diritura della rimessa dell'Arcivescovo verso la detta Capella del SS.mo Sacramento avanti la casa nova parochiale, che hora si trova in essere fatta fabricare dal medesimo Sig. Card.le Aldobrandini in distanza dalla medesima piedi quattordici in circa . . .

(Quoted in part by Mazzotti in *Corsi* [1961], p. 263.)

Document 9, January 22, 1741 [22, 28, 142, 157; 2.29]

"Inventario del Priore Grossi delli 22 Gennaro 1741 per la Chiesa Parochiale di S. Giovanni Fonte."

[The Orthodox Baptistery] è posta . . . in faccia alla porticella laterale della Metropolitana Chiesa a settentrione, e a ponente di essa tramezzando la strada, da mezzogiorno la casa Parocchiale, da tramontana il Cimitero, e da levante il cortile di M.r Arcivescovo . . . [The Baptistery was renovated by Neon] come consta dal monumento posto sopra la porta del Battistero con i sequenti versi: Cede vetus [etc.] . . . In questa chiesa evvi un altare con l'imagine di S. Gio. Batt.a che battezza Gesu Xto . . . dipinta sopra la tela in bona forma . . . [The font] è coperta con piano di tavole, e sopra coperta di tela dipinta ad olio con rabeschi alla chinese ed in mezzo l'immagine di S. Gio. Batt.a che battezza nostro Sig.re nel Giordano, da me infrascritto fatta interamente fare e dipingere 1733. [Description of the opus sectile.] . . . un grande ovato di porfido in faccia alla porta del Battistero e due piccoli ovati posti nel volto vicino all'altare a cornu Epistole di porfido con in mezzo una Lapide di serpentino, ed il restante tutto intrecciato vagamente di porfido e verde antico, benche alcuni di questi volti circondanti si vedano o in tutto, o in parte, spogliati . . . ed al presente solamente dipinti per dimostrare colla pittura la nobiltà che prima l'adornavano.

. . . Evvi in detta nicchia [Niche C] altro piccolo battisterio di marmo greco in forma rotonda adorno di varie figure a bassorilievo, posto sopra piedestallo pure di marmo greco, e questo serve solamente per fare la funzione del Battesimo il sabbato di Pentecoste. Questo vaso pure è coperto con coperchio di legno e sopra una piccola guglietta pure di legno con croce di ferro dipinta di color d'oro . . .

(Transcribed from "Raccolta," pp. 9–12. Quoted in part by Sangiorgi, *Battistero*, pp. 27–28, 76.)

Document 10, April 15, 1751 [22, 157]

"Prot. 2.0 pag. 56. Da una lista di spese fatto l'anno 1751."

Per far accomodare il Mosaico di marmo sotto il primo volto a Cornu Epistole il pr.o quadro vicino alla pr.a collonna [Zone I, Side A?] in gesso . . . per giornate due baj. 50 . . .

(Transcribed from "Raccolta," p. 20. Unpublished.)

Document 11, August 21, 1765 [22, 142, 157]

Idem (Prot. 2.0).

Dati al sig. Scaramello Campanaro per aver impresso su la Croce di metallo posto nel colmo del Battistero alla parte oposta questa iscrizione–Baptisterii hujus Tectum ex integro refectum fuit Anno Domini MDCCLXV–e per aver fatto l'agiunta al piombo posto sotto della Croce per diffesa del colmo di esso tetto in tutto s. 2:05.

(Transcribed from "Raccolta," p. 21. Unpublished.)

Document 12 (ca. 1780) [23, 26, 157; 3.15, 3.20]

From an inventory by the rector Giulio Varneri.

Ingresso antico   . . . si entrava in Chiesa [the Baptistery] per una porticina (o piccola porta) posta nella Nicchia dell'Altare a Cornu Evangelii e

Ingresso nuovo   per essere il piano del cortile più alto di quello della Chiesa si discendeva tre gradini, e metteva all'aperto del cortile e per molti inconvenienti che questa porta portava fu chiusa dal Varneri nel 1767 e in essa si aprì una finestra per dar lume all'Altare, dandosi l'ingresso dalla nuova Porta che si aprì nel mezzo all'arco attiguo all'altare a cornu Epistole . . . [In the process, the architrave of an older door was found, and was used as threshold for the new door.]

[Every year at Holy Sabbath] si vuotava e si riempiva [the font] di acqua per la benedizione e si scaricava l'acqua precedente nel Sacrario. [This Sacrario] era . . . contiguo alla prima colonna a mano sinistra entrando dalla porta Maggiore e si engeva sul suolo de Batt.o due piedi e mezzo a forma di catino terminanto con un marmo rettangolare a forma di catino incavato con in mezzo un foro, e si chiudeva con un coperchio a chiava. [Thus the Sacrario formed a well within the Baptistery, and the water in it gradually sank into the foundations damaging them.] Nel 1775 fu finalmente il Battistero liberato affatto dalla passiva servitù delle accennate acque. [For within the large font was put a new one] a forma di urna di sasso d'Istria, coperta di legno a forma di tomba . . .

Anche in q. anno (1775) si alzò l'architrave della Porta del Battistero che acquistò maggior luce . . . [The architrave was taken down and stabilized with iron clamps.] . . . si assicurò il muro di facciata con tirar un arco assai superiore allo stesso architrave (di scarico) ma appena che fu posto a terra l'architrave li due muri laterali della porta caddero a terra e si aprì tutta la facciata e questo disordine portò che si alzò la porta quanto si potè e la si mise in mezzo mentre prima era molto bassa, e piegava a destra di chi entrava. Ciò si eseguì colla direzione del Morigia, che pur pensò di aggiungere qualche adornamento alla stessa porta (gli stipiti o piedritti di marmo) . . .

Una volta non vi era certamente alcun altare nel Battistero . . . [but only the four niches]. Una [of the niches] fu tolta di mezzo nell'aprire la strada che ora abbiamo in faccia al Battesimo, l'altra probabilmente cadde per l'ingiuria dei tempi . . .

(Transcribed from "Raccolta," pp. 21 ff. Unpublished.)

Document 13, June 13, 1781 [23, 157]

Idem (Prot. 2.0).

. . . a Fabro Santini per spesa fatta in Chiesa per stringere li archi e rinnovarne uno, aprir due finestre e rifare il tetto del piccolo Battistero (Nicchia a Nord) . . .

(Transcribed from "Raccolta," p. 21. Unpublished.)

Document 14, June 8, 1785 [24]

[Source?]

8 giugno 1785, pagati al pittore Pietro Brandolini che dipinse a olio tutti li 8 pennacchi a musaico, le due nicchie a fresco e che ritoccò altre cose, ecc. Scudi 24.

(Published by Gerola in *Atti per la Romagna*, 4.7 [1917], 140. Quoted by Ricci, *Tavole*, 2, 14.)

Document 15, July 10, 1785 [23, 38, 75, 140, 141, 143, 165; 3.32]

"Inventario di Giulio Varneri."

In questo Battistero vi è un sol Altare di Marmo fatto da me engere [ingerire ?] secondo il pensiere del Nobil. sig. Cammillo Morigia dentro la Nicchia a mano destra (est), ed ha il lume da una finestra che guarda il cortile e prima era Porta, per cui dalla Canonica si aveva ingresso in Chiesa per ogni Funzione. Nell'altra Nicchia (allora eran due solo) vi è collocato sopra antichissimo Capitello di greco che forma piedestallo un vaso di Marmo Pario . . . In detto [Beltrami, *Il Forestiere instruito delle cose notabili della città di Ravenna* (Ravenna, 1783), p. 31] è scritto che tal vaso servì per urna ceneraria; ma osservato diligentemente nel 1784 dal P. Lodovico Pattuzzi Scolopio, fu di opinione che anzi ad uso servisse di purificazione . . . e perchè osservò in esso Vaso a basso rilievo sotto li suoi due Braccietti l'Aquila sedente, arguì che nel Tempio di Giove avesse luogo . . . [The *putti* and the arrows allude to matrimonial purification.] . . . e notò che quando avesse docuto servire per urna ceneraria, non dovevano li Bracetti piegare sul labro del vaso, anzi lasciarlo libero, onde portarne il copritorne; che ne sia di ciò, a me basta lasciarne di questo erudito Padre il pensamento.

[Describes the font.] Nell'anno 1775 feci intromettere nella predetta vasca l'altra piccola colla direzione del prefato sig. Cammillo, che resta chiusa con ben inteso copritore dipinto a marmo (porfido) portante sulla sommità un Agnello, entro cui si custodiscono i Sacri Olii ed il Sale Benedetto in vasetti d'argento da me rinnovati, e dal quel anno si levò dal Battistero la dannosa servitù di ricevere in ogni rinnovazione del Fonte la gran coppia d'acqua che scaniavasi [scan-savasi ?] dalla Vasca nel Sacrario vicino allora al Confessionale (a sinistra en-trando) e che poi perdendosi entro il corpo stesso della Chiesa rendeva tutto l'anno umidissimo il pavimento.

[There were originally two other niches at the Baptistery;] e se una [Niche A] fu tagliata nell'aprirsi la nuova strada detta del Battesimo, l'altra [Niche B] ruinò pregiudicata dal Cemeterio, che gli fu anticam.e costrutto vicino; qual Cemeterio era circondato da muri e per essere di fondo più alto assai del piano dello stesso Battistero, tante e tante volte vi scaricò le sue acqua, e non si sa spie-gare il pregiudizio e danno. [So he begs Archbishop Cantonio to open a new cemetery] sotto l'Atrio della Metropolitana. [This is done in 1781: see *Protoc. 2.o C.131.*]

Prot 2   [After the earthquake of 1781] si apriron quindi tre nuove finestre,
C 126:   chiuse, e chi sa da quanto tempo, si puliron le colonne che reggon
la Cupola, o sià Catino, ritrovate intonacate di gesso; si rilevarono le sedici figure a basso rilievo rappresentanti li dodici Maggiori e quattro Minori Profeti [a marginal note corrects this to read "li 12 minore e 4 magg."]; si riformarono le otto Penacchi; si rinnovarono li banconi, che si vedevano appogiati ai muri,
Prot 2   e si munì con Balaustra di noce la Nicchia dell'Altare; e molto
C 61   prima pensai di alzare la Porta del Battisterio assai bassa, a co-
e seg: struire nuovo Sacrario, e a render più decente il Confessionale . . .

Per dar corso felice alle acque e condurle alla chiavica esistente su la strada Morigia, furono obbligati [i Sigg. Deputati alle strade] di abbassar lo stradello del Battistero a qualche profondità; ed in occasione di questo abbassamento si trovò che porzione di questa casa ha per fondamento antico un muro in ghiarra e nello spurgo del cimitero su accenato e molto più nello scavo di cui ora parlo, si sono incontrati più muri antichissimi pure in ghiarra che attraversando il Cemeterio sudd.o andavano a finire col muro laterale della Metropolitana; quali avanzi di sepolta antichità danno a vedere, che dalla Metropolitana si passava al Battisterio con andito coperto, e che contiguo al Medesimo Battisterio erano fabbriche di qualche sua attinenza.

Si ha gran parte di questo Edifizio sotto terra; basta dire che nell'aprirmi l'ingresso colla porticella laterale al livello del piano del Battistero ritrovai l'Architrave di una porta ben capace formato di grossi e gran pradoni [?], anzi mi approfitai di alcuni e per la soglia del ingresso sudd.o e pel primo gradino della nuova scala; e nel demolire il vecchio Altare scoprì finestra antica, entra la quale collocai la sacra Pietra di cui parlo al Protoc. 2.o c. 141. Ciò sia detto per dar pascolo agli Antiquarii.

(Transcribed from "Raccolta," pp. 15 ff. Last part published by Sangiorgi, *Battistero*, p. 139, where the inventory is dated [mistakenly ?] 1783; and following him by Casalone, "Ricerche," p. 260 n. 20, and by A. Ghezzo in *FR, 86* [1962], 17. The originals of this and other inventories of the Baptistery are preserved in the Archivio Arcivescovile, in "Inventaria Paroch. Urbis et Suburb.," 2, folios 232–58. The reference to the "Sacra Pietra" found within Niche B, according to the last sentence of the document, reads as follows in the source cited by Varneri: "La pietra sacra si fece collocare entro il piccolo finestrino che si vede di dietro all'Altare, qual finestrino, sebbene si creda aperto dei secoli dopo la Fabbrica del Battistero, ciò non ostante ci fa conoscere quanto ne resti sepolta di questa Fabbrica dagli oltremontani specialmente stimata tanto e lodata" [Sangiorgi, *Battistero*, p. 46]).

Document 16, December 17, 1785 [24]

"Memorie storiche di Ravenna." In the Biblioteca Classense (MS Mob 31 N. no. 25).

D. GIULIO FRANC. MIO AMATISSIMO.

Non potendo il Governatore di Ancona ricevere alla sua Anticamera una Visita più gradita fra le tante che ne' presenti giorni si vedono comparire per sola formalità, quanto la Vostra . . . Non si perda dunque il prezzo dell'Opera, e giacchè con tanto lodevole impegno avete intrappreso il Restauro della preziosa sagra antichità di Codesto Battisterio colla generosa scorta fattavi dai Degni Cavalieri, che mi nominate, jo mi unisco a secondarla, colla promessa, che fin da ora vi assicuro di scudi 15, de' quali potrete far Capitale a tempo opportuno, giacchè presentemente sono un po' sfornito di denaro e Carico di Spese . . .

Vostro Servitore
DESIDERIO SPRETI

(Published in its entirety by Ricci, "S. Giovanni," p. 306.)

Document 17, May 13, 1788 [24, 141, 157]

"Inventario 13 Magg. 1788."

Una quota di scudi 50 fu data dai nob. Patr. Sign. Conti ed Abbati Luigi Sette Castelli, ed Agostino del Sale perchè fossero dal Varneri Priore di S. Gio. in Fonte impiegati a pulire il Musaico del Catino del Battistero, onde si uniformasse alli otto Pennacchi, quali furon si ben ridotti dal pittore Sig.r Pietro Brandolini . . . Il lavoro dei Pennacchi fu eseguito circa l'anno 1785.

Nel 1785 terminate da me (Varneri) l'Altare (di marmo presente) e ridotto in det.o anno a qualche pulitezza il Battisterio sud.to.

(Transcribed from "Raccolta," p. 19. Unpublished.)

Document 18, March 26, 1791 [24, 157]

"Inventario della 3.a Visita 26 Marzo 1791," p. 20.

Nel 1791 scrive il Varneri che . . . il ristauro fu affidato dal medesimo (Mr. Arcivescovo) al Can.co Giuseppe Lovatelli . . . così che dopo la festa del S. Precursore si pianterà l'armatura, e immediatamente si darà mano al sud. ristauro [of the cupola mosaics].

(Transcribed from "Raccolta," p. 20. Unpublished.)

Document 19, December 31, 1791 [24]

"Memorie storiche di Ravenna." In the Biblioteca Classense (MS Mob 31 N. no. 25).

Signor Paroco mio Amatissimo.

Sono sensibile e grato al cortese augurio di felicità natalizie, ch'Ella si è compiacciuto avvanzarmi . . . e per quello riguarda il ristauro del Cattino, Ella può intendersela con il Signor Canonico Lovatelli, il quale ha la necessaria ed opportuna intelligenza. Intanto sono perfettamente suo . . . [etc.]

Desiderio Spreti

Below the letter this postscript was added later:

Li 26 maggio 1792.
Dal Nob. Sig. Canonico Giusepe Lovatelli ho ricevuto io infrascritto scudi quindici, che Monsignor Ill.mo e Rev.mo Desiderio Spreti offrì nel ristauro del Cattino di questo nostro antichissimo Battistero fino dalli 17 Dicembre 1785 essendo allora il Prelato Governatore in Ancona—D. Giulio Francesco Varneri.

(Quoted by Ricci, "S. Giovanni," p. 307.)

Document 20, June 3, 1792 [24]

Letter of the painter Brandolini. [Source?]

Ravenna, 3 giugno 1792.

Dal signor Don Giulio Varneri Priore della Chiesa Parrocchiale di S. Giambattista ricevo scudi ottanta e questi per aver accomodata la volta della sua chiesa ed avere imitato il mosaico, e lavori di Essa, con avervi posto, del mio, oglio e colori, ed avere ridotto il vecchio Mosaico, quasi nuovo, come osservasi al presente, in fede di che dico scudi 80 obbligandomi di fare il resto con vero discreto emolumento.

(Published by Gerola in *Atti per la Romagna*, 4.7 [1917], 140, from which it is transcribed here. Published also by Ricci, *Tavole*, 2, 16–17.)

Document 21, 1792 [24, 157]

Inventory of Varneri in "Bona patrimonia," 2, 64.

Laus Deo, anno Domini 1792. A compimento del ristauro di questo battistero inalzato da S. Orso nostro arcivescovo . . . desideravasi riattare il cattino e mosaico, lavoro di cui ne fu autore Neone . . .

La spesa non è indifferente. La sola armatura non poteasi veder all'ordine che non sc. 50, somma esibitasi dal nob. signor Camillo Morigia, nostro celebre architetto, ed uno de' più discreti de' nostri capi muratori: trattavasi di doversi impegnare gran legname a lungo tempo e a troncarne per rendere detta armatura in tutte le sue parti comoda al pittore. Ed il pittore Pietro Brandolini non voleva meno di sc. 90.

Doveva egli non solamente pulire il vecchio musaico, coperto di oscura pattina, ma con scelti colori a olio accompagnarlo, comprendo tante e tante magagne e richiamando alla prima idea tanti e tanti pezzi o smarriti affatto o di molto pregiudicati, fors'anche da goccie d'acqua che dal tetto cadero sul volto o non avvertite o trascurate.

Il signor don Francesco Beltrami, ora priore di S. Adalberto, ch'era cappellano di questa chiesa a quel tempo in cui maneggiavasi questo trattamento, si adoperò co' nobili patrizi sign. conti ed abati Luigi Settecastelli e Agostino Del Sale, che offrirono sc. 50, immediatamente da me deposati nel Sacro monte. Passò però la cosa in silenzio per qualche anno, quando mi venne il pensiero di scriverne a mons. Desiderio Spreti, allora governatore di Ancona, in oggi presidente della Reverenda Camera. [Cf. Document 16.] Proposi anche alle nobildonne signora contessa Angelica Lovatelli vedova Ginanni e signora Antonia Fusconi il sospeso trattato e assicurai quasi intero l'emolumento pel pittore; quindi, dependendo questi dal nobile signor canonico Giuseppe Lovatelli, cimiliarca nella nostra metropolitana, lo pregai stringere il contratto, ed essendo portatissimo per la conservazione delle nostre sacre antichità, non solo abbracciò volentieri l'impegno, ma supplì anche al contante, da lui accordato col pittore, che fu in tutto di sc. 80.

Restava da stabilirsi la spesa dell'armatura; ma appena ne resi inteso il degnissimo nostro prelato mons. Antonio Codronchi, che si offrì avendo nei suoi magazeni abbondanza di legnami, piantarla a sue spese e a sue spese ancora impegnare un diligente e paziente muratore che rimboccasse con buona matteria le accennate magagne e stringesse que' pezzi che stavano per distaccarsi: non era di fatti infrequente il raccogliersi pietruccie cadute dal vecchio musaico nello scopparsi il battistero.

Sul fine di luglio 1791 fu formata per ordine di mons. arcivescovo detta armatura e per vari giorni travagliò il muratore per acconciare le già ennunciate magagne: il pittore poi il 16 agosto diede principio all'opera.

Aveva questi già abbracciati altri lavori prima del nostro accordo e dall'altra parte servendo le abazie de' canonici Lateranesi di S. Salvatore e de' monaci Camaldolesi, fu più volte e per settimane e settimane distratto dai rispettivi superiori, cosicchè non si vidde il fine del tanto sospirato ristauro che nel giorno 26 maggio anno corrente 1792, avendovi impiegate da 60 giornate da me notate giorno per giorno e venendo al lavoro a colori già preparati in sua casa e instancabile sull'opera sempre dal buono mattino al mezzodì e per quattro ore il dopopranzo.

Scopertosi questo ristauro, tolta in mezzo l'armatura, fu frequentissimo il concorso del popolo per osservarlo e universalmente fu applaudita la fatica del Brandolini, che seppe sì esattamente accompagnare il vecchio lavoro, che distinguendosi di fatti questo dalle tante aggiunte col pratico suo pennello su tal fare, mentre allorchè li monaci di S. Vitale fecero ristorare il lor mosaico del coro, il nostro Brandolini chiamato dal celebre signor Barozzi, che dipinse la cupola di quel insigne chiesa, a travagliare su detto mosaico, soddisfece pienamente e con sua lode alle premure dello stesso signor Barozzi che all'aspettativa dei monaci.

Viddi perciò compita anche quest'opera a spese della Divina provvidenza, cui laus et gloria in saecula saeculorum amen.

D. Giulio Francesco Varneri priore.

(Published by Gerola in *Atti per la Romagna, 4.7* [1917], 140–42.)

Document 22, August 26, 1793 [24, 157]

"Bona patrimonia," 2, 63.

. . . pagati al Signor Pietro Brandolini, che ritoccò tutto l'ordine di sotto piano del Battistero, che dopo li [?] Giugl. 1793, in cui dipinset come c. 63. t.o ave.a patito in ogni parte, tolti le pennacchi, e nel qual lavoro impiego pei giorni, lavorando ogni dì da ora dieci per ogni giorno 8 S:

(Unpublished.)

Document 23, 1895 [23, 157]

Note added by an unknown writer to "Raccolta," p. 26.

Il Commend. Faccioli Dirett. Regionale pei Monumenti nel 1895 rimosse dalla porta del Batt.ro due grossi gradini di marmo pei quali all'esterno si ascendeva e all'interno si discendeva. Erano stati questi messi dal Prior Varneri per impedire le acque che affluivano in troppa quantità, che non entrassero nel Battistero; aveva anche egli pensato di levare quella deformità nel 1793, ma per la detta ragione non pote farlo.

(Unpublished.)

BIBLIOGRAPHICAL NOTE

The following is a descriptive bibliography of the Orthodox Baptistery to date, including books, articles, newspaper excerpts, and unpublished manuscripts. It is selective only so far as it does not include routine descriptions of the monument in handbooks and guides; otherwise even brief comments in works of a general nature are noted. To list the many entries alphabetically by author's name would be less useful, in my opinion, than grouping them around subject headings which would correspond roughly with the organization of this book.

1. HISTORY

The earliest document is the ninth-century description of the Baptistery in Agnellus' "Life of Bishop Neon" in the Codex Pontificalis Ecclesiae Ravennatis; (see above, p. 11). For commentary on the description, see Testi-Rasponi's edition of Agnellus (*Codex*), pp. 77–78; and H. L. Gonin, *Excerpta agnelliana* (Utrecht [1933]), pp. 67–68.

Documents pertaining to early restorations are collected mainly in:

(1) "Raccolta da una miscellanea del Battistero," MS at the Biblioteca Classense of Ravenna, n.d.; a compilation of transcribed documents from the sixteenth century to 1895. See Documents 3–7, 9–13, 15, 17, 18, 23 in Appendix 2. See also Chap. 2, n. 2.

(2) "Bona patrimonia ecclesiae sancti Johannis in Fonte," MS at the rectory; a compilation of expense accounts, inventories, and similar documents. See Documents 21, 22 in Appendix 2.

(3) "Varia ad ecclesiam sancti Johannis in Fonte spectantia," MS at the rectory; a compilation of documents and pamphlets. See Documents 2, 8 in Appendix 2.

See also M. Fantuzzi, *Monumenti ravennati de' secoli di mezzo per la maggior parte inediti* (Venice, 1801–04); a compilation of medieval documents, some of which (vol. 2, p. 340; *4*, 380; *6*, 103, 237) contain passing references to the Baptistery.

For the restorations of the second half of the nineteenth century, the article by G. Gerola, "La tecnica dei restauri ai mosaici di Ravenna," *Atti per la Romagna, 4.7* (1917), 101–94, is essential. Reports contemporary with the restorations are the following:

(1) News items in *L'Adriatico, giornale delle Romagne, 2* (Jan. 18, 22, 1861); concerning the renovation of the arcade of Zone II.

(2) *Diario di Ravenna per l'anno 1863* (Ravenna, 1862), p. 93; item concerning the restoration of the mosaics in the arch soffits of Zone II.

(3) News items in *Il Ravennate, 20* (March 17, 1883); and *24* (Aug. 24, 1887).

(4) P. Sulfrini, "Miscellanea di cose spettante a Ravenna," MS in the possession of Monsignor Mario Mazzotti, n.d. Contains entries from 1860 to 1903. For the Baptistery note entries no. 48 (see Chap. 2, n. 62 above), no. 67 (on the nineteenth-century rectory abutting on the Baptistery), no. 468 (on the various pavements), and no. 479 (on an antique inscription found during Lanciani's excavations, and reburied; see above, p. 143).

(5) O. Gardella and R. Faccioli, *L'Atterramento di una parte dell'ardica della Basilica Classense di Ravenna* (Ravenna, 1890), pp. 18, 42, where the modern painting of the stuccoes of Zone II is severely criticized.

(6) O. Gardella, "Ancora del Battistero," *Il Faro romagnolo* (Ravenna, Oct. 24, 27, 1897); heated criticism of the restoration of the opus sectile by the Reale Opificio delle Pietre Dure in Firenze (cf. p. 28 above).

(7) C. Ricci, *Ravenna e i lavori fatti dalla sovrintendenza dei monumenti nel 1898* (Bergamo, 1899), p. 35; notes the restoration of the opus sectile and the painting of the stuccoes.

The controversy over the project of the "rialzamento" (see above, pp. 26–27) can be followed in these contemporary reports:

(1) Items in *Il Ravennate.* Editorial entitled "L'innalzamento del Battistero," in support of Lanciani's project (May 5, 1876); commentary entitled "Osservazioni intorno al progetto d'isolamento e innalzamento del Battistero di Ravenna," against the project (June 2, 1876); responding editorial, "Una polemica devoluta" (June 6, 1876); news items (March 8, 10, 1876).

(2) "Sollevamento dell'antico Battistero di Ravenna," *Monitore delle Romagne, 3* (Feb. 5, 1876); unsigned commentary.

(3) Editorial in *The Architect, 23* (1880), 365–66; see above, p. 27.

(4) Letter to the editor in *The London Times* (April 23, 1880).

(5) Unsigned commentary in *Il Secolo* (March 19, 20, 1883).

(6) C. Ricci, "Ristauri e ristauratori," *Fanfulla della Domenica, 5* (Nov. 18, 1883); against the project.

For the twentieth century we have the following notices:

(1) An editorial in *Il Risveglio, 4* (Dec. 28, 1907), proposes the demolition of remaining structures around the Baptistery.

(2) C. Ricci (ed.), "L'arte e la guerra. Protezioni dei monumenti. Ravenna: Battistero," *Bolletino d'arte 11–12* (1917–18), 265–69; describes measures taken to protect the monument during World War I. See above, p. 29.

(3) For the last major restoration of the mosaics (see above, pp. 29–30) the crucial account is by C. Calzecchi, C. Capezzuoli, L. Becherucci, and C. Gnudi, "Cronaca dei ritrovamenti e dei ristauri," *Le Arti, 1* (1938–39), 531–46. The progress of the restoration is reported in "Notiziario: Monumenti e scavi." *FR, 46* (1938), 63–64.

(4) The damage to the roof of the Baptistery during a bombardment on August 25, 1944, is reported in C. Capezzuoli, "Danni di guerra ai monumenti di Ravenna e restauri compiutivi," *FR, 52* (1950), 73.

2. ARCHAEOLOGY

The only excavations in and around the Baptistery (see above, pp. 13, 26, 36–37) were published, briefly and unsatisfactorily, by their director F. Lanciani in *Cenni intorno ai monumenti e alle cose più notabili di Ravenna* (Ravenna, 1871), pp. 7–8; and "Scoperte degli edifici cristiani di Ravenna: Battistero della Basilica Ursiana," *BAC, 4* (1866), 73, with a ground plan of the excavated area. For unpublished drawings, see my *Figs.* 20–25, and Chap. 3, n. 14. Seemingly independently of his finds, G. Berti, *Sull'Antico Duomo di Ravenna e il battistero e l'episcopio e il Tricolo* (Ravenna, 1880), pp. 47–55, proposed the theory of a connecting portico between the Baptistery and the Basilica Ursiana (see above, pp. 37–39 and Chap. 3, n. 23). The presence of an external ambulatory (see above, p. 39 and Chap. 3, n. 28) is discussed best by S. Bottari, "Il Battistero della Cattedrale di Ravenna," *Corsi* (1960), fasc. 2, 7–12.

3. MONOGRAPHS

There have been four. The oldest, C. Ricci's article "Il Battistero di S. Giovanni in Fonte," *Atti per la Romagna, 3.7* (1888–89), 268–319, is notable only for proposing that the Baptistery was originally a unit in a Roman bath complex (see above, pp. 12–17); in other respects it is negligible. An early summary of the article is given by F. X. Kraus in *Repertorium für Kunstwissenschaft, 17* (1894), 56.

C. Sangiorgi, *Il Battistero della Basilica Ursiana di Ravenna* (Ravenna, 1900), is descriptive and impressionistic; it is the first study to make generous use of unpublished documents, and useful also as an eye-witness account of contemporary restorations. A summary of the book appeared some years earlier in serial form in the Ravennate paper Corriere di Romagna ("Ancora del Battistero di Ravenna," Dec. 16, 1897; April 21–23, 27, 1898).

The two other monographs are recent. C. Casalone's article, "Ricerche sul Battistero della Cattedrale di Ravenna," *Rivista dell'Istituto nazionale d'archeologia e storia dell'arte, 8* (1959), 202–68, a perceptive and sympathetic study, is flawed by inaccuracies and some uncritical hypotheses; see above, pp. 5, 19, 39, 97 and Chap. 3, n. 30; 4, n. 155; 5, n. 13. A. Ghezzo's monograph ("Il Battistero degli Ortodossi di Ravenna, problemi ed aspetti architettonico-strutturali e decorativi," *FR, 86* [1962], 5–73) adds nothing to previous scholarship and is not a very discerning summary at that.

4. DESCRIPTIONS

The following descriptions are of interest because of their antiquity:

(1) *Hieronymi Rubei historiarum ravennatum libri* (Venice, 1589), p. 110. See above, p. 21.

(2) G. Fabri, *Le Sagre Memorie di Ravenna antica* (Venice, 1664), p. 214 (see above, p. 18); also idem, *Ravenna ricercata o vero compendio istorico delle cose più notabili dell'antica città di Ravenna* (Bologna, 1678), pp. 48–49.

(3) S. Pasolini, *Lustri ravennati dall'anno seicento doppo l'Universal Diluvio fino all'anno mille di Nostra Salute* (Bologna, 1678), pp. 124–25; important for a statement about the form of the Neonian inscription (see above, p. 17).

(4) G. G. Ciampini, *Vetera monimenta in quibus praecipuè musiva opera sacrarum* (Rome, 1690–99), pp. 178, 233–38. See above, p. 10.

(5) A. Zirardini, *De antiquis sacris Ravennae aedificiis liber posthumus* (Ravenna, 1908–09; original ed. Faenza, 1726), p. 21.

(6) G. L. Amadesi, *Metropolitana di Ravenna* (Bologna, 1748), pp. xviii–xix.

(7) F. Beltrami, *Il Forestiere instruito delle cose notabili della città di Ravenna e suburbane della medesima* (Ravenna, 1783), pp. 30–31. See above, pp. 19–20.

(8) B. Fiandrini, "Annali ravennati dalla fondazione della città fino alla fine del secolo XVIII" (Ravenna, 1794), MS in the Biblioteca Classense, 2, 264–66, section entitled "S. Giovanni in Fonte o Battesimo."

(9) G. Ribuffi, *Guida di Ravenna* (Ravenna, 1835), pp. 24–27.

(10) A. Tarlazzi, *Memorie sacre di Ravenna* (Ravenna, 1852), pp. 256–60.

G. Bard, *Dei Monumenti d'architettura bizantina in Ravenna* (Ravenna, 1844), pp. 26–27, is important for recording the niche inscriptions before their restoration by Kibel and Garrucci (see above, pp. 58–61); S. Busmanti, *Guida breve per Ravenna antica e moderna* (Ravenna, 1883), pp. 93–94, for mentioning the destruction of the stuccocs in the lunettes of the Zone II arcade. A good general description of the monument is that in F. Cabrol and H. Leclercq, *Dictionnaire d'archéologie chrétienne et de liturgie*, 2 (Paris, 1910), cols. 426–29 and Figs. 1337, 1347 (mislabeled). A good detailed description of the mosaics is in M. van Berchem and E. Clouzot, *Mosaïques chrétiennes du IVme au Xme siècle* (Geneva, 1924), pp. 97–102; and more recently the enthusiastic account by S. Bettini, "Ravenna: Battistero della Cattedrale," *Scuola italiana moderna* (Brescia, Feb. 19, 1938).

5. ILLUSTRATION

Earliest are the engravings in Ciampini, *Vetera monimenta* (see above, p. 22); and a very poor engraving of the interior in an undated edition of Fabri's *Ravenna ricercata,* probably ca. 1707, by Vincenzo Coronelli (see above, p. 10). Ribuffi, (9) above, contains a ground plan which includes the old rectory abutting on the Baptistery (see above, p. 22). Other early prints are in A. F. von Quast, *Die altchristliche Bauwerke von Ravenna vom fünften bis zum neunten Jahrhundert* (Berlin, 1842), Pl. I; L. Canina, *Ricerche sull'architettura più propria dei tempij cristiani* (Rome, 1846), Pl. 104; M. E. Isabelle, *Les Édifices circulaires et les domes classés par ordre chronologique* (Paris, 1855), Pl. 42, from which the ground plan is reproduced in Cabrol-Leclercq, *Dictionnaire d'archéologie, 2,* Fig. 1337; H. Hübsch, *Monuments de l'architecture chrétienne* (Paris, 1866), Pls. XIII.13 (ground plan), XIII.14 (plan of Zone

II), XV.2 (exterior view), XV.3 (cross section), and XXIX.4–5 (opus sectile); J. R. Rahn, *Ravenna: Eine kunstgeschichtliche Studie* (Leipzig, 1869), Pl. opposite p. 8, which shows the stuccoes of the Zone II lunettes already destroyed (see above, p. 28); F. de Dartein, *Étude sur l'architecture lombarde et sur les origines de l'architecture romano-byzantine* (Paris, 1865–82), Pl. 1; and R. Garrucci, *Storia della arte cristiana nei primi otto secoli della chiesa* (Prato, 1872–81), *4*, Pls. 226–28, and *6*, Pl. 406.1, 406.7. For early ground plans which show the niches as externally polygonal, cf. also Chap. 3, n. 19 above.

By far the most thorough illustration of the Baptistery is in F. W. Deichmann, *Frühchristliche Bauten und Mosaiken von Ravenna* (Baden-Baden, 1958), Pls. 36–95. Also useful are A. Colasanti, *L'Arte bisantina in Italia* (Milan, 1913), Pls. 1–3, 5; and W. F. Volbach and M. Hirmer, *Frühchristliche Kunst. Die Kunst der Spätantike in West- und Ostrom* (Munich, 1958), Pls. 139–43.

The earliest colored illustration of the interior is in H. Köhler, *Polychrome Meisterwerke der monumentalen Kunst in Italien vom V. bis XVI. Jahrhundert* (Leipzig, 1880), Pl. I. For this century, the hand-painted plates in J. Wilpert, *Die römischen Mosaiken und Malereien der kirchlichen Bauten von IV. bis zum XIII. Jahrhundert, 3* (Freiburg, 1916), Pls. 78–82, were the best available until quite recently. They have now been superseded by G. Bovini, *Chiese di Ravenna* (Novara, 1957), Pls. on pp. 46–61; and esp. idem, *Ravenna Mosaics* (New York Graphic Society, 1956), Pls. 6–12.

C. Ricci's *Tavole storiche dei mosaici di Ravenna, II; Il Battistero della Cattedrale* (Rome, 1931), is still indispensable for the Azzaroni–Zampiga plates showing the history of the restorations of the mosaics (see above, p. 29). Note also illustrations of mosaic reproductions of details from Zones III and IV for an exhibition in Paris, in *Musée des monuments français. Mosaïques de Ravenne: Repliques par les mosaïstes de l'Academie de Ravenne* (Paris, 1951), Pls. 2–6.

6. ARCHITECTURE

The single most important study of the building's fabric is still G. Gerola, "L'alzamento e la cupola del Battistero Neoniano," *Atti del reale instituto veneto di scienze, lettere ed arti, 76* (1916–17), 311–21; see above, pp. 39–40. Since then the only analytical description to take into account the import of Gerola's survey has been the recent article by M. Mazzotti, "Il Battistero della Cattedrale di Ravenna, problemi architettonici e vicende del monumento," *Corsi* (1961), pp. 255–78; three of the drawings prepared for this book are published there with the present author's permission. Cf. above, pp. 40–41. Shorter descriptions will be found in O. Mothes, *Die Baukunst des Mittelalters in Italien* (Jena, 1884), pp. 130–32; P. Verzone, *L'Architettura religiosa dell'alto medio evo nell'Italia settentrionale* (Milan, 1942), pp. 75–78; A. De Capitani d'Arzago, *L'Architetture dei secoli quarto e quinto in alta Italia* (Milan, 1944), pp. 44–45, with a ground plan that shows a reconstructed external ambulatory; and A. Khatchatrian, *Les Baptistères paléochrétiens* (Paris, 1962), p. 120 and Fig. 339.

An unpublished thesis by Gino Gamberini on the stages of building ("Il Battistero Neoniano," University of Venice, Scuola Superiore di Architettura, 1956) is in the main unreliable, but has some interest for its reconstruction drawings, three of which have been published by Casalone, "Ricerche," Figs. 2, 3, 9. Cf. Chap. 3, n. 30 above.

The question of the exterior blind arcading (see above, pp. 43–45) is discussed by G. Gerola, "L'architettura deuterobizantina a Ravenna," *Ricordi di Ravenna medioevale per il VI centenario della morte di Dante* (Ravenna, 1921), pp. 82–83; and idem, "Per la datazione dell'architettura deuterobizantina a Ravenna," *FR, 34* (1930), 6, 12. On the date G. Galassi's book, *Architettura protoromanica nell'Esarcato* (*FR* Supplement, *3;* Ravenna, 1928), esp. pp. 74–76, is crucial. A comparable date was suggested earlier by A. Kingsley Porter, *Lombard Architecture, 1* (New Haven, 1915–17), 224. G. T. Rivoira (*Lombardic Architecture, Its Origin, Development and Derivatives,* trans. by Rushforth, *1* [London, 1910], 37–39) and C. Calzecchi ("Sviluppi e influssi dell'architettura ravennate de V e VI secolo in Italia," *FR, 47* [1938], 5–21) both favor a Neonian date. Puig y Cadafalch (*La Géographie et les origines du premier art roman* [Paris, 1935], p. 113) is noncommittal. Cf. also Chap. 3, n. 40 above.

For the structure of the dome C. Capezzuoli's article ("Ravenna: Battistero di Neone. Indagini interessanti, la struttura muraria dell'edificio," *Le Arti, 2* [1940], 393–97) is essential; see above, Chap. 3, n. 5. The system of tubular vaulting is also discussed by P. Verzone, "Le cupole di tubi fittili nel V e VI secolo in Italia," *Atti del I convegno nazionale di storia dell'architettura, 1936* (Florence, 1938), pp. 10–11; and especially G. De Angelis d'Ossat, "Nuovi dati sulle volte costruite con vasi fittili," *Palladio, 5* (1941), 245–49, republished with a few additions in idem, *Studi ravennati: Problemi di architettura paleocristiana* (Faenza, 1962), pp. 137–55. G. Bovini, "L'impiego dei tubi fittili nelle volte degli antichi edifici di culto ravennati," *Corsi* (1959), fasc. 1, pp. 30–34, provides a useful summary of previous scholarship on the subject.

Some interesting remarks on the pulvins of Zone I are found in G. DeAngelis d'Ossat, "L'importanza architettonica del battistero di Fréjus," *Bulletino della commissione archeologica comunale di Roma, 63* (1935), 49–50.

Distant though it is, F. de Dartein's is still the most penetrating formal analysis of the architecture (*Étude sur l'architecture lombarde,* pp. 15–27). Links with sixth-century architecture are considered by H. Sedlmayr, "Zur Geschichte des justinianischen Architektursystems," *BZ, 35* (1935), 55–56; but cf. above, pp. 132–33. Also of some interest is the analysis in H. Koethe, *Der frühchristliche Nischenrundbau* (Marburg, 1928), pp. 23–26.

For the symbolism of the form, see R. Krautheimer, "Introduction to an 'Iconography of Medieval Architecture,'" *Journal of the Warburg and Courtauld Institutes, 5* (1942), 1–33 in general, and particularly the brief remarks on pp. 22–23, 28–29.

7. STUCCOES

Miss Casalone's treatment of the stuccoes of Zone II has been the most detailed ("Ricerche," pp. 246–53; see above, p. 97). Of earlier accounts, A. Melani's is a

confused note claiming that the stuccoes are not entirely original ("Stucchi a Ravenna nel Battistero Ursiano," *Arte e storia, 20* [1901], 53); and E. Tea's, a negligible
attempt to prove that the stuccoes and the mosaics were executed by the same artists
("Gli stucchi del Battistero e un passo di Agnello," *FR, 21* [1916], 939–41; cf. Chap. 5,
n. 12 above). Brief remarks in G. Galassi, "Scultura romana e bizantina," *L'Arte,
17* (1915), 40; A. Haseloff, *Pre-Romanesque Sculpture in Italy* (Florence, 1930), pp.
31–32; and C. Cecchelli, "La decorazione paleocristiana e dell'alto medio evo nelle
chiese d'Italia (Roma esclusa)," *Atti del IV congresso internazionale di archeologia
cristiana, 1938, II,* Studi di antichità cristiana, *19* (Rome, 1948), 185—are all unim-
portant.

8. Iconography

The early general accounts are R. Garrucci, *Storia dell'arte cristiana, 4,* 34–39, no
longer of much use; J. P. Richter, *Die Mosaiken von Ravenna. Beitrag zu einer
kritischen Geschichte der altchristlichen Malerei* (Vienna, 1878; see above, p. 81);
X. Barbier de Montault, "Baptistère de la Cathédrale," *RAC* (1896), pp. 73–86; and
F. Ficker, "Der Bilderschmuck des Baptisterium Ursianum in Ravenna," *Byzantinisch-neugriechische Jahrbuch, 2* (1921), 319–28. The affiliation of the decorative
motifs of the Baptistery to Roman iconography is considered by M. Mesnard,
"L'influence de l'iconographie romaine sur les mosaïques de Ravenne," *RACrist, 5*
(1928), 314–16 (worthless); and G. Bovini, "Rapporti fra l'iconografia romana e
quella ravennate," *Forschungen zur Kunstgeschichte und christlichen Archäologie, 2*
(Baden-Baden, 1953), 80–81.

Specifically: elements of Zone II are discussed by A. Grabar, *L'Empereur dans l'art
byzantin* (Paris, 1936), pp. 237–38, who comments on the imperial iconography of the
scene of Christ trampling the lion and adder; L. De Bruyne, "La décoration des baptistères paléochrétiens," *Miscellanea liturgica in honorem L. Cuniberti Mohlberg, 1*
(Rome, 1948), 212–15, with remarks on the Traditio legis; and O. Mitius, *Jonas auf
den Denkmälern des christlichen Altertums* (Freiburg, 1897), p. 103, with remarks on
the scene of Jonah and the whale. For Zone III, the following are of interest:

(1) Ciampini, *Vetera monimenta,* pp. 178–79, 236; see above, p. 79.

(2) G. B. De Rossi, "Del sarcofago, nella cui fronte e effigiato il monogramma di
Cristo pendente sopra un trono," *BAC,* 2.3 (1872), 137–38, discusses the thrones of
Christ.

(3) S. Beissel, *Geschichte der Evangelienbücher* (Freiburg i.B., 1896), p. 6; note
on the iconography of the open gospels; see above, p. 81.

(4) F. van der Meer, *Maiestas Domini: Théophanies de l'Apocalypse dans l'art
chrétien,* Studi di antichità christiana, *13* (Vatican, 1938), 236, on the thrones of
Christ.

(5) A. Grabar, *Martyrium. Recherches sur le culte des reliques et l'art chrétien
antique, 2* (Paris, 1946), 111–12; important; see above, p. 82.

(6) H. Stern, "Nouvelles recherches sur les images des conciles dans l'église de la
Nativité à Bethléem," *Cahiers, 3–4* (1948–49), 85–86.

(7) E. Dyggve, "Über die freistehende Klerusbank. Beiträge zur Geschichte des Bema," *Beiträge zur älteren europäischen Kulturgeschichte (Festschrift für Rudolf Egger, 1*; Klagenfurt, 1952), 48–49 and Fig. 4; see Chap. 4, n. 90 above.

(8) M. Mazzotti, "Gli altari paleocristiani degli edifici di culto ravennati," *Corsi* (1960), fasc. 2, pp. 237, 239–40.

The crown-bearing apostles of Zone IV are considered briefly by K. Wessel, "Kranzgold und Lebenskrönen," *AA, 65–66* (1950–51), cols. 111–13. Early commentaries on the baptism of Zone V are by C. Rohault de Fleury, *L'Évangile; Études iconographiques et archéologiques* (Tours, 1874), pp. 102–03 and Pl. 32; J. Strzygowski, *Ikonographie der Taufe Christi* (Munich, 1885), pp. 9–11; and J. Ficker, "Sitzunprotocolle: Sitzung am 23. December," *RM, 2* (1887), 296–98, on the original form of the scene.

There have been two recent attempts to find an iconographic unity in the three zones of the cupola scheme. S. Bettini's is the earlier ("Il Battistero della Cattedrale," *FR, 52* [1950], 41–59); see above, p. 90. The newest hypothesis, rejected here, is by C.-O. Nordström, *Ravennastudien. Ideengeschichtliche und ikonographische Untersuchungen über die Mosaiken von Ravenna* (Uppsala, 1953), pp. 32–54; see above, pp. 90–91. A criticism of Nordström's claim that the baptism should be understood as the investiture of Christ was provided by K. Wessel, "Zur Interpretation der Kuppelmosaiken des Baptisterium der Ortodoxen," *Corsi* (1957), fasc. 1, pp. 77–81. The following reviews of Nordström's hypothesis and his general methodology should also be consulted: C. Cecchelli in *FR, 71* (1955), 49–52; L. De Bruyne in *RACrist, 31* (1955), 111–12; F. W. Deichmann in *BZ, 48* (1955), 409–13; A. Grabar in *Cahiers, 8* (1956), 248–53; E. Schäfer in *Zeitschrift für Kirchengeschichte, 66* (1954–55), 172–75; G. de Francovich in *FR, 79* (1959), 147–51.

9. STYLE OF THE MOSAICS

The finest analysis remains that by G. Galassi, *Roma o Bisanzio: I musaici di Ravenna e le origini dell'arte italiana, 1* (2d ed. Rome, 1953), 33–42. Others which contain suggestive or interesting remarks are:

(1) A. J. C. Hare, *Cities of Central Italy, 2* (London, n.d. [ca. 1880]), 21–23; an appreciation signed by "Kugler."

(2) J. A. Crowe and G. B. Cavalcaselle, *Storia della pittura in Italia, 1* (Florence, 1885), 28–30.

(3) J. Kurth, *Die Wandmosaiken von Ravenna* (2d ed. Munich, 1912), pp. 65–81.

(4) P. Toesca, *Storia dell'arte italiana. I. Medioevo* (Turin, 1927), pp. 110–11, 184–87, 256–58.

(5) H. Peirce and R. Tyler, *L'Art byzantin, 1* (Paris, 1932), 84–86, 89.

(6) A. Grabar, *Byzantine Painting* (Skira, 1953), pp. 56–57.

The eastern aspects of the mosaics have been stressed by:

(1) D. Ainaloff, *The Hellenistic Origins of Byzantine Art* (St. Petersburg, 1900, in Russian; now also English ed., trans. by E. and S. Sobolevitch, New Brunswick,

1961), Chap. 3. For a summary of the work, see O. Wulff in *Repertorium für Kunst-wissenschaft, 26* (1903), 35 ff., esp. 49.

(2) E. Bertaux, *L'Art dans l'Italie meridionale* (Paris, 1901), pp. 57–58.

(3) J. Strzygowski, *Altai-Iran und Völkerwanderung* (Leipzig, 1917), pp. 169, 266 (see above, p. 114); the same author's comments on the didacticism of the program (*Origins of Christian Church Art,* trans. O. M. Dalton and H. J. Braunholtz [Oxford, 1923], p. 163) have been evaluated above, p. 89.

(4) C. R. Morey, *Early Christian Art* (2d ed. Princeton, 1953), pp. 157–58.

The Roman-ness of the mosaics is most recently defended by S. Zanella, "I mosaici di Ravenna," *FR, 61* (1953), 12–15. The following authors have tended instead to underline the proto-Byzantine qualities of the mosaic program: see E. K. Redin, *The Mosaics of the Churches of Ravenna* (in Russian; St. Petersburg, 1896), Chap. 1, summarized by E. Dobbert, "Zur Geschichte der altchristlichen und der byzantinischen Kunst," *Repertorium für Kunstwissenschaft, 21* (1898), 95–111, esp. 96–98; C. Diehl, *Ravenne* (Paris, 1907), pp. 33–40; and P. Muratoff, *La Peinture byzantine* (Paris, 1928), pp. 63–64.

The efforts, first, of A. W. Byvanck ("De Mozaieken te Ravenna en het Liber pontificalis ecclesiae ravennatis," *Mededeelingen van het Nederlandsch historisch Instituut te Rome, 8* [1928], 61–82; short summary in *Byzantion, 5* [1929–30], 829) and later of S. Bettini ("Il Battistero della Cattedrale," *FR, 52* [1950], 41–59; short summary in *Fasti archeologici, 5* [1950], no. 5662) to prove that the cupola mosaics are earlier than the episcopate of Neon can no longer be considered valid; see above, pp. 100–01.

On the disposition of the cupola scheme, the following are of interest: O. Demus, *Byzantine Mosaic Decoration* (Boston, 1955), pp. 46–47; C. Mango, *The Brazen House: A Study of the Vestibule of the Imperial Palace at Constantinople,* Arkaeologisk-kunsthistoriske Meddedelser, *4.4* (Copenhagen, 1959), 32–34 (see above, p. 113); and G. de Francovich in *FR, 79* (1959), 147–48.

10. FURNITURE

J. Corblet, "Des lieux de baptême," *RAC, 24* (1877), 143, claims that some columns and the urn in Niche C come from the Temple of Jupiter at Caesarea (cf. Document 15); unconvincing. The altar in Niche B is described by C. Rohault de Fleury, *La Messe; Études archéologiques sur ses monuments* (Paris, 1883–89), p. 137 and Pl. 7; and the font by C. F. Rogers, "Baptism and Christian Archaeology," *Studia biblica et ecclesiastica, 5,* part 4 (Oxford, 1903), 345–46.

INDEX

ILLUSTRATIONS

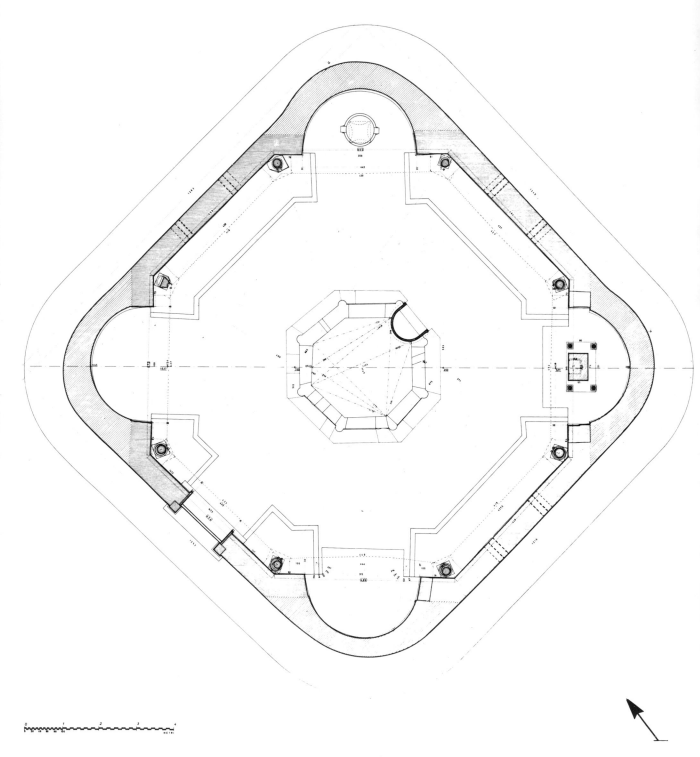

Fig. 1. Ground plan

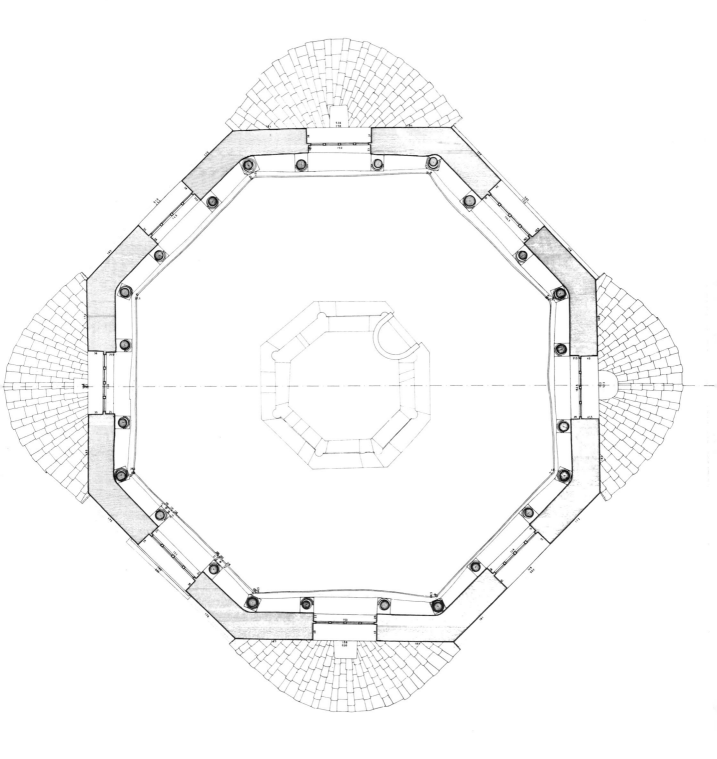

Fig. 2. Plan at the level of Zone II

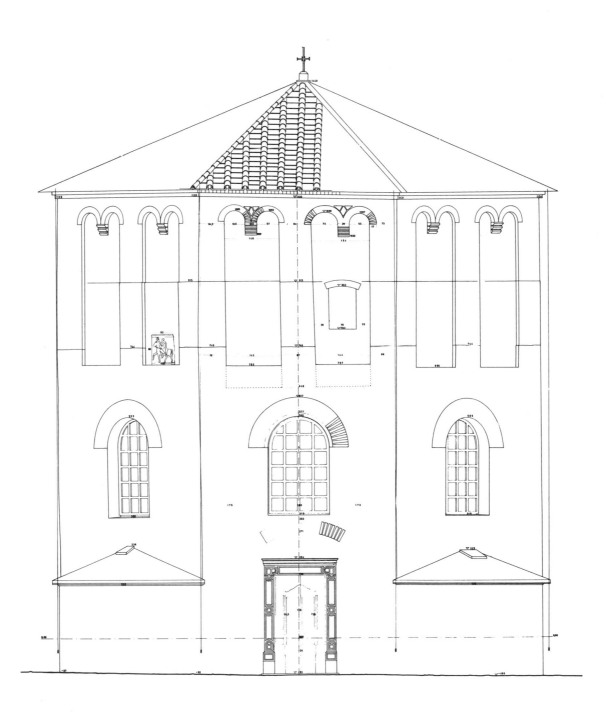

Fig. 3. Elevation: Sides D, D', and A

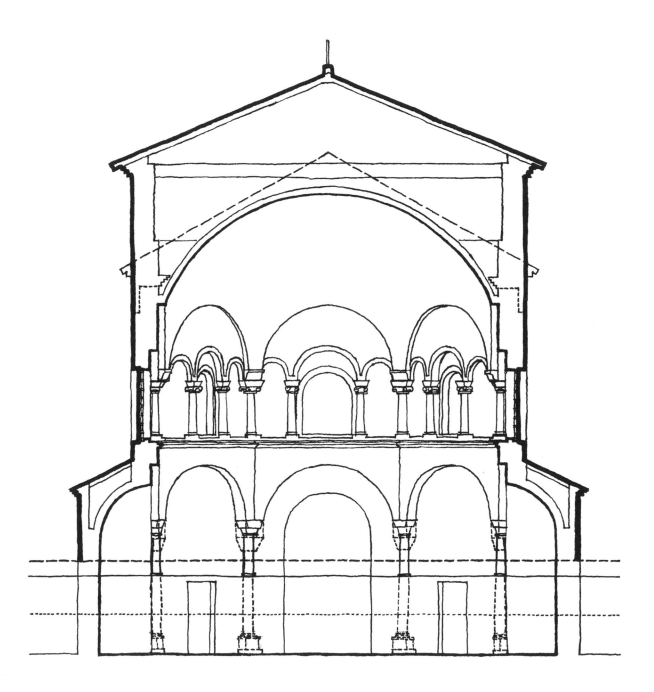

Fig. 8. Interior, tentative reconstruction of the original fifth-century scheme, with the subsequent floor levels

Fig. 9. The Baptistery and surrounding buildings, air view

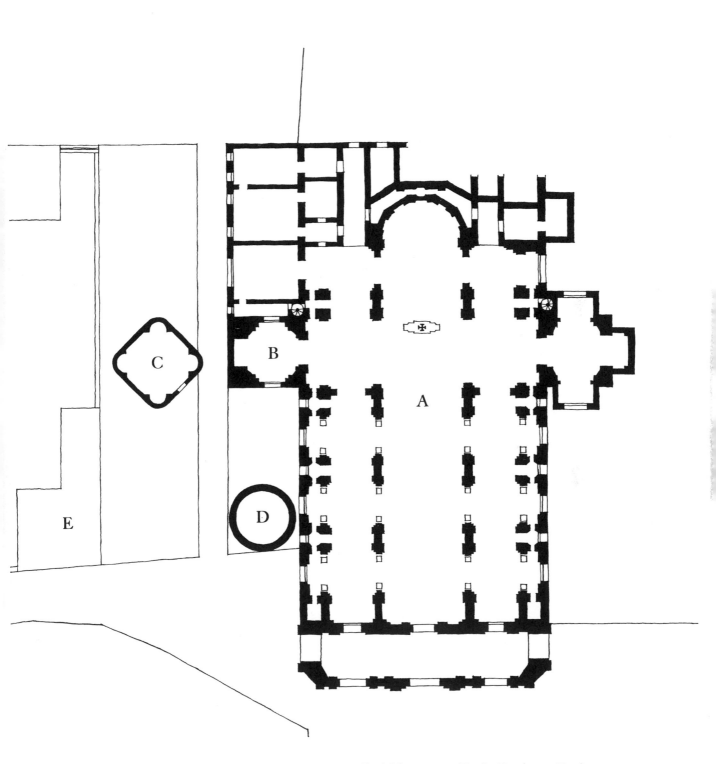

Fig. 10. Site plan with the cathedral (A), the Cappella del Sacramento (B), the Baptistery (C), the medieval campanile (D), and the rectory (E)

Fig. 11. The Baptistery and abutting structures, nineteenth-century view (prior to 1880)

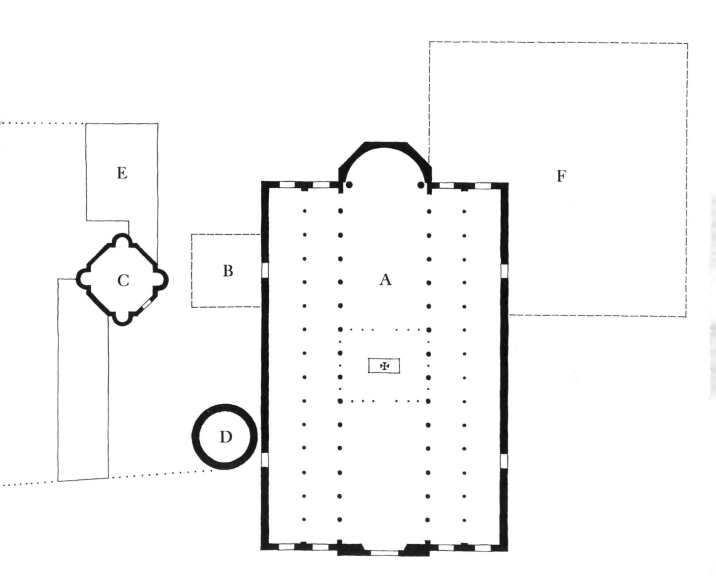

Fig. 12. Site plan before 1750, showing the relation of the Baptistery (C) to the Basilica Ursiana (A) and the old rectory (E). B marks the Cappella del Sacramento, and F the site of the episcopal palace

Fig. 13. Exterior view from the east

Fig. 14. The Baptistery from above

Fig. 15. Exterior, detail of Side B'

Fig. 16. Exterior, detail of Side B showing the masonry of the Lanciani restoration of the 1860s (left) and the restoration of the 1930s (right)

Fig. 17. Detail of the upper masonry, showing the change in mortar between the original structure and the later medieval renovation

Fig. 18. Bounding wall, below ground level, before the restoration of the 1930s

Fig. 19. Bounding wall, below ground level, after the restoration and coating of the 1930s

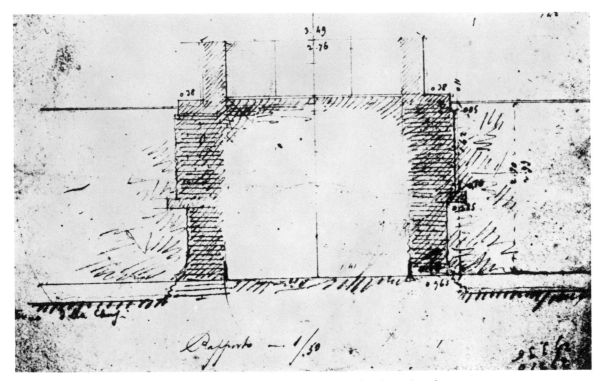

Fig. 20. Drawing from the excavations of F. Lanciani in the 1860s, showing the ancient font

Fig. 21. Drawing from Lanciani's excavations, showing the bases of the antique columns, the arches for the "rialzamento," and the remnants of the ancient font

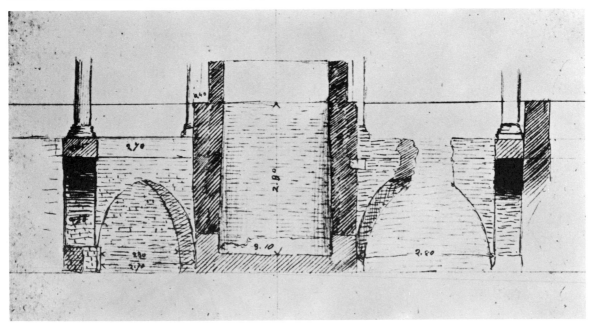

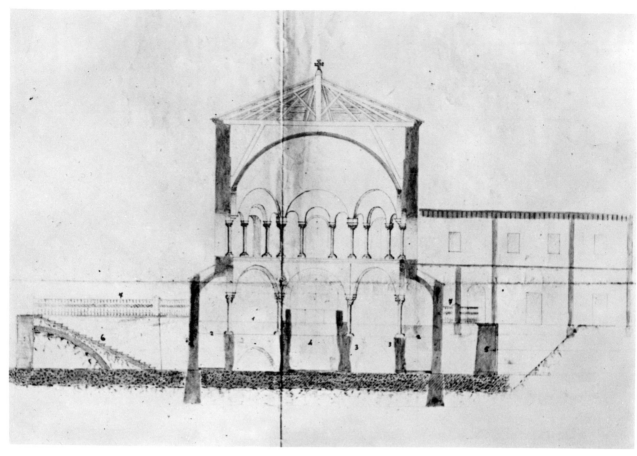

Fig. 22. Sketch for the project of the "rialzamento"

Fig. 23. Plan of the Baptistery site, dating from ca. 1870

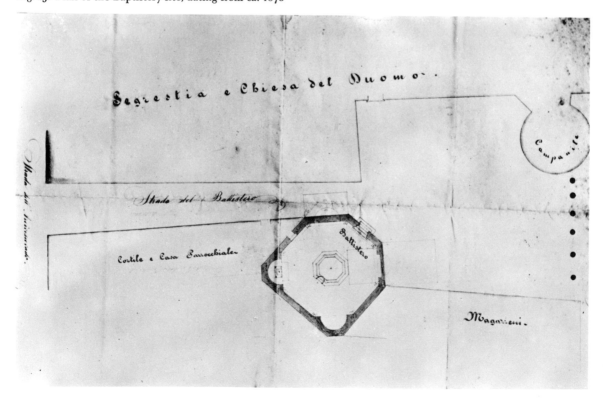

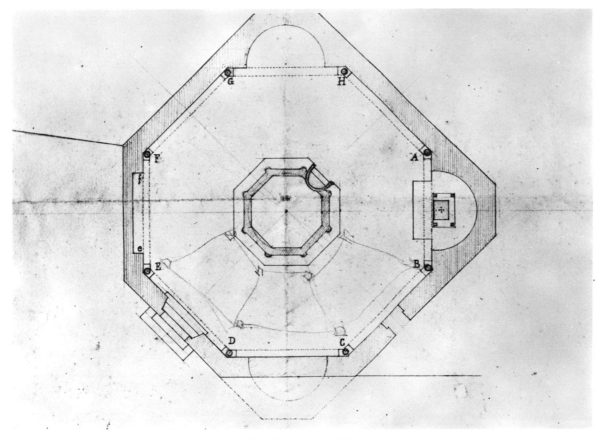

Fig. 24. Sketch by Lanciani (?) for the reconstruction of the corner niches

Fig. 25. Sketches by Lanciani, signed and dated (February 10, 1863), showing the two excavated niches (right), a scheme of reconstruction (left), and a plan of the Baptistery at the level of Zone II

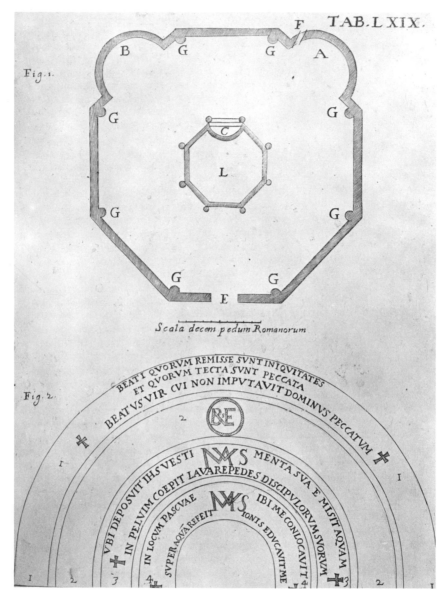

Fig. 26. Ground plan and niche inscriptions of the Baptistery, from the seventeenth century

Fig. 27. Monogram on Niche D (left), compared with two monograms of Archbishop Maximian from the ivory throne in the Museo Arcivescovile (center), and from a pulvin in the same museum (right)

Fig. 28. The cupola: detail of the extrados

Fig. 29. The cupola: detail of the intrados, showing the
change from tubular vaulting to pumice blocks

Fig. 30. The cupola: detail of the intrados (area in
pumice blocks is outlined)

Fig. 31. The cupola: structural detail

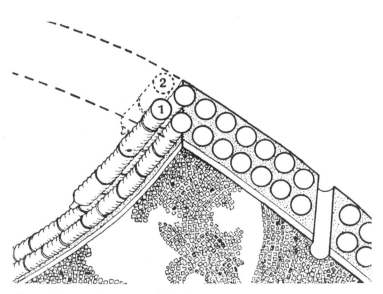

Fig. 32. The cupola: structural drawing

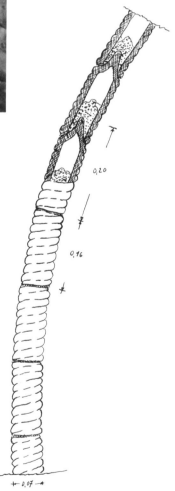

Fig. 33. The cupola: structural
drawing of tubular vaulting

Fig. 34. Area between the extrados of the cupola and the bounding wall, showing part of the stucco cornice in situ

Fig. 35. Fragment of stucco cornice after cleaning

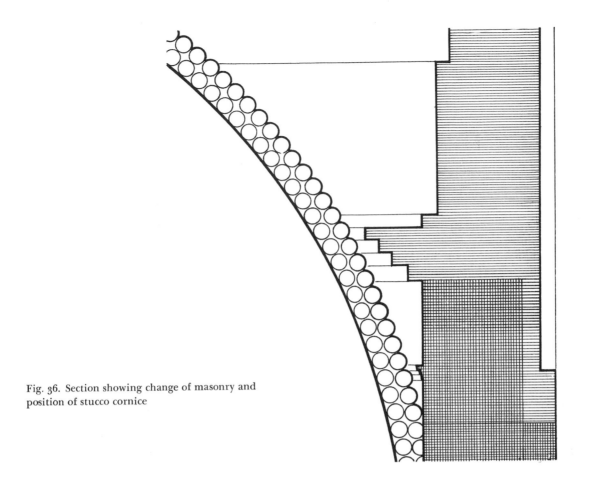

Fig. 36. Section showing change of masonry and position of stucco cornice

Fig. 37. Interior view: eighteenth century

Fig. 38. Interior view: nineteenth century, before the restorations of the 1890s

Fig. 39. Interior: present view

Fig. 40. Interior: present view

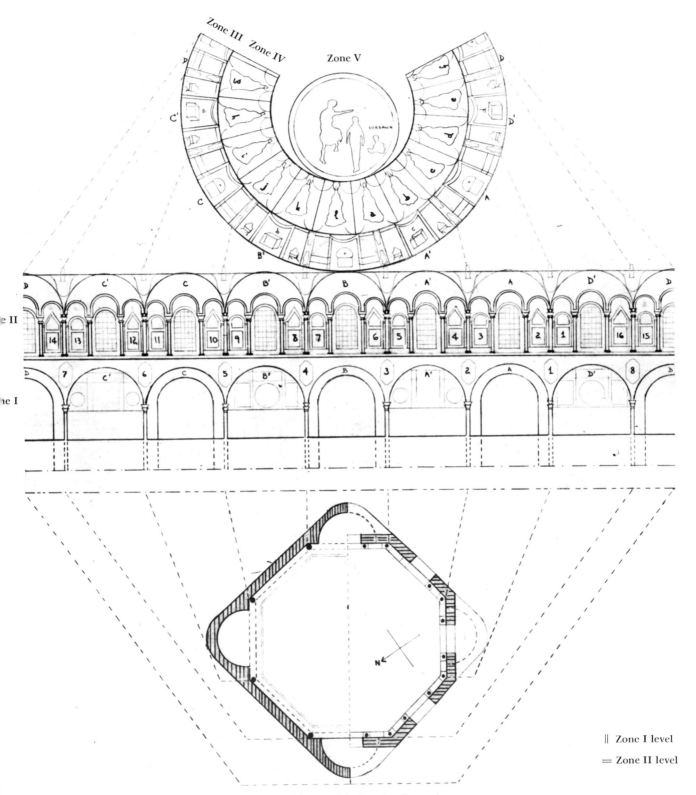

Fig. 41. Schema of the interior decoration

SCALE 1/100

Fig. 42. A. General view of the cupola mosaics

Fig. 42. B. Same view; blank areas indicate modern restorations

Fig. 43. The mosaics of Zone V: baptism of Christ

Fig. 44. Detail of Zone V: the river god Jordan

Fig. 45. Zone IV: Sts. Thomas and Paul

Fig. 46. Zone IV: St. Andrew

Fig. 47. Zone IV: St. James of Zebedee

Fig. 48. Zone IV: St. Philip

Fig. 49. Zone IV: St. Bartholomew

Fig. 50. Zone IV: St. Simon

Fig. 51. Zone IV: St. Matthew

Fig. 52. St. Peter

Fig. 53. St. Andrew

Fig. 54. St. James of Zebedee

Fig. 55. St. John

Fig. 56. St. Philip

Fig. 57. St. Bartholomew

Fig. 58. St. Jude

Fig. 59. St. Simon   Fig. 60. St. James of Alphaeus

Fig. 61. St. Matthew

Fig. 62. St. Thomas

Fig. 63. St. Paul

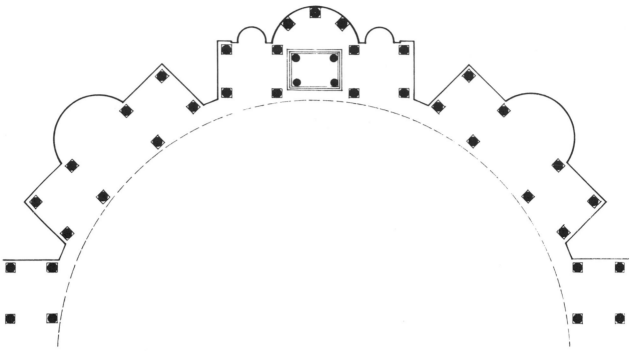

Fig. 64. Reconstruction of the architecture of the mosaics of Zone III, ground plan

Fig. 65. Zone III: altar panel with Gospel of St. Luke

Fig. 66. Zone III: altar with Gospel of St. John

Fig. 67. Zone III: the throne of Christ (Panel C)

Fig. 68. Zone III: parapet with symbolic bough (Panel B)

Fig. 69. Zone III: plant-candelabrum with birds

Fig. 70. Zone II: view

Fig. 71. Zone II: view

Fig. 72. Zone II, Side A: Prophets 2 (right) and 3 (left)

Fig. 73. Zone II, Side C: Prophets 10 (right) and 11 (left)

A

B

C

Fig. 74. Reconstruction of the architectural scheme of Zone II:
three possible readings and their ground plans

Fig. 75. Zone II, detail with the relief of the *Traditio legis*

Fig. 76. Zone II, detail with the relief of Christ trampling the lion and adder

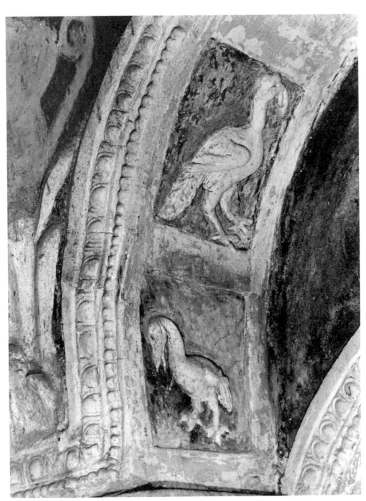

Fig. 77. Zone II, detail: birds in an arch soffit

Fig. 78. Zone II, detail: confronted goats (Side D', above aedicule 1)

Fig. 79. Zone II: Jonah and the whale (Side C', above aedicule 12)

Fig. 80. Zone II: Christ trampling the lion and adder (Side C' above aedicule 13)

Fig. 81. Zone II: *Traditio legis* (Side D, above aedicule 14)

Fig. 82. Zone II: Daniel and the lions (Side D, above aedicule 15)

Fig. 83. Zone II, Prophet 1 (Side D′)

Fig. 84. Zone II, Prophet 1, detail

Fig. 85. Zone II, Prophet 2 (Side A)

Fig. 86. Zone II, Prophet 3 (Side A)

Fig. 87. Zone II, Prophet 4 (Side A′)

Fig. 88. Zone II, Prophet 4, detail

Fig. 89. Zone II, Prophet 5 (Side A′)

Fig. 90. Zone II, Prophet 6 (Side B)

Fig. 91. Zone II, Prophet 7 (Side B)

Fig. 92. Zone II, Prophet 7, detail

Fig. 93. Zone II, Prophet 8 (Side B′)

Fig. 94. Zone II, Prophet 9 (Side B′)

Fig. 95. Zone II, Prophet 10 (Side C)

Fig. 96. Zone II, Prophet 11 (Side C)

Fig. 97. Zone II, Prophet 12 (Side C')

Fig. 98. Zone II, Prophet 13 (Side C')

Fig. 99. Zone II, Prophet 14 (Side D)

Fig. 100. Zone II, Prophet 14, detail

Fig. 101. Zone II, Prophet 15 (Side D)

Fig. 102. Zone II, Prophet 16 (Side D')

Fig. 103. Zone I: view of the altar niche (Side B)

Fig. 104. Zone I: view toward Niche C

Fig. 105. Zone I: view of Niche D

Fig. 106. Zone I: view of Niche A

Fig. 107. Zone I, Side C': *opus sectile* and Prophets 6 (right) and 7 (left)

Fig. 108. Zone I, Side B': *opus sectile* and Prophets 4 (right) and 5 (left)

Fig. 109. Zone I: brickwork exposed during the restorations of 1938

Fig. 110. Zone I, detail showing that the *opus sectile* does not continue under the arches

Fig. 111. Drawing for the restoration of the *opus sectile* of Zone I, 1897–1906

Fig. 112. Drawing for the restoration of the *opus sectile* of Zone I, 1897–1906

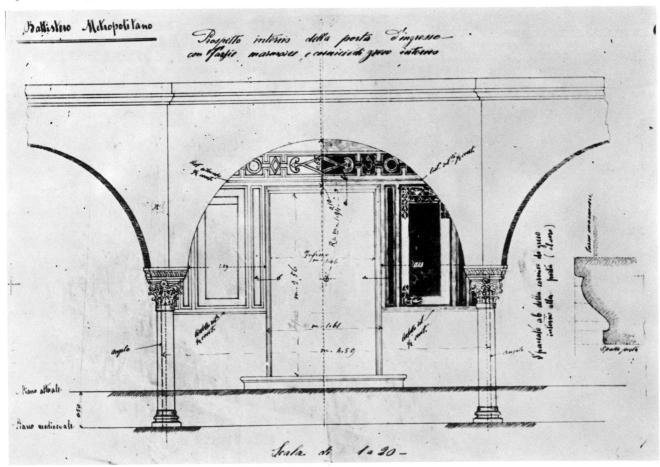

Fig. 113. Zone I: Prophet 2 (corner of Sides A–A′)

Fig. 114. Zone I: Prophet 3 (corner of Sides A′–B)

Fig. 115. Zone I: Prophet 5 (corner of Sides B'–C)

Fig. 116. Zone I: capital at corner A–D'

Fig. 117. Zone I: capital at corner A'–B

Fig. 118. Another view of capital shown in Fig. 117

Fig. 119. Zone I: capital at corner
B–B′

Fig. 120. Another view of capital
shown in Fig. 119

Fig. 121. Zone I: capital at corner D–D′

Fig. 122. The font and the pulpit, after the removal of the smaller eighteenth-century font in 1960

Fig. 123. The altar in Niche B

Fig. 124. The classical urn in Niche C

Fig. 125. Relief of a man on horseback in blind arcade of Side D

Fig. 126. Cast of a fragmentary Roman epitaph, first century A.D. (uncovered during nineteenth-century restorations)

Fig. 127. Fragment of a sarcophagus (?), used in the font, probably sixth century

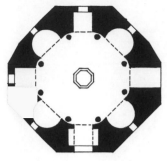

Albenga

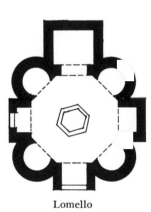

Ravenna, Arian

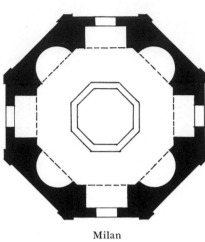

Milan

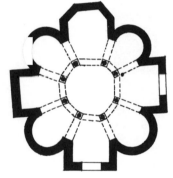

Nevers

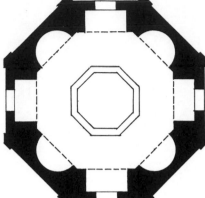

Lomello

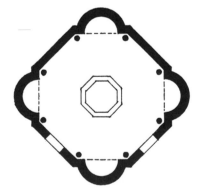

Ravenna, Orthodox

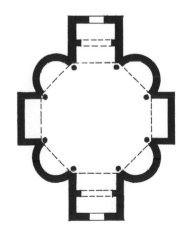

Como

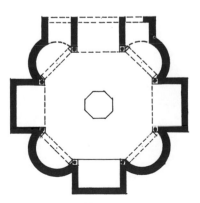

Novara

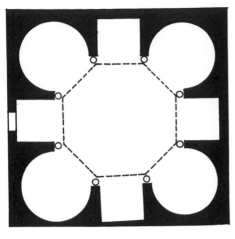
Brescia

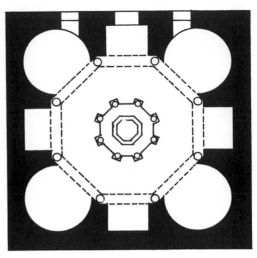
Fréjus

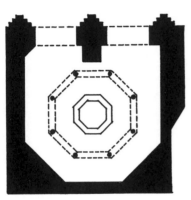
Aix-en-Provence

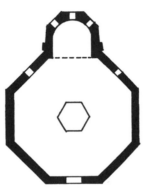
Grado

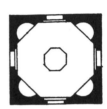
Riva San Vitale

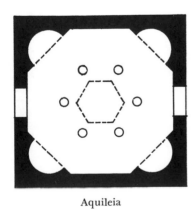
Aquileia

Fig. 128. Sketch plans of Early Christian octagonal baptisteries in North Italy and southern France.
Scale about 1/330

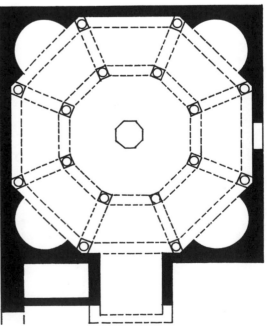
Marseille

Fig. 129. Rome, the Lateran Baptistery, as rebuilt by Pope Sixtus III (432–40)

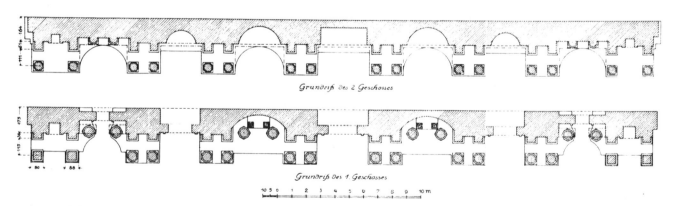

Fig. 130. Ephesos, Roman theater, plans of the first two stories of the *scaenae frons*

Fig. 131. Ephesos, Roman
theater, reconstruction of the
scaenae frons

Fig. 132. Roman relief of a
theater scene from Castel S. Elia,
ca. A.D. 50

Fig. 133. Ravenna, Archiepiscopal
Chapel: Christ trampling the lion and
adder, ca. A.D. 500

Fig. 134. Ravenna, Archiepiscopal
Chapel: St. Philip

Fig. 135. Ivory throne of Archbishop Maximian, detail: baptism of Christ

Fig. 136. Ravenna, Arian Baptistery: mosaics of the cupola

Fig. 137. Rome, catacomb of Domitilla: vault painting, mid-fourth century (?)

Fig. 138. Bevsan, mosaic pavement with a calendric scheme, sixth century

Fig. 139. Naples, Baptistery of S. Giovanni in Fonte: scheme of the mosaic decoration of the vault

Fig. 140. Thessaloniki, St. George: mosaics of the cupola, late fourth century

Fig. 141. Milan, S. Aquilino, apse mosaic: Christ and the twelve apostles

Fig. 142. Rome, Lateran Museum: gladiator mosaic from
the Baths of Caracalla, early third century

Fig. 143. Milan, S. Vittore in Ciel d'Oro: St. Maternus,
fifth century

Fig. 144. Boston, Museum of Fine Arts: Coptic stele, seventh—eighth century

Fig. 145. Cluny Museum, ivory panel: St. Paul, sixth century

Fig. 146. Ravenna, the so-called Mausoleum of Galla Placidia, view of the interior

Fig. 147. Baouit, Chapel 17: wall painting, fifth century.